Public Reactions to Jack the Ripper

Published by:

Dan Norder, Inklings Press
2 N. Lincoln Ridge Dr. #521
Madison, WI 53719 USA

www.inklings.com

ISBN: 0-9759129-7-6

Collected contents copyright © 2006 by Stephen P. Ryder, All Rights Reserved

Proceeds from sale of this book go to the *Casebook: Jack the Ripper* press project, **www.casebook.org**

This title is printed simmultaneously in the United States and the United Kingdom by Lightning Source, Inc.

Public Reactions to
Jack the Ripper

Edited by Stephen P. Ryder

- Inklings Press -

Introduction

For the past ten years I've moderated an online discussion forum at *Casebook: Jack the Ripper* [www.casebook.org], so in a way, my fascination with these Victorian "Letters to the Editor" seems only natural. They were, after all, the 1888 equivalent to a modern day Internet message board. Slower, yes, but just as effective – and oftentimes, just as contentious.

The Whitechapel murders forever altered London society, and nowhere can these changes be better seen than in these letters sent by the reading public to the major newspapers of the day. Some of these letters were penned by familiar names such as the Reverend Samuel Barnett, Albert Bachert, George Lusk and Sir Charles Warren. But for the most part these names will be unfamiliar to the average researcher. These were in large part normal, everyday Londoners who had an opinion to share or a complaint to voice. And it's through their letters that the modern researcher can really come face-to-face with the various social issues raised by the Whitechapel murders.

You will notice several recurring themes throughout these letters. Many severely criticized both police and government officials for their failure to act swiftly and decisively to stop the murders. A large portion offered suggestions on how to capture the killer. Some were extraordinarily insightful, such as the one which suggested examining the "corrugated surface of a thumb," many years before fingerprinting would ever be used as an accepted means of criminal detection. Many suggestions, however, seem just plain silly when viewed with modern sensibilities.

And for every suggestion, there was a theory. Was the Ripper a Frenchman? A Malay? An American? Surely a foreigner of some sort? (As one correspondent wrote, the celerity of the killer's movements simply didn't jibe with the "phlegmatic nature" of an Englishman.) Was he a butcher? A seaman? A clerk? Was it more than one person? Could a clairvoyant reveal his true identity?

But perhaps the most interesting letters are those which embrace reforms to improve the lives of those who were being brutally slaughtered in London's East End. Ideas were proposed on how best to "clear the rookeries" of Whitechapel and Spitalfields. Was it best to just demolish these "dens of vice" and replace them with well-built, artisans dwellings which could provide their inhabitants with clean, healthy living space? Was religion the answer? Should prostitution be institutionalized and regulated? Or would shelters for fallen and inebriate women provide enough of a social crutch to stem the tide of vice and immorality? And what about the incredibly lenient sentences generally offered to men who engaged in violence against women? (Be sure to check out the "Woman Killing No Murder" series from the *Daily News* for more on this controversy.) Anti-Semitism? Lodging houses? Inquest reform?

You'll read about all of that and more in this compendium of letters sent to the editors of the major London newspapers between August and December 1888. I hope you enjoy reading them as much as I have.

Stephen P. Ryder
Editor, *Casebook: Jack the Ripper*
March 2006

The Letters

Sir Charles Warren

8 August, 1888

THE TOWER GARDENS.
TO THE EDITOR OF *THE EVENING NEWS*.

SIR -

Perhaps it is not generally known that since the opening of the Tower Gardens free to the public, the H Division[1] police band performs a selection of music in the grounds every Saturday afternoon from five to seven, which will continue till the end of September. The expense of this is borne by Samuel Montagu[2], Esq., M.P. Might not this example be copied by many of our philanthropists in other of the open spaces of the metropolis?

I am, &c.,

M. VAN THUL.
9, Great Alie-street, E., August.

SIR CHARLES WARREN'S APPOINTMENT.
TO THE EDITOR OF *THE EVENING NEWS*.

SIR -

Under the original Police Act the appointment of Sir Charles Warren as Chief Commissioner[3] is clearly illegal, as the Act specially enacts that the Chief Commissioner must be "a barrister of seven years' standing." I write these few lines, having read the letter signed "Ratepayer" in your issue of Saturday last.

I am, &c.,

AN OLD POLICE-CONSTABLE
UNDER SIR RICHARD MAYNE.[4]

---

[1] H Division was the Metropolitan Police designation for Whitechapel.

[2] Samuel Montagu was a well-known Jewish activist and Liberal Member of Parliament for the Whitechapel division of Tower Hamlets (1885-1900). After the murder of Annie Chapman, Montagu personally offered to raise a reward of £100 for the capture of the killer. See also his letter to the editor of the *Echo* "The Jews and Animal Killing," October 11th 1888.

[3] Sir Charles Warren (1840-1927) was appointed Commissioner of Police in 1886. He was widely criticized for his tendency to employ military tactics in the execution of police duties and for his stormy relationship with Home Secretary Henry Matthews. Warren's handling of the "Bloody Sunday" riots in November 1887 drew even more ire from the Radical press.

[4] Sir Richard Mayne (1796-1868) served as Commissioner of Police of the Metropolis for thirty-nine years (jointly from 1829-1855 and then as the sole Commissioner from 1855-1868).

31 August 1888

IN PRAISE OF "THE SILLY SEASON."
To the EDITOR of the *PALL MALL GAZETTE*.

SIR,

Can you tell me why it is that the newspapers are always so interesting at this season of the year? I have often noticed that in August and September the articles begin to grow fresher and more varied; the hackneyed political subjects are dropped; anecdotes, descriptions of new scientific inventions, pretty accounts of the country, and deep thoughts about life take the place of the ordinary routine matter which no one ever reads. Is it because the gentlemen who write go away for autumn? Because, if it is, I am sure we should be quite content if they stayed away altogether, though no doubt they are thought very clever in their own set. I never enjoy the papers so much as in August; and I am sure there are plenty of people who think just the same. I hope you won't mind my saying so; but I feel certain that a great deal of money is wasted by newspaper proprietors on literary refinements and cleverness that only bore commonplace people like yours truly,

AMELIA MACKINTOSH.

5 September 1888

WHITECHAPEL-ROAD MURDER.
TO THE EDITOR OF *THE ECHO*.

SIR,

I have read with painful interest the account of the Whitechapel-road murder recorded in *The Echo* last night, and beg to call your attention to the sad state of the road, as stated in the enclosed paper. Thousands who read *The Echo* have not the faintest idea of the terrible state of things which exist in these parts. Every night all through the year I have to pass through this road, and I am forced to say the poor fallen women and the girls are increasing greatly. From New-road to Stepney-green, on the London Hospital side, there are scores of characters similar to those who met their death in George-yard and Buck's-row. The drink houses are the great attraction for these wretched women. Is it not high time that something be done to check this sad state of things?

Faithfully yours,

JAMES SHARPLESS

6 September 1888

TO THE EDITOR OF *THE EVENING NEWS*.

SIR -

Permit me, as an inhabitant of twenty years in Whitechapel, to express on behalf of a number of tradesmen and shopkeepers in Whitechapel our deepest regret and indignation at the shocking and revolting murders which have further diagnosed the unfortunate district of Whitechapel of late. The question that now arises is what is to be done, and what can be done to check and prevent the further spreading of such dastardly crimes. In the first place I would suggest that the police force should be strengthened in the East End, and secondly that there should be more gas lights in our back streets, courts, and alleys. There is no doubt but that these unfortunate women were butchered by their bullies (men who gain their livelihood from these unfortunates) and were the police to watch the haunts and dens of these villains and thieves, no doubt in a short time we should have a decrease of these crimes which have disgraced the capital of England. There are several supposed clubs in Whitechapel which these villains frequent, which are open all night for the sale of wines, spirits, and beer, and where any non-member can be admitted and served with as much drink as he or she can pay for. It is in these vile dens that the seed of immorality and crime is sown which brings forth the fruits we have just witnessed. The police must know of these places; if not, I am prepared, if required, to give the names of these places to any person in authority. The East End police are, with a few exceptions, a good and noble body of men who at all times have a hard and difficult duty to perform, and I feel sure that the heads of these police, such gentlemen as Arnold, Final and West will do their uttermost to stop the breeding of further crimes by these ruffians. In the second place I suggest more gas lights in our bye-streets, courts, and alleys. We pay rates and taxes, and have a right to have our district properly lighted. Only a little while back a City manufacturer living opposite me was knocked down, beaten, and robbed of a valuable gold chain within a few yards of his own street door, the villains escaping because the spot is dark. My sister also a short time ago was knocked down by some cowards. They also got away, the place being dark. Now, Sir, I hope and trust that the Whitechapel Board of Works and the Commercial Gas Company will awake to their duty, and do their best to have this grievance removed. Apologising for trespassing upon your valuable space,

I am, &c.,

ALBERT BACHERT[5]
Gordon House, Newnham-street, Whitechapel,
September 5.

---

[5] Bachert was involved (or possibly involved himself) in numerous ways with the investigation of the Whitechapel murders. He reported witnessing a suspicious-looking man at the Three Nuns Hotel and receiving two or more threatening letters signed "Jack the Ripper." Bachert had at least two run-ins with the law in 1887 and 1893, and was described by the *Times* as an "agitator."

7 September 1888

Crime in Whitechapel
TO THE EDITOR OF *THE STAR*.

SIR,

As a resident in the neighborhood of Whitechapel for the last 25 years, I wish to express my opinion as regards the terrible crimes of late at the East-end. I have had it brought under my notice several times. No later than a month back a female friend of mine was attacked by ruffians outside her own residence, a burglary taking place the same night a few doors off. A week later an elderly male friend was knocked down, assaulted, and robbed at the corner of the same street. In neither case has any clue yet been found. Last week myself and a colonial friend were passing through Commercial-street when we were assailed by a gang of six ruffians, but succeeded in getting away without injury. The robberies with violence are so frequent in the district in broad daylight, as well as night time, that it makes you ask the question, "Where are our police?"

Yours, &c.,

A WORKING MAN.
3 Sept.

9 September 1888

LETTER FROM THE HUSBAND.
TO THE EDITOR OF *LLOYD'S NEWSPAPER*

DEAR SIR,

I hope you will correct an error in your Sunday Edition in reference to the Whitechapel murder. It is stated that I did not know my own son.[6] That is not so. He left home of his own accord two years and a half ago, and I have always been on speaking terms with him. Only two or three months ago I saw him, and last week received two letters from him, asking me if I knew of any work for him. I did not leave my wife during her confinement and go away with a nurse girl. The deceased woman deserted me four or five times, if not six. The last time she left me without any home, and five children, the youngest one year and four months. I kept myself with the children where I was living for two and a half years before I took on with anybody, and not till after it was proved at Lambeth police-court that she had misconducted herself.

Yours respectfully,

W. NICHOLLS[7]

---

[6] Edward John, eldest son of William and Mary Nichols, was subsequently raised by Mary's father, Edward Walker. Some papers reported that William bumped into his son outside the mortuary when both had gone to identify the body, and didn't initially recognize who he was.

[7] William Nichols married Mary Ann Walker in 1864. The marriage lasted until around 1880. When he viewed his estranged wife's body at the mortuary William remarked, "Seeing you as you are now, I forgive you for what you have done to me."

10 September 1888

THE WHITECHAPEL MURDERS.
TO THE EDITOR OF *THE ECHO*.

Sir,

As usual, Drink seems to be intimately associated with these crimes, as with a great many more of a similar character, and yet Parliament legalises the trade, Magistrates grant licences, some medical men recommend the dangerous stuff, hundreds - aye, thousands - hourly drink it, and to excess; ministers of religion sanction its use at the sacramental table, parents send their young children to the public-houses and gin palaces to purchase it, with results too awful to contemplate. How much longer is this to go on? "Remove the cause, and the effect will cease!" Fortunately, *The Echo* is a valuable help to this end.

Yours faithfully,

REFORMER.

The Police and the Murders.
TO THE EDITOR OF *THE STAR*.

SIR,

As a reader and agent of your paper I should like to hear some of your readers' opinions what they think of the police proceedings at the East-end in respect of this heartless murder. It seems to me very strange that the authorities lay themselves out to prosecute the clubs where there is any chance of getting a conviction, while all the most barefaced robberies and murders take place week after week, and they are supposed to make elaborate arrangements to effect a capture of the culprit, but nothing seems ever to come of it, and it all seems to drop.

Yours, &c.,

RATEPAYER.
6 Sept.

11 September 1888

SLAUGHTERING THE JEWS.
TO THE EDITOR OF *THE EVENING NEWS*.

SIR - with reference to the above heading, on Saturday, evening last, I found it difficult to traverse the streets in the vicinity of the Whitechapel, without observing in almost every thoroughfare, knots of persons (consisting of men, women and children), and overhearing their slanderous and insulting remarks towards the Jews, who occasionally passed by. With justice to my countrymen, I mention that the foul epithets was made use of by people of the most ignorant and dangerous class, promoted by the information they had casually obtained that a man known as "Leather Apron" had a Jewish appearance, and was wanted for the recent Whitechapel murders. Even were it the case that the actual perpetrator belonged to the Hebrew class, is it not cowardly and unjust that in the extreme to calumniate a sect for the sins of one? Spotless indeed would be the flock entirely minus of black sheep. The Jew predominates in the neighbourhood where I am and have been residing for years, but notwithstanding the crimes committed by the members of our so-called Christian race average at least 99 per=8cent, in excess of those imputed by the Jews. Therefore if there were base enough to take a mean advantage of this knowledge, and impugn and molest every respectable Christian pedestrian they chanced to meet, no doubt riot and disorder would be the result daily. "Hard words break no bones," but often they lead to that end. The Jew is certainly no coward when on the defensive and if such conduct as I personally witnessed on Saturday last is not suppressed, the consequences may be serious indeed. My knowledge of the Jews impresses me with the belief that they are a persevering, thrifty and generous race. Clannish they may be, and it is a pity there is not more of such brotherly feeling existing among Christians; again, seldom have I seen a subscription list opened for the benefit of a deserving Christian that has not been contributed to by the Jews. Those who forget themselves so far as to insult them in the manner I have stated should put the query to each other, "What would our Christian labour market be (especially in this district) without the industry introduced by the Hebrew race? If your space will admit of giving publicity to the remarks made from a lover of fair play, it may be the means of deterring the self-imagined, pure-minded Christian, in abusing the people I have mentioned, and also teach him to endeavour "to pick the mote from his own eye," instead of molesting a harmless and industrious fraternity.

I am, &c.,

G. H. H.
48 and 49, Bishopsgate-street, Without
September 10.

11 September, 1888

THE WHITECHAPEL HORRORS
TO THE EDITOR OF *THE EVENING NEWS*

SIR - I have read your leader of to-day with great interest, especially the portion of it suggesting that the crimes were possibly committed by an epileptic[8], whose seizures take the form of homicidal impulses. There are many circumstances connected with these murders which support this hypothesis.

With the ordinary criminal it may be assumed that the police are quite capable of dealing; for in the cases of murder which run on general lines, some motive for their commission can be found, and a clue, of course, to the perpetrator may, in consequence, be discovered. Avarice, revenge, jealousy, and so forth, are instances of average motives for murder. Acting on the assumption of the existence of any of these, the police can almost always trace the crime to the criminal. Where, however, superior intelligence is possessed by the murderer, detection, of course, becomes, as a rule, more difficult. The ingenuity in the planning and executing of murder by a person of this class may occasionally baffle the skill of experts in crime investigation. But it may be generally assumed that the accumulated experience of our detectives is equal to the cunning of the most intelligent criminal.

In the case of the Whitechapel murders, however; the police are evidently at fault, since no intelligible motive can be ascribed to the perpetration of any of these crimes. It is well, therefore, to consider them as absolutely without motive.

Taking it for granted that they are the work of one man - and many circumstances point to this - then, on the assumption that they are motiveless, it is clear that they are the deeds of a lunatic. In support of this conclusion, the frenzied manner of the slaying and mutilation of the victim will go far. That the murderer is not a furious homicidal maniac, whose mania is continuous, may be assumed, else he would have betrayed himself before this. And the fact that his butcheries were restricted to a certain class would put out of question homicidal mania pure and simple.

Let us consider the question of monomania[9]. It is quite possible that monomania could be directed towards the commission of such crimes as we are considering. But here, again, the monomaniac would be almost certain to betray himself. Both in furious homicidal mania and monomania it is in the highest degree probable that the murderer's plans would be abortive because in the chaotic condition of mind which is the invariable attendant on both these manias, he would be unable to construct any consecutive course of conduct that would ensure success.

The third consideration is that of recurrent mania. What I have said above will dispose of this in so far as it is connected with the two manias I have been discussing. But a recurrent mania in the form of epileptic mania will account most adequately for the known facts relating to these crimes.

---

[8] In Victorian times, epileptics were often housed in asylums with the mentally retarded and the criminally insane.

[9] Monomania is defined as a mental or emotional fixation on any one thing (an object, a person, an urge, etc.). Its use in a criminal context was popularized in the 19th century by Edgar Allan Poe, whose characters often suffered from a form of monomaniacal paranoia that eventually led to their downfalls.

You have pointed out, Sir, that a homicidal impulse may take the place of the ordinary epileptic seizure, and the connection of epilepsy with erotic excitation is too well known for me to discuss at length here.

Now, it may be assumed that the same privacy would be required for the commission of an immoral act as for the commission of a deed of blood. A homicidal maniac would not seek privacy. He would, of course, slay, whenever he happened to find his victim. In the Whitechapel case there is, to my mind, no doubt that complete seclusion was a necessary condition for the purposes, whatever they may have been of the murderer.

Now, it is quite probable that the murderer's intentions in seeking an out-of-the-way place were nothing else than to commit an immoral act, and being on the point of committing this act, his excitement became epileptic with homicidal impulses.

I am therefore convinced of the excellence of your suggestion that "an inquiry as to the epileptic patients in Whitechapel and Spitalfields might afford more fruitful results than are to be attained by a mere wandering up and down streets, and asking householders whether they have heard 'unwanted noises'."

There are many things I might add in support of this deeply interesting theory, but I feel that I have already encroached too largely on your space.

I am &c.,

MEDICUS.

To the Editor of *The Daily News*

Sir,

Although it is hardly true to say that the inhabitants of Whitechapel are in a state of panic, yet no doubt excitement does exit, and the committee which I represent think that the present moment is advantageous for turning the feeling which has been aroused into action. They hope, therefore, that your kindness in publishing this letter may lead others to take steps to do what private citizens can do to better the state of our streets. A few days after the murder of the woman in George yard last month a meeting of about 70 men residing in the buildings in the immediate neighbourhood was held, and after discussion a committee of twelve was appointed to act as watchers, whose duties should be to observe the state of certain streets, chiefly between the hours of 11 and 1, and not only try to support the action of the police, when necessity arises, but also take careful note of disorderly houses and causes of disturbance. This committee has since met once a week to receive reports, which are carefully preserved, and to decide on future plans. It must not be supposed that we have in any way attempted to supplant the regularly constituted authorities, or that we are concerned merely with particular outrages or their perpetrators. But it does not need a long residence in this district to convince any one that many of the social conditions of the neighbourhood distinctly favour the commission of such crimes as those which have lately startled London. The police, whom we have found courteous and ready to allow us to work with them, must remain practically powerless as long as the apathy of the neighbourhood tolerates the scandalous scenes of daily and nightly occurrence. We have at present no definite suggestion, but we feel strongly that until the deeply rooted causes of these evils are known and attacked, the action of police courts, School Boards, and philanthropic institutions can do little to stamp out the disorder and crime which disgrace our city. The space which our committee is covering is very small, and must needs be so to secure efficiency, and as there is, at least, equal need for such district committees, for the better regulation of our streets elsewhere, we wish to suggest to those who feel as we do that steps should be taken in this direction without loss of time. If some communication could be set up between these committees when constituted, our powers would be strengthened and our opportunities improved.

I am, Sir, yours truly,

The Secretary of
the St. Jude's
District Committee.

TO THE EDITOR OF *THE TIMES*

Sir,

I would suggest that the police should at once find out the whereabouts of all cases of "homicidal mania" which may have been discharged as "cured" from metropolitan asylums during the last two years.

Your Obedient Servant,

September 9
A COUNTRY DOCTOR.

MORE POLICE WANTED.
TO THE EDITOR OF *THE ECHO.*

Sir,

In reference to the recent horrible atrocities committed in the Whitechapel-road, allow me (and old resident) to make a few remarks. Has it never occurred to the police to make any inquiries into the antecedents of the groups of loafers hanging about the public-house doors, day after day, and week after week, all the year round? They are never at work, but still can find money for drink and tobacco.

These wretches live by levying blackmail on the poor unfortunate women infesting the neighbourhood. There is quite a colony of these vagabonds living in the slums facing the London Hospital.

The fact is, I think, the police are not half strong enough to tackle them. In such localities there ought to be twice as many police on duty as in quiet neighbourhoods. I see that there has been another attempt at murder in an open market place at Spitalfields. The poor women are getting panic-stricken, and afraid to leave their homes after dark. I am sure the police will do their duty, and try all they know to bring the perpetrators of these cruel murders to justice.

I am, Sir, yours faithfully.

W.J.W.
Temple, Sept. 7

A DISGRACEFUL SCENE.
TO THE EDITOR OF *THE ECHO*.

Sir,

Will you kindly allow a little space in your paper to call the attention of your readers to what may be considered a public nuisance and disgrace? I refer to several low penny shows at the corner of Thomas's-street, Whitechapel-road, nearly facing the London Hospital. These sinks of iniquity are at the present time doing a roaring trade by exhibiting horrible pictures representing the poor victims who have been so brutally murdered of late. Great crowds stand gazing at these blood-stained pictures, blocking up the pavement. Meanwhile, the pickpockets are making the best use of their opportunity. Moreover, our young lads and lasses are being morally corrupted by visiting these tragic scenes. While walking along the streets it is truly painful to hear the jesting and trifling talk about things so awful. Is it not a wonder that the respectable shopkeepers (and there are many) in the road have not done something to put down these shows, which must be a hindrance to their business houses? Trusting this matter may be taken up by those whose business it is to remedy such evils, I enclose my card, and beg to remain, yours faithfully,

An East-Ender
Sept. 10

12 September 1888

THE EAST END HORRORS.
To the Editor of *The Evening News.*

Sir -

As a tradesman of many years standing in Whitechapel High-street, one of the finest thoroughfares in London, I protest (and I am sure I am expressing the feelings of my fellow-tradesmen) against the Press placarding the reporting in their various editions of Saturday and Monday (to-day) "Horrible murder in Whitechapel," when in reality it took place in the parish of Christ Church, Spitalfields. As about half the trade is done with persons residing out of the district, such misrepresentations are very misleading, and persons, especially females, are afraid of coming into Whitechapel to shop, thereby ensuring a very serious loss to traders. Whitechapel by many persons resident in the country and West-end, is looked upon as being a horrible place. I would advise such ladies and gentlemen to pay a visit to the parish: I think they would then come to a very different conclusion. I might say to those ladies and gentlemen who do not, or cannot, pay a visit to Whitechapel, that we have a fine, wide, handsome thoroughfare one mile in length, and that during the last seven years upwards of one million pounds has been spent in improvements for the benefit of the working classes. The whole of the houses surrounding and formerly known as Petticoat-lane have been pulled down and fine blocks of buildings for the artisan have erected in their place. Much remains to be done in the neighbouring parish of Spitalfields, when, I am assured, the new London Council will do justice to that long-neglected parish.

I am, &c.,

REFORMER.
September 10.

THE MURDERS IN WHITECHAPEL
TO THE EDITOR OF *THE ECHO.*

Sir,

It being everyone's duty to assist in any way possible the elucidation of the above dreadful tragedies, may I, through you, ask the police whether they have given a thought to the possibility of the crimes having been committed by a woman or a man disguised as such!

Yours obediently,

F.H.H.
Sept. 11

L. Forbes Winslow

12 September, 1888

TO THE EDITOR OF *THE TIMES*.

Sir,

My theory having been circulated far and wide with reference to an opinion given to the authorities of the Criminal Investigation Department, I would like to qualify such statements in your columns.

That the murderer of the three victims in Whitechapel is one and the same person I have no doubt.

The whole affair is that of a lunatic, and as there is "method in madness," so there was method shown in the crime and in the gradual dissection of the body of the latest victim. It is not the work of a responsible person. It is a well-known and accepted fact that homicidal mania is incurable, but difficult of detection, as it frequently lies latent. It is incurable, and those who have been the subject of it should never be let loose on society.

I think that the murderer is not of the class of which "Leather Apron" belongs, but is of the upper class of society, and I still think that my opinion given to the authorities is the correct one - viz., that the murders have been committed by a lunatic lately discharged from some asylum, or by one who has escaped. If the former, doubtless one who, though suffering from the effects of homicidal mania, is apparently sane on the surface, and consequently has been liberated, and is following out the inclinations of his morbid imaginations by wholesale homicide. I think the advice given by me a sound one - to apply for an immediate return from all asylums who have discharged such individuals, with a view of ascertaining their whereabouts.

I am your obedient servant,

L. FORBES WINSLOW[10],
M.B. Camb., D.C.L. Oxon.
70, Wimpole-street,
Cavendish-square, W.
Sept. 11.

---

[10] Lyttleton Forbes Winslow (1844-1913) had a formidable education both in medicine and in law and considered himself to be one of the utmost authorities on the Ripper crimes. At one time he proclaimed that it was solely because of his own conclusions on the case that the murders had ceased. Modem researchers now note that certain letters Winslow produced as evidence for his theories had had their dates altered so as to coincide with the atrocities. In 1910 he published a book titled *Recollections of Forty Years*, which includes a chapter devoted to the Jack the Ripper murders.

POLICE INCOMPETENCE.
To the Editor of *The Evening News.*

SIR –

Another ghastly, heartrending and horrible murder in Whitechapel, this morning. When is Sir Charles Warren, the incapable and incompetent, to be roused from his lethargy? The police are not allowed to do any duty now, they are all posted at street corners and there they stop. The street roughs, rowdies, cut-throats and assassins well know this and have the thoroughfares to themselves and commit all sorts of outrages with impunity, and without fear of detection or even interference. The streets, outside the City boundary, even in broad daylight, are positively unsafe. You may walk from Goswell-road to the top of Stamford Hill any day you like and never meet a policeman. The police never find anything out; they are not allowed! What do we want with a military man at the head of the police - especially a psalm-smiting, Gospel-grinding, and Bible punching specimen like Sir Charles Warren, who, by the bye, was a Gladstonian appointment?

I am, &c.,

RATEPAYER.
September 8.

NUISANCES IN WHITECHAPEL.
TO THE EDITOR OF *THE ECHO.*

Sir,

Being a tradesman of Whitechapel, I wish to have a few words on the article in your paper of the 11th, about the disgraceful scenes that have been going on lately at the corner of Thomas-street and its neighbourhood. It is not safe for a respectable person to walk the streets while such nuisances are going on. Another great nuisance which I think the police ought to put a stop to are those Italian organs which infest our streets day and night. They cause a large crowd of boys and girls, men and women, to assemble for the purpose of dancing. I was passing through a street only last Friday evening, when I noticed a drunken woman, with a baby which appeared about five months old, running round and trying to dance to one of those organs, the poor child half naked and crying, while a drunken lot of men and women were enjoying the fun. I am sure the police will do their best to quell these disturbances. Hoping this matter will be taken up by the inhabitants of Whitechapel,

I remain, yours faithfully,

A. Laing.
210, Oxford-street, W.
Sept. 11

12 September, 1888

The Non-Detection of Crime
TO THE EDITOR OF *THE STAR*.

SIR,

Your remarks on the ignorance of the police of the metropolis of the haunts of criminals are perfectly just. Further, this ignorance is virtually encouraged. It is well known that the common lodging-houses are the haunts of the lowest and vilest criminals, and of their abandoned female associates. Nests of thieves and prostitutes in most cases. The office of the lodging-house inspector is sanitary, not detective, nor repressive. Further, he can enter only at certain times, even for the enforcement of sanitary regulations, requisite air space, &c., without special permission. It is thus possible for many more persons to occupy the house than are allowed by the licence. Single men, single women, and "doubles" may occupy one house by permission of the Commissioner of Police, and the whole moral atmosphere is foul in the extreme. Casual laborers become tramps and beggars, and then thieves; and the women who, in their destitution, enter these portals, usually "leave hope behind." But unless in hot pursuit of a criminal the ordinary policeman may not enter, nor may the detective without warrant if the keeper objects. The slaughter ground of the East-end abounds with lodging houses, each victim of the last six months being an inhabitant of one or other, and their murderer is probably at this moment sheltered in the Alsatia of the East. The police of Whitechapel and Spitalfields are practically powerless to deal with the ruffianly population crowded into long, narrow streets, where nine out of 10 men are the policemen's natural enemies.

Yours, &c.,

AN EAST-ENDER.

13 September 1888

A DISGRACEFUL SCENE.
TO THE EDITOR OF *THE ECHO*.

Sir,

Referring to the letter under the above heading in your last night's issue, we beg to be permitted to place the real facts before you. There are only two houses at the corner of Thomas-street, Whitechapel, and they are next door to one another. The one belongs to Mr. Barry, who holds a lease of the premises, and this has for seven years been carried on by him as a wax-work show. The other premises are leased to his daughter, Mrs. Roberts, and here she has, in conjunction with her husband, carried on a similar show to that of Mr. Barry for the last twelve months. These places, we are informed by the proprietors, so far from being "sinks of iniquity," as alleged by your Correspondent, simply serve at the East, at the cheap rate of one penny for admission, the highly useful purpose that the deservedly well-patronised exhibition of Madame Tussaud serves at the West. There are wax figures of celebrated persons, a chamber of horrors, an exhibition of ghosts (according to the plan of Professor Pepper). As regards the pictures at which your Correspondent is so horrified, we are informed that there are only two, the one single and the other double in the events depicted, and that their character has been greatly exaggerated. Trusting you will find space for this explanation in the next issue of your valuable paper.

We are, Sir, yours faithfully,

Abbott, Earle, and Ogle
Solicitors for Mr. Barry and Mrs. Roberts
11, Worship-street, Sept. 12

PLAIN CLOTHES DETECTIVES.
TO THE EDITOR OF *THE ECHO*.

Sir,

I have watched with great interest the movements of our plain clothes detectives in search of the unknown murderer, and must give them due credit for zeal and shrewdness. But I venture to think one great mistake they are making is thing. They are in appearance too much the gentleman, and they carry with them too much the ordinary policemen walk. This will not do for the sharp, eagle-eyed characters in the East of London, who live by their wits. They can smell them, so to speak, at a distance. In my humble opinion they should assume more of the ordinary working man's dress and manners, and then push in and out among the so-called common people, who generally get to know what has happened long before it appears in the papers, and by this means they might possibly hear something to their advantage. The police must be careful they do not get their minds filled with the idea that the murderer must be a dreadful, wild-looking man, for I have had dealings in my time with white oily-tongued villains, as well as black ones. In fact, there are characters about who can keep up a decent appearance, and pass off as swells, yet they can do desperate deeds, and at the same time smile with a sweet air of innocency.

Yours, &c.,

Watch.

Sept. 12

TO THE EDITOR OF *THE EVENING NEWS.*

SIR -

I have read with great interest your article, and the letter of Dr. Forbes Winslow, on the Whitechapel murders; and as far as I can judge, the opinions therein expressed have met with the approbation of the great majority of newspaper readers - viz., that the murders are the work of one man, and he epileptic or a homicidal maniac. In the East-end, however, the scene of these tragic mysteries, the majority of the population are not newspaper readers. At least, there is a very large class who cannot, or at any rate do not, read the newspapers, and whose opinions are to a very large extent formed independently of newspapers. Moreover, those people of whom I speak have the advantage of the profoundest and most accurate local knowledge. They know the scene of the crimes intimately, and they know all the characters who frequent the neighborhood. Now, amongst those people the opinion is general that the murders are not the work of one man, but of several, acting probably, more or less in concert. Those people assert that in that neighborhood there is, notoriously, a set of low fellows-whom they could point out-who systematically live on the earnings of the poor unfortunates who there ply their wretched trade, one man levying blackmail from several women, and affording them in return his "protection." And those people believe that the murders are the work of some of these "bullies," acting probably, more or less, in concert. According to this theory, the murders were deliberately planned and executed; what led to them was the inability or unwillingness of the poor women to continue to satisfy the incessant demands of these blood-suckers - the women, it may be, acting more or less in concert; and the motive for the crimes is to be found in, first, a desire for revenge, and, second, a determination to read a terrible lesson to the others. The disemboweling and the other diabolical accompaniments were (according to this theory) dictated by the second part of the motive. If this should prove to be the true theory of the crimes, it would indicate a very serious state of things-far more serious, from one point of view, than even the presence among us of a lunatic at large, homicidal mania in his head, and a butcher's knife in his hand. I express no opinion upon the theory. I merely state it for the consideration of those who have not the same opportunities as myself of hearing it.

I am,

P. Q. R. S.

The Whitechapel Murders.
TO THE EDITOR OF THE STAR.

SIR,

It may interest your readers to learn in connection with the Whitechapel murders that a number of parallel cases occurred some seven years ago near Bochum in Westphalia. The murderer was in the habit of lassooing women, and treating them in exactly the same manner as his confrère of Spitalfields. After many fruitless efforts on the part of the police to catch the perpetrator of the outrages, they at last arrested a gipsy, who was duly sentenced to death and beheaded. Unfortunately, a few days after his execution the murders recommenced! The assassin had the impudence to write to the magistrate of the district that he meant to kill a certain number of victims and would then give himself up. The papers applied to such a murder the expressive term of *lustmord* (pleasure murder).

My German friend, who reminds me of this case would not feel astonished to hear that the Bochum *lustmörder* has put in an appearance at Whitechapel.

Yours, &c.,

S.
London, 10 Sept.

14 September 1888

BLOODHOUNDS AS DETECTIVES
TO THE EDITOR OF *THE MORNING ADVERTISER*

SIR,

Knowing by experience the sagacity and keen sense of smell of the bloodhound, I would strongly urge upon the Government the propriety of testing their powers in discovering crime. It could be done without cruelty, such as biting or tearing human beings, by running the dogs in the new muzzle, in which they can open or shut their mouths without being able to bite or pick up poison, but they will run the scent of a man or horse, or anything else you like to put them on, in a chain, led by hand, just as well. You only want them to point out the criminals.

About the year 1844, my brother-in-law had two bloodhounds in Huntingdonsire, and a clergyman, a friend of his, about ten miles off, one night had two sheep killed. He sent his man servant over, requesting my brother-in-law to bring one of his dogs. He at once mounted one of his hunters, and rode over to where the sheep had been killed and their carcasses carried off some fourteen hours previously. There had been a severe frost during the night. The police were waiting and could make nothing of the case, the dog was laid on the trail, and without a break she ran the men three miles to where the sheep had been carried off by boat. The police, without further troubling the dog, crossed the canal and went straight to the house where they found the mutton and arrested the men, who got six months' imprisonment for the possession of meat for which they could not satisfactorily account. My brother-in-law gave the young dog to a friend in Cambridge, and to show him what the dog could do started his manservant across country on his best hunter, giving him twenty minutes' start, and running two other horses across the track to try and break the scent. The horses were from the same stable, but in forty minutes the young dog was alongside the manservant. Give the police two or three brace of bloodhounds in each county, and it will greatly prevent undetected crime.

I am, Sir, yours, &c.,

L.F.S MABERLY
71, Wellington-road, Dublin,
Sept. 12, 1888.

P.S.- It may be remembered that in London some years ago the body of a murdered woman was discovered through the sagacity of a dog.

THE WHITECHAPEL MURDERS.
TO THE EDITOR OF *THE ECHO.*

Sir,

At the risk of appearing irrelevant and an alarmist, will you allow me to point out that the tragedies in Whitechapel, which have so shocked civilisation, have occurred between midnight on Friday and 6 a.m. on Saturday. We are clearly not dealing with an ordinary criminal, and may he not, therefore, have a predilection for the accomplishment of his fiendish purpose on especial days and between especial hours? And does it not, therefore, behove the police to be additionally active and alert on the periodical recurrence of those days and hours? yours, &c.,

C.F.A.G.
Stoke Newington, Sept. 13

TO THE EDITOR OF *THE TIMES.*

Yesterday, at 11 A.M., a gentleman was seized and robbed of everything in Hanbury-street. At 5 P.M. an old man of seventy years was attacked and served in the same manner in Chicksand-street. At 10 A.M. to-day a man ran into a baker's shop at the corner of Hanbury-street and King Edward-street, and ran off with the till and its contents. All these occurred within 100 yards of each other, and midway between the scenes of the last two horrible murders.

J.F.S.

Our Detective System
TO THE EDITOR OF *THE STAR*

SIR,

You certainly hit the right nail on the head in your Saturday's issue on our detective force. The inefficiency of our detectives is quite clear. Hundreds of our police never see London till they come up to join the force. Hence the ignorance amongst them of London and its people. Again, why should men be compelled to perform duty in uniform for several years before being permitted to do plain-clothes duty? The idea is ridiculous. What we want in London is men whose knowledge of London is most extensive. Why not leave the detective force open to men who are willing to go on trial. Men who are known to possess sound knowledge of London and the criminal classes. But under the present system men are kept out not because for want of skill, or knowledge; but because they are below the standard, 5ft. 9in. To-day the public are made to pay for height and not for brains. Surely it is time men who are ready and efficient for the work had a chance of proving the same.

Yours, &c.,

AN OBSERVER WAITING.

15 September 1888

THE BLOODHOUND AS A DETECTIVE.
TO THE EDITOR OF *THE MORNING ADVERTISER,*

SIR,

The letter of a Huntingdonshire correspondent in your issue of to-day reminds me of a circumstance that took place under my own observation in the same and adjoining county, Beds, in either 1852 or 1853. At that time the late Duke of Manchester (Kimbolton) had in his possession several bloodhounds. Sheep had been stolen several times from outlying farms and villages. At length a farmer at Little Staughton, Beds, three miles from Kimbolton, lost a sheep, and after searching fruitlessly for four days, asked Mr. Bollard, the Duke of Manchester's keeper, if he would take over one of the hounds and try if anything could be found. Mr. Bollard, myself, and hound were in the field next morning at three o'clock. The dog, on being put on the trail, bore almost direct homeward, not by the road, but across country, and kept our horses at full speed. After running about two miles he stopped at an open drain, in which, after a search, we discovered the skin and entrails of a sheep. The dog, one being put on the trail again, ran nearly a mile on the hard road to a cottage at Stoneley, near Kimbolton, where the greater part of the sheep was found. I feel sure that, had the police been provided with a hound and a good horse, the Whitechapel murderer would have been found within six hours.

I am, Sir, yours, &c.,

E.P.
27, Northumberland-place
Bayswater, W.
Sept. 14, 1888.

The Dangers of Whitechapel.
TO THE EDITOR OF *THE STAR.*

SIR,

As the above-named district is now in a state of ferment in consequence of the recent atrocities, I think it not out of place to state my own experience respecting the Whitechapel-road. A few months since myself and a friend were on our way home, walking, and speaking about business matters, and when midway between the London Hospital and Cambridge-road, a man suddenly turned the corner of a street and immediately made a snatch at my watch chain. I may mention I was carrying with me a small cash book, and I at once clasped my hand containing the book to my vest pocket in order to protect my watch, &c. Luckily for me, the scoundrel missed his mark, as he seized my chain near the bar fastened in the button-hole. He at once ran down a street which leads behind the London Hospital. Myself and friend immediately gave chase; but, as the ruffian turned into a dark street, and knowing it to be a dangerous part, we threw up the chase reluctantly. On our return, I called a policeman's attention to the matter, and he at once spoke to two plain clothes officers who happened to be near by. I laid the attack before them; but, in answer to their queries, I could give no information as to the fellow's identity except that he was tall and young. The only remedy I can see is that the authorities send more police to assist those already in Whitechapel, as I consider they are insufficient in number to cope with the roughs. There should also be several detectives employed and make themselves thoroughly acquainted with all the gambling dens, houses of ill repute, lodging houses and beer shops in the many back slums abounding the East-end. In conclusion I may add that it is almost impossible for any female to walk along the road from Aldgate to the Bow and Bromley railway station, without being insulted by a pack of hulking ignorant jackanapes.

Yours, &c.,

J. E. WALLER.
26, Raverley-street,
Bromley-by-Bow,
10 Sept.

[Editor's Note: The following short summations of letters to the editor of the Star were published immediately following the above letter from J.E. Waller.]

W. GEARON. - The term "common lodging-house" means a house common to or usable by anybody. It is not intended as a reproachful word.

H. M. HAREWOOD thinks one of the causes of undiscovered crimes in London is the fact that the police are frequently changed from one district to another.

"WORKING MAN" refers to the fact that John Davis had to lose his time to attend the inquest on the Whitechapel victim. He thinks the Treasury should guarantee to indemnify working men for loss of time while giving evidence.

The Whitechapel Atrocities.
To the Editor of the *East London Observer*.

SIR,

As the above lamentable affair is creating vast exciting interest in this end of London, it may not be known to many of your readers how inadequately the streets of the East End are lighted. My professional duties frequently call me out at midnight, and during the early hours of the morning, when the streets are almost entirely deserted save by the guardians of the peace; and how it is possible for them to keep proper guard over life and property under the existing dingy lighting, does not seem difficult to surmise. Under the present system it is impossible to discern objects, even at a near distance. Such sad occurrences as the above should in some way arouse the latent energies of our local Boards in adopting an adequate and scientific system of lighting by means of reflectors and otherwise, and thus lucubrate all courts and turnings likely to afford obscurity. The more reliance we place in the police, the more likely we are to remain unprotected, unless we assist in adopting individual care, and thus help to maintain a social protection. Increase of punishment must necessarily bring about increase of wanton and dastardly crime. In order to remedy this, our moral and intellectual faculties should be strengthened, instead of placing so much reliance upon physical force. I am sure we East Enders can boast that our police protection does not equal that of other parts of London, especially the City and West End, with its military array.

I am, sir, yours obediently,

M. CURSHAM CORNER,
113, Mile End-road, E.

WHITECHAPEL MURDER.
TO THE EDITOR OF *THE ECHO*.

SIR,

Is the treatment the man Davis[11] received on Monday from the Coroner calculated to induce others to offer any evidence they may hold? Remarking that he had lost a day's work, he was told that he would probably lose many more before the inquiry finished. Asking who was to pay for his day, was curtly told the Treasury might do something, but he (the Coroner) had no power. Seeing that a day's wage means so much to this hard-working class, would it not be desirable to let it be known that loss of time in the interests of Justice will be paid for? Another suggestion from Dr. Phillips'[12] evidence yesterday. The throat of the deceased was cut from left to right. Now, from the position of the body, the purpose, presumably, of her visit to the yard, is it not most likely the victim was attacked from the front, in which case, judging from the force of the blow, it would appear to be the work of some left-handed person? Is this point overlooked by the police?

Respectfully yours,

H.E.W.
Sept. 14.

---

[11] John Davis was an elderly resident of 29 Hanbury Street, and the first to discover the body of Annie Chapman on September 8th 1888. He attended the Chapman inquest as a witness.

[12] Dr. George Bagster Phillips (1834-1897) was the police surgeon for H Division. He performed the post-mortem on the body of Annie Chapman.

18 September 1888

POLICE ORGANIZATION.
TO THE EDITOR OF *THE TIMES*.

Sir,

The occurrences in Whitechapel are being made the opportunity for the raising a cry against the metropolitan police. This is on every account to be regretted, for whatever imperfections there may be in the administration of that force a cry by people who know nothing about administration is not a good means whereby to reach its reform. Neither is a cry directed against its chief.

Sir Charles Warren is not to be blamed for those alterations in general management which were initiated, I believe, as long ago as 25 or 30 years before the present time. He has carried out, with some additions of detail, a system that began under Colonel Henderson. That system differs from what preceded it in two particulars chiefly. My opinion, which I have formed from practical experience of police government in a large town during several years, is that both deviations from the old system have impaired the efficiency of the metropolitan force, and that from their nature they could not do otherwise than impair it.

It was formerly the practice to keep a well-behaved policeman - and nearly all policemen are well-behaved - on the same beat, without shifting, for a very long time; and a man was seldom or never removed from his beat without some reason. It is now the practice to shift men sometimes once a month, sometimes at the end of two months, and nearly always at the end of three months. I may be told that there is no rule or order on the subject. I have no means of knowing what the rule, if any, may be, but I know what the practice is, about which any Londoner may satisfy himself by asking any policeman that he may have acquaintance with, or, indeed, any policeman whom he may address civilly. Sir Edward Henderson's other innovation was to separate, far more than had been before, the police on ordinary duty from the detective police in as it were two departments. I do not know the particulars, I only know the heads, of this change; and I strongly suspect, though I cannot prove from facts, what its working has been. The two alterations are based it will be evident to all acquainted with police management on the idea of treating the force as a machine. Many minor details that have arisen under the same idea look like militarism. While I do not want to impute militarism to either the late or the present chief, I am of the belief that what I would prefer to call the mechanical idea has dominated both of them too much.

A policeman who knows his beat - being not merely a beat the duty of which is attending to traffic - is worth three who do not know the beat. This applies to the whole of a city, and it applies with double force to such parts as Whitechapel. A man will know the streets of his beat in a day - or may do so if he chooses; although I have asked my way to a street, naming it, which was part of a man's beat, without his having heard of it. But a man will not, till after a very considerable time, know the people who live in a beat; nor will he know, as an old hand will, every house and its doors and windows. A policeman who has attained thorough knowledge, who knows the people, and is known to them, becomes a kind of referee, especially in the poorer neighbourhoods. Knowledge of him produces confidence in him; and he becomes without his knowing it an embryo detective. He is able to put down street rows with a mere glance when a stranger would be unheeded. I need not enumerate the particulars in which the old policeman is and must be the superior of the stranger. If it be said that he will become too intimate with the population, it is not so; he cannot be too intimate. He may abuse his intimacy, which is another thing. Last year, there was much talk of blackmail in connexion with the Regent-street affair. I believe perhaps one-hundredth part of it. But it would be a more difficult thing for a policeman, known by hundreds of neighbours, to pursue a system of blackmail, such as was imputed, than for a man transferred once a month from one beat to another.

The school of detectives, which the metropolitan police was till recently, is now not in existence. Hence I believe the practical separation of the two departments of the force, a separation that tends to the efficiency of neither.

If I be thought to be giving my unsupported opinion, I have authority, the very highest, for my views; indeed, I think the following two authorities amount to proof. Every one that I know holds that the City police is superior in effectiveness to the metropolitan. The only difference, but the slightest, in their organisation is that the City men are kept without a break on the same beats for a *minimum* period of three years; never being removed during those three years except for misconduct; and often, at the end of the term, being placed on day duty instead of night duty on their old beats. My other authority is Paris, the best policed city in the world. There the *Regents de ville* are never removed. I knew one who had been in the same district for 30 years. He knew every man, woman, and child, dog and cat, door, window, shutter and spout in his six or seven streets; and burglary and disorder were most difficult.

Sir Charles Warren inherited the traditions of his predecessor. It is not, as I said, so much the military as the mechanical conception of the force that is erroneous, though these two ideas may have something in common. The military idea is that soldiers, to be effective, must act as bodies; the policeman must nearly always act alone. Such occasions as occurred last winter in Trafalgar-square are quite exceptional.

Yours truly,

EDMUND LAWRENCE.

AT LAST.
TO THE EDITOR OF *THE TIMES*.

Sir,

The tilled garden is fast producing the crop sown; it is ripening, it affords ample evidence of the nature of the seed, its fruit is just that which such seed, under such tillage, was certain to produce.

However abhorrent in all cruel, filthy detail are the murders to which public attention is now so painfully called, however hard it may be to believe that they could occur in any civilized community, the fact remains that they have been so committed. Whatever the theories to account for them, whether or no the perpetrators may be yet discovered, they have been the means of affording to us a warning it will be at our extreme peril to neglect.

We have far too long been content to know that within a walk of palaces and mansions, where all that money can obtain secures whatever can contribute to make human life one of luxury and ease within homes, from infancy to old age, surrounded with all that can promote civilized life, there have existed tens of thousands of our fellow creatures begotten and reared in an atmosphere of godless brutality, a species of human sewage, the very drainage of the vilest production of ordinary vice, such sewage ever on the increase, and in its increase for ever developing fresh depths of degradation.

What pen can describe, what mental power can realize the nature of the surroundings of child life under these conditions? Begotten amid all that is devoid of the commonest decency, reared in an atmosphere in which blasphemy and obscenity are the ordinary language, where all exists that can familiarize the child with scenes bestial - thus reared in home life, it can scarcely itself walk or talk, when first introduced to outside life, the street life, such as it is, where these tens of thousands have to dwell. It is already so far morally corrupted that it is hard to conceive that this in itself can be in any way repulsive to it, for to it the home has been a school in all things preparatory; it is the seedling thus transplanted to grow to adolescence as it grew from infancy; be the growth that of male or female, so far as any one feature moral of sex obtains, there is no one distinguishing characteristic; as is the boy so is the girl, what the one has witnessed and heard within the home has been objectively and orally familiar to the other. We may choose to ignore the fact, but there is not a shadow of doubt in the minds of those who have made this deprived race a study, that of both sexes it may be said they scarce have passed childhood before they fall into the grosser sins of that adult life which is their daily street example.

We hear much of the sufferings of those who come under what is called the "sweating" system of employment, and we are told that it is the fierce competition in the labour field that has produced it. What about competition in harlotry? What a text has been given us from which we may draw a sermon, which should go home to every Christian heart, in the evidence of that "unfortunate" who desired a bed to be kept for her, for she would go at once to earn the eightpence! If the wages of such sin have fallen so low we have proof afforded us of the competition in this foul market; can human nature find a greater depth of degradation? But, further, where such competition thus exists, can we be surprised that in this bestial life the jealousies which surely will be begotten of it beget murders, outrages of a character such as scarce the most heathen nation could find in its category of crime, and this in the metropolis of a land ever boastful of its Christian creed.

I believe nearly half a million pounds is yearly raised in this country by societies having their head-quarters in London to propagate the Gospel in foreign parts, to support our Established Church system, to send missions to convert the heathen in other lands, to bring the Bible cheaply in all sorts of languages within reach of people of other nationalities; the Non-conformists on their own lines acting in the same spirit. We are raising large sums for a Church Institute to be a rallying-point for Church work; very lately we have had a conference of bishops of the Established Church, at which a large number of the colonial bishops were present and the greatest zeal was shown in regard to the spiritual life and working of the Church Episcopate; and all this within cheap cab hire of that portion of eastern London which for many years has been known to have been in a social condition utterly devoid of the commonest attributes of civilization, so saturated with all that can contribute to heathenize as to be a standing shame to the nation.

We seem to have needed at last some home stroke to awaken us to the fact that we have at our very doors an element of danger threatening consequences which may prove, but too late, that we have suffered, with little attempt to arrest it, the growth of a large and increasing portion of our population to live, move, and have their being under a condition of things tending to the utter subversion of the very commonest principles of civilization; leading to the commission of crimes which hitherto would have been held to have been so abhorrent as to be inconceivable even where all ordinary crime had full sway. I am quite prepared to give all praise to the efforts of the very many excellent, pious, hard-working volunteers of both sexes who for years have quietly and earn-estly devoted themselves to the work of Christian salvage amid this wreckage of our common humanity; they will have their reward where alone they so devotedly seek it. But although they may here and there rescue a few of those wretched beings and bring them into the habits of civil-ized life, the masses to whom they owe their existence, the homes in which they were reared remain untouched; and, such as the homes are, so will from them filter forth into street life the same race of beings, bred and reared in all that can make them ignorant of God, defiant of all law, revellers in the profligacy which taints the scenes where they congregate with crimes which, however repulsive to the ordinary mind, are in their own estimation just the issues of the life they best enjoy.

As far as I can see, the great object of the philanthropist of the day is to create a multitude of institutions, societies &c., as a sort of hospitals in which morally-maimed humanity is to be treated, as if these soul and body poisoned beings were merely under some mental and physical disease, for which we had a Pharmacopoeia with prescriptions for each form of it, treating the disease with educational and religious formulae, but ignoring, as far as they can, the fact that much of it is hereditary, the patients so treated healthy as regards their race, only diseased as judged by the ideas regarding health entertained by those who thus seek their cure.

Just so long as the dwellings of this race continue in their present condition, their whole surroundings a sort of warren of foul alleys garnished with the flaring lamps of the gin shops, and offering to all sorts of lodgers, for all conceivable wicked purposes, every possible accommodation to further brutalize, we shall have still to go on - affecting astonishment that in such a state of things we have outbreaks from time to time of the horrors of the present day.

All strange, Sir, as it may appear to you and the generality of your readers, it is within the range of my belief that one or both these Whitechapel murders may have been committed by female hands. There are details in both cases which fit in well with language for ever used where two of these unfortunates are in violent strife; there is far more jealousy, as is well known, between such women in regard to those with whom they cohabit than is the case with married people where one may suspect the other of sin against the marriage vow.

There are, I have no doubt, plenty of women of this class known for their violent temper, with physical power to commit such a deed. As to the nature of their sex forbidding belief that they could so act, how many of them are altogether unsexed, have no one element in character with female feeling? It is now many years ago; when writing in your columns on these guilt gardens, I had procured for me some specimens of the kind of printed matter circulated among this class. From the nature of much which is now open to readers of a very different class, I can well conjecture what manner of cheap reading is open to the poorest class in the present day. The first of these murders was, I have no doubt, served up after a fashion with every horrible detail exaggerated, and may well have had the suggestive effect to produce others.

I can only hope that "at last" we may awaken to the fact that, quite outside the political arena which seems to absorb all our interest, there are causes at work, close at hand, which undealt with may develop into a form of danger far more serious than any political disturbance. Sewer gas will sometimes explode, but this work of hand can remedy. Where will be found the remedy when this moral sewage attains the full development of which these murders are a mere passing sample?

S.G.O.[13]

---

[13] Reverend Lord Sydney Godolphin Osborne (1834-1889), noted London philanthropist. Wrote many letters to the *Times* as S.G.O.

18 September, 1888

PERIL IN EAST LONDON
TO THE EDITOR OF *THE DAILY TELEGRAPH*

SIR -

The terrible Whitechapel tragedies, with their lurid revelation of the condition of life amongst the East-end poor, emphasise the need of getting more amongst the massed population. We want, it is true, better police protection, and for this I would suggest the use of our idle military for many public police duties. This arrangement would allow of a much larger unmilitary police for patrol and inspection work, at no additional cost.

But the people themselves need to be got at, and got at in their own homes. The homes of the poor should be regularly and frequently visited by level-headed, trained Christian men and women, who, by counsel, sympathy, encouragement, temporal help judiciously administered, action in matters sanitary, and by other good and practical means, might largely purify the moral atmosphere, and keep the unfortunate in life's fray from running into excesses in their despair. This is a kind of work which several of us in East London are endeavouring to carry on, but we get scant sympathy and help from the affluent classes. Our funds are allowed to exhaust themselves, and the work, which sorely needs rapid development, is checked, if not arrested. I employ eight such men and women as those I have described, but with a practically empty exchequer I cannot take a single step forward, whatever may be the urgency. It is well for the peace of mind of many of the prosperous that they are ignorant of the real condition of the poor and also of the sentiments of many of the destitute. Next year Paris celebrates the centenary of her great revolution. My deep conviction is that the French are more than a hundred years ahead of us in revolutionary experience. It needs but for suitable leaders to be forthcoming, and the impoverished multitudes of London will rise as one man. Ten thousand may be driven out of this square or that, but when half-a-million people spring to their feet, there will be another kind of reckoning. Why not deal with the matter whilst there is time? Those of us who are doing our best in East London will most gladly give up our posts to any who can do the very trying work better; but whilst we stand in the breach let us not be forsaken.

Faithfully yours,

W. EVANS HURNDALL,
Minister of Harley-street Chapel, Bow.
16, Cottage-grove, Bow, London, E.,
Sept. 17.

19 September 1888

TO THE EDITOR OF THE *TIMES*.

Sir,

Is it not time that the inquest on Annie Chapman should close, and a verdict of "Wilful Murder against some person or persons unknown" be given?

The question which the jury are soon to determine - viz., how, when, and where the deceased met with her death, and who she was - is virtually solved.

The discovery of the murderer or murderers is the duty of the police, and if it is to be accomplished it is not desirable that the information they obtain should be announced publicly in the newspapers day by day through the medium of the coroner's inquiry.[14]

J.P.

AT LAST.
TO THE EDITOR OF THE *TIMES*.

Sir,

Whitechapel horrors will not be in vain if "at last" the public conscience awakes to consider the life which these horrors reveal. The murders were, it may almost be said, bound to come; generation could not follow generation in lawless intercourse, children could not be familiarized with scenes of degradation, community in crime could not be the bond of society and the end of all be peace.

Some of us who, during many years, have known the life of our neighbours do not think the murders to be the worst fact in our experience, and published evidence now gives material for forming a picture of daily or nightly life such as no one has imagined.

It is for those who, like ourselves, have for years known these things to be ready with practical suggestions, and I would now put some forward as the best outcome of the thought of my wife and myself. Before doing so, it is necessary to remind the public that these criminal haunts are of limited extent. The greater part of Whitechapel is as orderly as any part of London, and the life of most of its inhabitants is more moral than that of many whose vices are hidden by greater wealth.

---

[14] Wynne Baxter (1844-1920) served as coroner for the inquests of Mary Ann Nichols, Annie Chapman and Elizabeth Stride. On average these inquests lasted between four and five days, during which time witnesses would be brought forward to answer questions not only about how the victim was killed, but about who may have been responsible. Some believed Baxter was overstepping his boundaries – that the purpose of an inquest was simply to determine cause of death. He received some criticism in the press for his "overly thorough" inquests, which may explain why subsequent inquests held by Samuel Langham (Catherine Eddowes, lasted two days) and Roderick Macdonald (Mary Jane Kelly, wrapped up in one day) were much shorter by comparison.

Samuel A. Barnett

Within the area of a quarter of a mile most of the evil may be found concentrated, and it ought not to be impossible to deal with it strongly and adequately. We would submit four practical suggestions: -

1. Efficient police supervision. In criminal haunts a license has been allowed which would not be endured in other quarters. Rows, fights, and thefts have been permitted, while the police have only been able to keep the main thoroughfares quiet for the passage of respectable people. The Home Office has never authorized the employment of a sufficient force to keep decent order inside the criminal quarters.

2. Adequate lighting and cleaning. It is no blame to our local authority that the back streets are gloomy and ill-cleaned. A penny rate here produces but a small sum, and the ratepayers are often poor. Without doubt, though, dark passages lend themselves to evil deeds. It would not be unwise, and it certainly would be a humane outlay, if some of the unproductive expenditure of the rich were used to make the streets of the poor as light and as clean as the streets of the City.

3. The removal of the slaughter-houses. At present animals are daily slaughtered in the midst of Whitechapel, the butchers with their blood stains are familiar among the street passengers, and sights are common which tend to brutalize ignorant natures. For the sake of both health and morals the slaughtering should be done outside the town.

4. The control of tenement houses by responsible landlords. At present there is lease under lease, and the acting landlord is probably one who encourages vice to pay his rent. Vice can afford to pay more than honesty, but its profits at last go to landlords. If rich men would come forward and buy up this bad property they might not secure great interest, but they would clear away evil not again to be suffered to accumulate. Such properties have been bought with results morally most satisfactory and economically not unsatisfactory. Some of that which remains might now be bought, some of the worst is at present in the market, and I should be glad, indeed, to hear of purchasers.

Far be it from any one to say that even such radical changes as these would do away with evil. When, however, such changes have been effected it will be more possible to develop character, and one by one lead the people to face their highest. Only personal service, the care of individual by individual, can be powerful to keep down evil, and only the knowledge of God is sufficient to give the individual faith to work and see little result of his work. For men and women who will give such service there is a crying demand.

I am, truly yours,

SAMUEL A. BARNETT[15]
St. Jude's Vicarage, Whitechapel,
Sept. 18.

---

[15] Samuel Augustus Barnett (1844-1913) was a clergyman active in social reform and the erection of model dwellings. He served as the first warden of Toynbee Hall and wrote several books on social issues in the East End.

20 September 1888

THE EAST END ATROCITY
To the Editor of *The Evening News*

Sir -

I am glad you have raised your voice against the senseless abuse of the police. As well blame the murderer or murderers for not having left a good clue. A reward, however, should have been offered ere now by the Government, and the police allowed to earn it. Also it is very doubtful whether the force is really strong enough for its duties; and the gait and bearing of detectives drawn from it must often tell against them. There is, moreover, one fact which should not be lost sight of in connection with the horrible butchery of the last two unfortunate women. Both were homeless. They had not sufficient to pay for a night's lodging, and rather than have recourse to some casual ward or charitable institution they wandered about the streets until they fell into the fangs of some human tiger or tigress. Had they gone to some charitable institution they would probably have been tortured with questions relating to their past. Had they gone to the workhouse for a night's shelter they would have been kept prisoners the following day until they had more than paid with their labour for what they had received. If that is relief, every employer relieves, and his belief does not taint and degrade the recipient. But the employer does not profess to relieve, nor does he tax the ratepayer. A few days ago a poor old soldier (who, it may be supposed, had risked his life over and over again for his country) was brought before a magistrate for having refused to break 12 cwt. of stone. This was the price exacted for his night's shelter. He very naturally refused to submit to this extortion, and his grateful country made him a criminal. Depend upon it, Sir, the Poor Law system is largely responsible not only for the late shocking crimes but for many others.

I am, &c.

ONLOOKER
September 18.

To the Editor of *The Evening News*

Sir -

May I be permitted to add a few lines to those already appearing in your columns with regard to the Whitechapel murders? I do not suppose those in charge of the case would for one moment tolerate the interference or advice of the outside public in the mod of procedure, but if some more feasible theory or suggestion than that hitherto advanced were to be the means of aiding the course of the law, I believe it would not be the first time the community at large were indebted to a private individual for help in unravelling a seemingly complicated and brutal crime. I believe the suggestion put forward by your correspondent of Saturday last, that the same cause may furnish the motive as in that of the Cambridge murderer, to be very probable, and a clue. But I cannot by any means agree with your correspondent (A.W. Hux) as to his theory that searching inquiry in that direction might lead to a possible way in which the deed was carried out. To carry any practical weight, we should have to assume that the murderer also found the other unfortunate victims under similar circumstances, or, supposing the deed to be the work of a wretch who had no hand in the previous crimes, that he had studies the means and methods to such perfection as to utterly mislead the judgement of medical and criminal detective experts, who I believe unhesitatingly describe the three crimes as the work of one hand, or rather one fiend. With regard to supposition that the murdered woman, if in company with the man, being able to give some outcry, how would it be possible, unaware of her danger, no doubt in a perfectly helpless position, in the back yard of a house, without the slightest glimmer of light, to warn her of the terrible end in store? One slash of the deadly instrument carried by the cunning imp from hell, and the victim past all outcry. My opinion is that in the event of any crime, such as that under discussion, all supposed unoccupied houses, tenements, and ruins, such as are to be found where buildings have been pulled down for improvements, and vaults left standing, and where it well known hundreds of outcasts slink away during the night for shelter, should be surprised and all those found therein be called upon to give account of themselves. Supposing the man wanted to be of the vagrant class, sane in all things but that of the fearful desire to shed blood for some real or fancied wrong, what is more probable than that he is in hiding during daylight, and stealing out for two or three hours during the night seeking fresh victims, or, failing that, to procure the means to prolong a terrible existence? For I feel positive that no one would shelter a man who must carry such unmistakable signs of bloodshed upon his person as the one wanted must do.

Yet another theory and I have done. If the crime has been committed by a man, who, after accomplishing his fearful work, there can be only one or two classes of men who would be able to escape detection in the manner that has been done in the present instance, and they are either meat market porters or slaughtermen, who would be able by means of their ordinary trade garb to walk away right under the nose of a policeman without arousing suspicion. I sincerely hope that no one following the above callings will feel unnecessarily hurt at the above suggestion, and, to give them credit, I do not believe they would for a moment hesitate to place information in the hands of the police if they had reason to suspect any of their calling of the crime.

Apologising for troubling you, I am, &c.

E. SWABEY
September 18.

20 September, 1888

SOLDIERS AS POLICEMEN
To the editor of *The Evening News*

Sir -

Will you allow me a small space in your paper with reference to a letter in Friday's *Evening News*, a Valuable Suggestion, signed "B.F." I don't think "B.F." can know very much about a soldier's duties or he would not make such a suggestion. It is not because a soldier is taking a walk of an afternoon that he has nothing to do. It's very probable that that soldier was on duty all the previous night, and very likely the twenty four hours previous, as soldiers that do day guards do twenty four hours before being relieved. I don't mean to say that they are walking sentry all that time, but they have to keep on all their clothes and accoutrements that time, and in many instances where duty is heavy a man has to go on guard, with, what is termed in the army, only two or three nights in bed, that means two or three nights between coming off guard and going on again. I have never done duty in London, but in Dublin I have often gone with only two or three nights in bed, and I should think duty is quite as heavy in London as there, and much more so than in a good many places. Then again there is the patrol duty to do; that means marching about the streets preventing soldiers creating disturbances and running in absentees, &c., that is from about 7 p.m. till midnight. That does not count a turn of duty at all, only a fatigue. If it was a man's turn to go on guard the next day, he would have to go; so I consider a soldier gets plenty of night duty without doing police duty. It could be done by knocking off some of the guards and sentries; but then a soldier should do soldier's duty, and a policeman do policeman's duty. If there are not enough who not get more?

I am, &c.

A Time Expired
September 15.

21 September 1888

A SAFE FOUR PER CENT
TO THE EDITOR OF *THE DAILY TELEGRAPH*

SIR -

In consequence of the serious and dreadful crimes recently committed in the East-end of London, public attention seems at least to have been aroused to the shameful neglect on the part of constituted authorities with regard to the deplorable condition of tens of thousands of citizens, who are housed more after the manner of wild beasts than of human creatures. This apathy is the more astounding because there is abundant evidence to prove that it would pay capitalists and small investors to form companies to erect buildings suitable not simply for the artisan and respectable working classes, who have hitherto been chiefly considered, but for the accommodation particularly of those who are regarded as outcasts and semi-criminal. With the present value of money great difficulty is often experienced in finding a security which gives a really safe guarantee with a dividend of 4 per cent. In the poorer parts of London, on the most selfish grounds, the people who are herded together have a right to appeal for the assistance of the wealthier classes of society in order to have the land cleared of dirty hovels to make room for open spaces and plain, substantial, well-built habitations. If the objection be raised that directly a company came into existence and wished to obtain a particular site for such purpose all the owners of property so-called would at once make demands which would render it impossible to carry out the plans in view, in that case the public would have a right to demand that Parliament should confer upon the proper authorities, or, failing them, then upon private capitalists, under due restrictions, the same powers of acquiring freeholds compulsorily which the railway companies possess and exercise. It is significantly hinted in East London that the blame for the continuance of the present disgraceful state of things in Whitechapel rests upon the Metropolitan Board of Works. The Artisans' Dwellings Acts[16] have been put into partial operation only. To a great extent they have been inoperative, although something has been done in Royal Mint-street and in Goulston-street[17]. In connection with the Goulston-street and Flower and Dean-street[18] scheme, which included two large areas covering 312,000 square feet, the land had been sold at various times for the erection of artisans' dwellings, and accommodation has been given for over 3,500 persons. As compared with its condition of, say, ten years since, Whitechapel has certainly much improved, but the clearance effected has been as

---

[16] Passed in August 1875, the Artisans' Dwelling Act empowered local and municipal authorities to demolish decaying and unsafe structures in their communities, to be replaced with buildings with required amounts of space and sanitation.

[17] The Wentworth Model Dwellings in Goulston Street would become infamous just over a week after this letter was published, as the location where the infamous Goulston Street Graffito was discovered soon after the "double event" of September 30th 1888.

[18] The Rothschild Dwellings in Flower and Dean Street opened in April 1887. They were built by The Four Per Cent Industrial Dwellings Company, formed by Baron Nathan Meyer de Rothschild in 1885.

much due to the extension of the railways and to the activity of private persons as to the authorities representing the rate-payers. Why, it is asked, did the Metropolitan Board of Works abolish the one half of Thrawl-street and of Flower and Dean-street and leave the other half still standing? Why did they stop short in pulling down a portion and not the whole of Wentworth-street? For how long will the Fashion-street scheme remain "under consideration?" As far back as 1877 the Sanitary Officer reported that an area of 19,886 square yards with a population of 2,307, should be rebuilt, and this would have entailed the wholesale demolition of Bell-lane, Coburg-court, Little Montague-street, Bell-court, Artillery-passage, Artillery-lane, Sandys-row, Rosetta-place, Frying-pan-alley, Tripe-yard, Tuson's-court, Fisher's-alley, Cox-square, Paradise-place, Cobb's-court, Middlesex-street, Bull-court, Wentworth-street, New-court, and Short-street. In this area each person has, or had at that time, just a little over eight square yards to live and to breathe in. This Bell-lane scheme and another, the Pearl-street scheme, were scheduled together under the Artisans' and Labourers' Dwellings Act. Five years since Great Pearl-street and Little Pearl-street, Vine-court, Vine-yard, Crown-court, New-court, Wilk-court, Diamond-court, and a portion of Great Eagle-street were condemned, and yet nothing has been done. Eight thousand and odd square yards to house a population of over 1,000, with a death rate of 33.3 per 1,000 as compared with 26.4 per 1,000 for the rest of the district! These broad facts have been staring the authorities in the face for years, and yet nothing has been achieved. In the part of Thrawl-street which still exists the population is of such a class that robberies and scenes of violence are of common occurrence. It is a risk for any respectable person to venture down the turning even in the open day. Thieves, loose women, and bad characters abound, and, although the police are not subject, perhaps, to quite the same dangers as they were a few years ago, there is still reason to believe that a constable will avoid, as far as he can, this part of his beat, unless accompanied by a brother officer. The district, in short, is one of common lodging-houses, and it is believed by some that if the mysteries of their ownership were exposed to the public eye much would be made clear which now puzzles the uninitiated, and which would serve to explain why the march of improvement is so slow in Whitechapel. But nothing short of a Royal Commission would accomplish this object.

Taking the sub-district known as the Commercial-street Division, which is bounded by Baker's-row on the east and Middlesex-street on the west or City side; with Whitechapel-road on the south, there are no less than 146 registered lodging-houses, with a number of beds exceeding 6,000. Of these 1,150 are in Flower and Dean-street alone, and nearly 700 in Dorset-street. Some of the houses contain as few as four beds, whilst others have as many as 350. At a few of these men only are received, and at others women only, but in the majority there are what are known as "double-doss beds." If no other testimony were needed than that tendered before Mr. Wynne Baxter, coroner, there is little room to doubt the truth of the assertion that when these double beds are let no questions are asked, and the door is opened for the most frightful immorality. The prosecution of a registered lodging-house as a disorderly house is never heard of, and the reason is said to be the fact that the lodging-house keeper takes refuge behind the licence granted to him by the police. Under the Act of 1851 the keepers of common lodging-houses have to register their names and addresses, to give the police inspector appointed for the duty free access at all times, to cleanse the premises, to limewash the walls and ceilings twice a year, and to give immediate notice of an outbreak of infectious disease. The police also require that the house should provide 300 cubic feet to every bed, and they demand of the keeper a certificate of character. In addition to these regulations which concern the lodging-house keeper, the local District Board of Works looks carefully after the drainage and sanitary arrangements, for which the owner is responsible. From the observation of independent witnesses there seems no ground for supposing that the inspector delegated by the Commissioner of Police fails in his duty, or that the District Board officials evade theirs; and, so far as outward cleanliness goes, and compliance with the Act in this respect, the common lodging-houses of to-day are, no doubt, superior to those of a few years ago, before the footrule and whitewash brush were brought into constant use. But what the police and the local body appear to disregard is the moral condition of the inmates of these dens. They admit that they are often of a dangerous class, but their argument is that if they are hunted from their known resorts in one quarter of the metropolis they will only overcrowd another. Thus it happens that the common lodging-house keeper is seldom asked to furnish the name of every person who has frequented his house during the preceding day and night, and, further, steps are rarely taken under the "Prevention of Crime Act, 1871," which prescribes that it is an offence to harbour thieves or reputed thieves, or knowingly to permit them to assemble, or to allow the deposit of goods suspected of having been stolen. Indeed, when the police do make a raid and search the place upon complaint being made, the thieves and their confederates contrive with great effrontery to conceal their plunder unseen. The permanence of these hotbeds of crime has become recognised, and yet the police are not in sufficient force to keep them well under supervision. At any rate, they do not seem able to prevent ruffians from wilfully damaging surrounding property, and from injuring people by throwing brickbats from behind hoardings. If the police argument were strictly true that the houses were inhabited by the criminal classes merely, there might be a justification for not wishing to disperse the infecting units all over London, where they would be more difficult to deal with than when congregated, but in the common lodging-house may be met all sorts of people, many of whom owe their degradation to the life which it entails upon them. As a respectable artisan remarked, "A man who goes into a lodging-house is cursed: he can never get out of it." Happily the demoralising effects upon children are not so great since the Vigilance Societies, empowered by the Criminal Amendment Act of 1885, have been busy in removing young people under age from the pernicious atmosphere; but there are far too many boys and girls who are dragged by their parents into the worst of temptations and associations.

It was with a view to ameliorate the condition of the poor that Lord Radstock and other gentlemen, with a purely philanthropic motive, acquired two years since a warehouse of four floors in Commercial-street, at the corner of Wentworth-street, and converted it into a model lodging-house. The success of the venture led to the acquisition of the adjoining premises, and the number of beds now provided is 500. In every respect this lodging-house - the only one of its sort in London - deserves to be imitated. First, its charges are low - viz., 4d for a single bed, or 2s per week; and 6d for a "cabin," or 3s per week. Each bed has two blankets, two sheets, and a quilt; the bedstead is of iron, and a kind of shield at the head affords a certain degree of privacy. The floor space is partitioned into rooms, containing each ten or a dozen beds; whilst in the "cabins" there is only one. A "casual" ward for the reception of newcomers has lately been added, and probationers are transferred thence to floors above. Many of the lodgers are regulars, but some are birds of passage purely. The lavatory, ventilating, and sanitary arrangements are on an enlightened scale. In the common kitchen food may be cooked at the great fire, or obtained at low charges at the bar, a dinner with vegetables for fourpence, or a bowl of soup for a penny. No known bad characters are admitted. Tickets for beds are issued from five p.m. until 12.30 midnight, and after that hour if a man wants to get in he must have a pass. It is by these rules, especially, and by the exclusion of women, that the Victoria Home is so greatly to be preferred to the most modern and "improved" of the lodging-houses which are strictly commercial undertakings. There are establishments which comply with every requisition of the police, where the beds are made regularly at a certain hour, and the kitchen closed from two a.m. to four a.m., and where uncleanliness is not tolerated, but which, nevertheless, perpetuate the old system of the doss-house, with many of its most glaring evils. The success that has attended the Victoria Home will lead, it is said, to the formation of a similar retreat for women, who are indeed badly off. It is in this direction that there is an opening for enterprise. From Lord Radstock's programme bible class teaching and such influences are inseparable; but is there not room even for a business movement which, dispensing with any aim of this special character, shall, first, provide the homeless poor with good lodgings at a minimum cost per night, free of all the abuses which belong to the existing system of profit-making at an exorbitant rate; and, secondly, assure to investors furnishing the necessary capital a fixed dividend of four per cent. per annum?

There is already a company in existence which proceeds on parallel lines to this suggestion. Lord Rothschild is at the head, and the block of buildings owned by it is in Thrawl-street. It cost £40,000 to build 198 tenements and thirty workshops. A single room can be had for 2s 3d per week, but the chief feature is what may be termed "flats," each complete and self-contained. A sitting-room, bed-room, scullery, and lavatory can be rented from 4s to 6s 6d per week; and if two or three bed-rooms be wanted the rates are respectively from 6s 6d to 6s 9d and from 7s 3d to 7s 6d. Whatever the income, the dividend is not to exceed 4 per cent, and, as the first year's working has shown, it is never likely to be less. The plain question is, What reason, apart from the difficulty of purchasing sites at a reasonable outlay, is there to prevent the application of the same principle to the erection of lodging-houses for the lowest classes? It may be pleaded, from the investor's point of view, that 4 per cent. is not enough to be very tempting, but, on the other hand, we must include the consideration of safety, and the difficulty experienced nowadays in associating that with anything over 4 per cent. is known to all capitalists, big and little. The last report of Lord Rothschild's company distinctly says that the directors are convinced "there will always be, after making all due allowances for depreciation and repairs, a safe dividend of 4 per cent. per annum." Here, then, leaving philanthropy apart, is the investor's desideratum - an interest on his capital exceeding what he can now derive from any English railway securities of average standing. I am not sufficiently acquainted with the financial arrangements of this particular concern to be able to say whether the directors went to work in the most economical way. Probably, not being practical men, they did not. I see they paid £7,000 - more than a sixth of their capital - for a freehold site of three-quarters of an acre. This is a heavy deduction at starting. But under the provisions of the Artisans' Dwellings Act, 1875, land might be acquired by the local authority on much better terms, and with subsequent good management 4 per cent. might safely be taken as the minimum yield. Thus, helped by the existing Acts, a well-considered scheme, amply provided with capital, should pay as a mere commercial speculation. Why is not the attempt made?

Yours, &c.,

London, Sept. 19.
RATEPAYER.

LONDON DETECTIVE FORCE.
TO THE EDITOR OF *THE DAILY TELEGRAPH.*

SIR -

I have read with considerable interest your very able article in yesterday's issue, which closes with the expression of most just strictures upon the present inadequacy and incapacity of the detective department.

I think that it may not be inappropriate or irrelevant to state my experiences as a candidate for enrolment on the staff of that department, which will tend to prove, in my humble opinion, that the conditions imposed upon applicants virtually bar the admission of men of superior education, intelligence, and address. I stated in my letter to the then head of the department that I was a man of good attainments, a gentleman by birth, of mature experience, speaking French, and, in addition to knowing London and England well, had travelled all over the Continent and knew Paris perfectly. In my ignorance of the working of the department, I naturally supposed that officers other than those one may readily recognise in the streets, and at our various railway-stations, exhibitions, &c., from their very carriage and the listlessness of their behaviour, were employed, at any rate, for tracing superior criminals of the Benson class - men who must be sought in the haunts of gentlemen (in which the men indicated above would be out of their element and conspicuous at once), and not necessarily at Whitechapel or in the purlieus of Shadwell. I, unfortunately, destroyed the stereotyped form of letter I received in reply to my application, but I can quote from memory. Firstly, I was required to serve for a term of, I think, three years in the police force as an ordinary constable and of course to wear the uniform. This was a *sine qua non!* Secondly, there was a standard of height, one's intelligence was to be gauged by one's inches. A man, say of 5 ft 10 in, regardless of his qualifications, could possibly be enrolled in that select corps; whereas a pigmy of say 5 ft 8 in would have to put up with his *conge* for no other cause. I only instance the height, as I forget the exact standard.

Surely, Sir, reform is needed, and I trust that your influential voice will not be silenced until we see our detective force as effective as that of France and other countries, and not as it at present stands, a laughing stock to all men of ordinary 'cuteness and intelligence.

I enclose my card, and am, Sir, your obedient servant,

Essex-street, W.C.,
Sept. 19.
REFORM.

THE WHITECHAPEL MURDER.
THE EDITOR OF *THE ECHO*.

Sir,

As the question has once or twice arisen, in connection with the last murder in Whitechapel, as to whether an image of the murderer might be found on the retina of the victim[19], perhaps you will allow me to say that, under the circumstances, such a thing would be impossible.

I have gone somewhat deeply into the subject of the effect of light and colour on the retina, and I know, from repeated experiments, that an impression of an object can only be retained on the retina by fixing the eye immovably on one particular point in the object for several seconds; and, even in that case, the object must be strongly illuminated. It is not conceivable, in the terrible struggle which must have taken place, that the woman's eye could have been immovably fixed for any appreciable period; but even if it had been, the retina would require to be chemically treated almost instantly to retain even a faint impression.

I am, Sir, your obedient servant,

Sydney Hodges
19, Pont-street
Sept. 20

---

[19] At the inquest into the death of Annie Chapman the jury foreman asked if the police had photographed her eyes, in the hope that the last image she saw (presumably, the face of her killer) would be preserved in the retina. Dr. Phillips expressed his opinion that such a photograph would serve no useful purpose, and we have no evidence that this was ever done. Walter Dew suggested that such a procedure was performed on Mary Kelly, but again, no evidence survives to support this claim.

22 September 1888

A SAFE FOUR PER CENT
TO THE EDITOR OF *THE DAILY TELEGRAPH*

SIR -

I quite agree with your correspondent, "Ratepayer," that "the erection of lodging-houses for the lowest classes" might prove a profitable and safe investment, that is, that a capitalist might earn 4 per cent. on his outlay with nearly absolute security; but there are difficulties in the way which should be pointed out and which can only be avoided by careful management. I do not refer to the question of sites, for there should be no difficulty here. If ground is not procurable in the ordinary way and on reasonable terms the local authorities, by carrying out the provisions of the Artisans' Dwellings Act - which are very imperious and sweeping - can get rid of existing slums, block by block, and hand over the land thus cleared to any company or individual on any terms they think fit. Whatever reluctance there might be to enforce this act on the part of existing bodies, no such feeling is likely to actuate the London Council which will shortly come into existence, the members of which are more likely to err on the side of new-born zeal than of caution or timidity. Sites will always be procurable in the East-end on fair terms. The difficulties I have in view are those of the after-management, and on that point no existing investigations supply us with quite the guidance we want. The Radstock Victoria Home is a philanthropic effort which involves the separation of the sexes and the infusion of a religious influence. The Rothschild company is for a superior class of lodgers to the lowest, and is not intended, so far as I can make out, for the wandering outcasts who might manage to pay their 4d, 6d, or 1s a night for shelter and a bed, but who could not afford to take a room for a week, and who would also certainly be repelled by any attempts at inquisitorial supervision or well-meant lectures on the error of their ways. Both of these undertakings may pay, while others, looking for support to a different class of inmates, might not. The main question, it appears to me, to be decided is the nature and extent of the restrictions to be enforced - on that will depend the measure of success. With all their dirt, noisome associations, and relatively high charges the low lodging-houses which it is sought to clear out of the way suit those who frequent them, because they impose no check whatever and ask no questions beyond the night's rent. Any man or woman, together or separate, may "claim kindred there, and have their claims allowed" if they can pay their footing. As they come, so they go, unvexed by supervision of any kind. They may be virtuous poor, or roving beggars, or criminals laden with "swag" and preparing for another "plant." To multitudes in such a city as London these houses are a convenience and a necessity. But the improved low lodging-house which is to supplant them must be better than these, and in order to do any good its conductors must begin with restrictions. It must be something else than a brothel; some check would have to be put on the indiscriminate intercourse of the sexes; cleanliness would need to be enforced; and the desperate criminal be excluded, if possible, altogether. Unless, in fact, the company as well as the building be purified we may as well leave the present festering dens alone. Now the first difficulty, I apprehend, will be to draw the line of distinction clearly between the vicious and the casual poor. The former are not wanted in the improved lodging-house - the latter are, and plenty of them, too, if the scheme is to pay. It will not do to limit the admission to one sex, or to prevent couples from hiring a room for the night - this would often mean the exclusion of deserving persons who are temporarily in trouble, and whom it is desirable to keep free of the demoralising associations of the low lodging-house. Here, then, is the dilemma - you must make the house attractive enough to draw a constant influx of inmates from the inferior "dens," and yet you must shut out an entire class, whose contributions go far to make the existing houses so profitable a source of income. The difficulty, however, is very far from insuperable. It is entirely a question of management, and the right men can, I have no doubt, be found with experience of the kind of work required. It is certain that could they feel sure of escaping debasing associates and associations the very poor would in all cases prefer the improved lodging-house; and it is also clear that if in course of time the virtuous and the vicious elements could be kept entirely separate the duties of the police would be much facilitated, as the habitat of the latter would be confined within narrower limits. Allowing, then, that the primary obstacle I have mentioned is surmounted, I see no reason why a scheme to establish lodging-houses for the lowest class of inmates on a strictly business basis should not be a complete success - at once a boon to the poor creatures concerned and a safe investment to shareholders who may provide the capital. Rents on even cheaper terms than those exacted at the "dens" should yield a large profit. There need be no bad debts; the outgoings need be only small after a start is fairly effected, for we do not want the professional promoter with his charges and commissions. I see more than 4 per cent. in it, but it is well to be moderate, and one need not excite too high expectations at first. One element of success I should add, and that is the multiplication of the improved lodging-houses. They should be, if possible, numerous enough to form a feature in more than one locality, to attract notice, and to provoke imitation. The West-end needs them as well as the East, and the South, perhaps, more than either.

I am, Sir,

A PRACTICAL PHILANTHROPIST
London, Sept. 20.

TO THE EDITOR OF *THE DAILY TELEGRAPH*

SIR -

Your correspondent, "A Ratepayer," has raised a very large and complex question when he virtually demands that all slums shall be swept out of the Metropolis. He, moreover, suggests that this noble work could be accomplished by the capitalist who is content with a "Safe four per cent." for his money. In the discussion of the difficulties which beset the road of improvement in this direction I notice that a good deal of the responsibility for inaction, particularly in Whitechapel, is thrown upon that moribund body, the Metropolitan Board of Works. In the whole of London that authority has provided accommodation for 35,000 persons of the labouring class, under the Artisans' Dwellings Acts. This total may seem a large one, but taking into consideration the magnitude of the work accomplished by other agencies the effort of the Metropolitan Board of Works appears miserably small. In the face of the urgent representations placed before them the Board have, indeed, displayed great apathy. Their powers under the amended Acts are said to be sufficiently strong, and their resources fully adequate to the discharge of the duty entrusted to them by the Legislature, but the secret of their inertness in many instances has been the fear which the Board have had of the ratepayers. To put the Artisans' Dwellings Acts into operation has been a costly proceeding, and the Board has been reluctant to ask the ratepayers for the funds. That is the root of the difficulty. Thus, it is calculated that the Board have never been in a position to lease freeholds suitable for artisan dwellings under 6d per foot ground rent, which in most cases would represent the market value of the land. But it has been contended that dwellings to be let at rents within the reach of the working-man's pocket cannot be saddled with a higher ground rent than 2d or 2½d per foot. The Board have had to dispose of sites on those terms at Whitechapel and elsewhere. The difference between the price which they paid for the land, under the award of the Government arbitrator, and the value at which they have been obliged to sell, has been equivalent to the loss which the ratepayers have had to meet. There is no wonder that the operation has been unpopular, and that the Board has been careful to reduce this head of expenditure to its minimum. If the public really desire that the hotbeds of disease and crime such as exist, to the danger of the State, not alone in Whitechapel but in other parts of London, shall be cleared away, and their outcast population provided with better quarters, they must be prepared to meet the outlay in one form or another. It is not now a question of helping the respectable working classes. For them, at the present time, there is to be had in many districts a great variety of accommodation; indeed, in the last report of the Metropolitan Association for Improving the Dwellings of the Industrial Classes, it is stated that the directors did not propose to erect more dwellings, on the ground that a very considerable number built by other companies were unoccupied. Quite ten millions of money, it is estimated, are invested in this class of property. A return compiled three years ago then showed that 60 private individuals, 132 chartered associations and companies, 11 corporations and parochial authorities, and 51 builders and contractors had embarked in the business. These figures have, since 1885, been largely increased. Upon the experience of the three leading companies - the Artisans', Labourers', and General Dwellings, the Metropolitan Association, and the Improved Industrial Dwellings Company - it is possible to earn even more than five per cent. But the classes provided for do not belong to the lowest orders. It is open to question even whether the East-end Dwelling Company, which is satisfied with four per cent., and lets single rooms at as low as 1s 8d per week rent, caters for the semi-criminal. For the pauperised, shiftless, and outcast population of London nothing has been done. They have been left to sink lower and lower in the scale of civilisation, to wander from common lodging-house to lodging-house, to live low and vicious lives, surrounded by whitewashed wretchedness. Whitewash often conceals dirt. Hearthstoning is not a cleansing process. Neither whitewash nor hearthstoning render the rotting tenements, huddled together in close courts, and denied air and sunshine, fit habitations for men and women, albeit the police and the district surveyor are satisfied with the cubic measurement of the houses. The problem stated by "A Ratepayer," then, is this: "Can we get rid of these eyesores and these centres of disease and crime, and, if so, by what means?"

If there had been a way of solving this problem surely it would have been done. There has been at least one attempt to do it. It was in 1850 that the Metropolitan Association, whose secretary, Mr. Charles Gatliff, was the pioneer in the work of the better housing of the poor, put up in Spitalfields a building of four floors, providing 234 separate sleeping compartments, 8 ft by 4 ft 6 in, each with a locker and half a window. The tenants received were single men, and they paid 3s a week, which charge included the use of a coffee-room 45 ft by 35 ft, kitchen 46 ft by 21 ft 9 in, lecture room 35 ft by 21 ft 9 in, and reading room 25 ft by 21 ft 9 in. There were also a cook's-shop and bar, with baths and lavatories. The total cost was a little over £13,000, but after eighteen years' trial the whole place was converted into dwellings for families, the single men never having fully occupied the beds. In fact, the average annual return did not exceed 1 per cent. upon the outlay. It appears that the cause of failure was the surveillance which was exercised, and which, at that time, labouring men resented. In many respects the attractions offered to them resembled those of the Victoria Home, now flourishing in Commercial-street, where quite as much supervision is enforced. Too much importance must, therefore, not be attached to the want of success which was experienced twenty years ago, for since then the habitual frequenters of the common lodging-houses have grown accustomed to having their privacy intruded upon by unexpected visits of the police, and the rules which the deputy has to see observed are somewhat stringent.

From the purely commercial standpoint, the main point to be considered is whether a company could afford to acquire sites, either leasehold or freehold, and build upon them lodging-houses of a superior type to the majority of those which survive in Spitalfields and Whitechapel. The plain answer to this question appears to me to be simply this: That if the present owners contrive to maintain such houses at a profit, then the capitalist, with a fresh start, could at least do the same, and charge no higher rent. That the common lodging-house of the ordinary kind yields no more than 4 per cent. is by no means certain; the probability is that the profit is very much more. But what the net profit would be is a matter for estimate. There are no data to guide a comparison. None of the dwellings which are now paying 4 or 5 per cent. stand in the same category exactly, nor will they serve the same purpose. Rooms at so much per week rental are not what the semi-criminal classes require; and if they wished to obtain them they could not. Objection may be taken to perpetuating the barrack system, the great kitchen, and other features of the common lodging-house. Yet it is the mode of living with which the lowest orders are familiar; and it is idle to expect that they will quickly adopt other habits. If you clear away the worst of the common lodging-houses, of which the slums are chiefly composed, the law says that you must supply house room for the inmates. It may be hoped that the more respectable will find their way into rooms of their own, obtainable at low rents. For the rest and refuse population some other kind of accommodation is needed. If capital cannot furnish it, and I believe it can, then capital and philanthropy should jointly undertake the work. Excuse for further delay there is none, and it will be a disgrace if the work be left unaccomplished until the County Councillors and the successors of the members of the Metropolitan Board of Works are called upon to use their new brooms.

Yours, &c.,

AN INQUIRER.
London, Sept. 20.

THE METROPOLITAN POLICE
TO THE EDITOR OF *THE DAILY TELEGRAPH*

SIR -

Some time ago, when the incapacity of a Royal Engineer as chief of the metropolitan police[20] had been amply demonstrated, a vacancy occurred, and it was generally supposed that there would be an efficient reorganisation of the leading personnel of the force. As a retired military officer taking interest in civil matters, I applied for a subordinate office. By some mistake it was supposed that I sought the post of Chief Commissioner, and this gave me the opportunity of explaining the views held, as I believe, by a large portion of the public, that the Chief Commissioner should not be a soldier, but a sharp civilian, with a knowledge of criminal law and experience of criminal classes. But the powers that be thought differently, and the mistake was made of appointing another soldier and Royal Engineer, to boot. The continuance of a drilled and disciplined military body in disguise is the natural result. Is it what is wanted in London?

No doubt London mobs are formidable, but it is their nature to be good tempered unless worried by the police. When the police had, by a series of blunders, angered the mob in Trafalgar-square, and made it dangerous, who cleared the ground and dispersed the irritated people? Was it not the cavalry of the guard? Then, so long as we have such cavalry in London, we don't want a military police. The classes hate the police, and like soldiers and sailors. They will cheer a soldier doing police duty, and hiss a policeman. The conscious power of drilled numbers seems to have inspired the force with a growing desire to irritate and then punish civilians for "resisting the police." No one doubts the strength of brute force, and that a few hundred armed and drilled men can disperse a mob. But when it comes to a game of skill the police are useless - the brains are all on the other side; and we have at present an instance of one cunning criminal successfully defying for at least a month the collective intelligence of 12,000 policemen, with a Royal Engineer at their head.

What is wanted is less drill and more intelligence, less brute force and more brains. A sort of staff college for the police would soon produce the article required. The calling of a detective will seem

---

[20] A reference to Sir Charles Warren, who was an officer in the British Royal Engineers.

to many persons a detestable one. But in the interests of society at large it is necessary that we should have an efficient corps of criminal hunters.

Your obedient servant,

CIVIS
King's-road, Brighton, Sept. 19

AT LAST
TO THE EDITOR OF *THE TIMES*.

Sir,

Referring to the fourth paragraph of Mr. Barnett's letter[21], published in *The Times* of to-day, and the comments thereon in your leading article, allow me to suggest that a practical solution of the control of tenement houses, at present dedicated to vice and crime, by a responsible landlord, would be found were a limited liability company formed for the purpose of buying up and improving such property as Mr. Barnett describes.

This need not be a matter of much difficulty if men of means who take an interest in the welfare of this great city could be induced to co-operate to form such a company, and my individual opinion is that from the improvement that would be wrought in the neighbourhood where such property was bought up, and its character transformed, a very good pecuniary result might be looked for.

Let a number of rich philanthropic gentlemen decide to underwrite the necessary capital, and then float such a company, taking up the shares not subscribed for by the public, and giving their services as directors gratuitously until a 5 per cent dividend could be paid. The operations of such a company might be extended to any extent by obtaining mortgages on the property acquired, or issuing debentures against it.

There are doubtless many men in London who would subscribe largely, by the actual gift of money, were any well considered scheme set on foot to abolish these rookeries of vice. I am not asking so much of them; let them simply invest the money in a company that would have every prospect not only of being self-supporting, but of paying a good dividend.

Yours faithfully,

GAMMA.
International Club, Sept. 19.

---

[21] Revered Samuel A. Barnett's letter was published in the *Times* on September 19th 1888, and is reprinted in this book.

STORIES OF CRIME.
TO THE EDITOR OF *THE TIMES*.

Sir,

It has long been the custom for provincial newspapers to publish serial stories in their weekly issues, generally of a more or less sensational character. These stories of late have in many instances taken the form of the lives and actions, most highly exaggerated, of notorious criminals - *e.g.*, "A Race to Ruin; or, the History of William Palmer the Poisoner," "Charles Peace, the King of Criminals," "Dick Turpin, the Prince of Highwaymen," "Pritchard, the Poisoner of Glasgow."

It is only those whose duties cause them to be mixed up with the lower and criminal classes who can really appreciate how great is the evil influencing of this pernicious literature and how eagerly it is sought after.

Not long since some lads, children of honest parents, committed two burglaries; it was clearly shown by their own confession that they had been instigated to do so by reading "Dick Turpin, the Prince of Highwaymen." A youth of about 18, of miserable physical power, when arrested for larceny bit the constable's thumb and said, "I am as game as Charlie Peace, and I will do as much as him before I die." The history of the "King of Criminals" was being published at the time by one of the local papers. Many similar instances could be furnished.

It is, to my mind, quite possible that the Whitechapel murders may be the fruit of some pernicious seed falling upon a morbid and degraded mind.

Although the law is powerless to repress such publications, they might be brought into disrepute and contempt if the attention of the better class of newspapers and the respectable portion of the community was drawn to this evil and its results by your powerful aid.

Your obedient servant,

K.T.A.

TO THE EDITORS OF *THE LANCET*.

Sirs:--

Possibly before your next issue the theories as to the sanity or insanity of the perpetrator of perpetrators of the Whitechapel murders will be set at rest. I venture to trespass on your valuable space to express most emphatically my opinion that these murders were committed by some person or persons who were perfectly sane. Some years ago I was consulted as to the state of mind of one

Frederick Hunt. This man had murdered his wife and two children. It was proved beyond doubt that the prisoner was on terms of the greatest affection with the victims of his impulse He had nothing to gain by the act, and he had at the time a balance of over £150 at his bankers. After the deed was done, he attempted suicide by placing his head on the line of a railway, from which position he was rescued by a guard and immediately given up into the hands of the police. He made no attempt to escape, or to conceal his crime, the details of which he [illegible] described to the authorities. I had several interviews with him in Horsemonger-lane Gaol, and I had no doubt whatever from symptoms, which it would take too long here to enumerate, that the man was a victim of a homicidal impulse. He was tried before Justice [illegible] at the Croydon Assizes, and found not guilty by the jury, on the ground of insanity. Subsequently, Dr. Orange, of the Broadmoor Asylum, confirmed my diagnosis in a paper he communicated to a medical contemporary on criminal responsibility, in which Hunt's case was described at length.

Now as to the Whitechapel murderer. He was most probably a stranger to his victim, and not bound to her by ties of blood as was the criminal Hunt. In all probability he was a poor man. The fact that the jewellery he stole from the woman was false goes for nothing. It is not unlikely that at such a time even an expert would be nice as to these distinctions. The deed of the first Whitechapel murderer was complicated by a subsequent mutilation of the body of his victim which was of so barbarous a nature as to make one of our own profession shrink from describing it. And this statement would also apply to the second murderer. It is well known to experts in insanity that although the anticipation of the deed may be long cherished, yet the act itself is sudden, unexpected, uncomplicated by any subsequent mutilation, or attempt to conceal the act, and very frequently followed by some suicidal attempt. As far as we have yet heard, there have been no suicides in Whitechapel lately. And any reader of the daily papers must be well aware how common is this tendency when an insane person has committed a murder.

From these data, imperfect as they must necessarily be, I have no hesitation in giving an opinion that should the Whitechapel murderer or murderers be apprehended, it will be proved that he or they are of perfectly sound mind, that at the time the act was committed they were evidently in want of money, which they imagined could be obtained from the sale of their victims jewellery, and that if there be any necessity to explain away the mutilation of the corpses, it will be found in the fact that such mutilation was effected with a view to the concealment of the crime, which there is every reason to believe was committed before the murders took place.

I am, Sirs, your obedient servant,

HENRY SUTHERLAND, M.D.
Richmond-terrace,
Sept, 16th 1888.

TO THE EDITORS OF *THE LANCET*.

Sirs,

Being more or less responsible for the original opinion that the individual who committed the wholesale slaughter in Whitechapel was a lunatic, I beg to trouble you with this communication.

In the interview I had with the officials at Whitehall-place I gathered that this was also their theory. In your issue of the 15th inst. you say, "The theory that the succession of murders which have lately been committed in Whitechapel are the work of a lunatic appears to us to be by no means at present well establish." Of course, it is impossible to give a positiveness to the theory unless some more evidence can be established; nevertheless, to my mind the case appears tolerably conclusive. the horrible and revolting details, as stated in the public press, are themselves evidence, not of crimes committed by a responsible individual, but by a fiendish madman. You go on to add that "homicidal mania is generally characterised by one single and fatal act." Having had extensive experience incases of homicidal insanity, and having been retained in the chief cases during the last twenty years, I speak as an authority on this part of the subject. I cannot agree with your statement. I will give one case which recalls itself to my recollection. A gentleman entered my consulting-room. he took his seat, and, on asking what it was he complained of, replied, "I have a desire to kill everyone I meet." I then asked him for further illustration of his meaning. He then said: "As I walk along the street, I say to myself as I pass anyone, 'I should like to kill you'; I don't know why at all." Upon my further pressing him on the matter, he jumped up and attempted to seize a weapon from his pocket, and to give me a further, more practicable, and more realistic illustration. I was enabled, however, to frustrate him in this desire. Another case in which I was retained as expert was that of Mr. Richardson, who committed murder at Ramsgate (his homicidal tendency was not confined to one individual) and was tried at Maidstone this year; and there are many others that I could mention. Homicidal lunatics are cunning, deceptive, plausible, and on the surface, to all outward appearances, sane; but there is contained within their innermost nature a dangerous lurking after blood, which, though at times latent, will develop when the opportunity arises. That the murderer of the victims in Whitechapel will prove to be such an individual is the belief of your obedient servant

L. FORBES WINSLOW,
M.B., LL.M.Camb, D.C.L. Oxon.
Wimpole-street, W.,
Sept. 19th, 1888

24 September 1888

BLOOD MONEY TO WHITECHAPEL.
TO THE EDITOR OF *THE STAR.*

SIR,

Will you allow me to make a comment on the success of the Whitechapel murderer in calling attention for a moment to the social question? Less than a year ago the West-end press, headed by the *St. James's Gazette*, the *Times*, and the *Saturday Review*, were literally clamoring for the blood of the people -- hounding on Sir Charles Warren to thrash and muzzle the scum who dared to complain that they were starving -- heaping insult and reckless calumny on those who interceded for the victims -- applauding to the skies the open class bias of those magistrates and judges who zealously did their very worst in the criminal proceedings which followed -- behaving, in short as the proprietary class always does behave when the workers throw it into a frenzy of terror by venturing to show their teeth. Quite lost on these journals and their patrons were indignant remonstrances, argument, speeches, and sacrifices, appeals to history, philosophy, biology, economics, and statistics; references to the reports of inspectors, registrar generals, city missionaries, Parliamentary commissions, and newspapers; collections of evidence by the five senses at every turn; and house-to-house investigations into the condition of the unemployed, all unanswered and unanswerable, and all pointing the same way. The *Saturday Review* was still frankly for hanging the appellants; and the *Times* denounced them as "pests of society." This was still the tone of the class Press as lately as the strike of the Bryant and May girls. Now all is changed. Private enterprise has succeeded where Socialism failed. Whilst we conventional Social Democrats were wasting our time on education, agitation, and organisation, some independent genius has taken the matter in hand, and by simply murdering and disembowelling four women, converted the proprietary press to an inept sort of communism. The moral is a pretty one, and the Insurrectionists, the Dynamitards, the Invincibles, and the extreme left of the Anarchist party will not be slow to draw it. "Humanity, political science, economics, and religion," they will say, "are all rot; the one argument that touches your lady and gentleman is the knife." That is so pleasant for the party of Hope and Perseverance in their toughening struggle with the party of Desperation and Death!

However, these things have to be faced. If the line to be taken is that suggested by the converted West-end papers -- if the people are still to yield up their wealth to the Clanricarde class, and get what they can back as charity through Lady Bountiful, then the policy for the people is plainly a policy of terror. Every gaol blown up, every window broken, every shop looted, every corpse found disembowelled, means another ten pound note for "ransom." The riots of 1886 brought in £78,000 and a People's Palace; it remains to be seen how much these murders may prove worth to the East-end in *panem et circenses*. Indeed, if the habits of duchesses only admitted of their being decoyed into Whitechapel back-yards, a single experiment in slaughterhouse anatomy on an aristocratic

George Bernard Shaw

victim might fetch in a round half million and save the necessity of sacrificing four women of the people. Such is the stark-naked reality of these abominable bastard Utopias of genteel charity, in which the poor are first to be robbed and then pauperised by way of compensation, in order that the rich man may combine the idle luxury of the protected thief with the unctuous self-satisfaction of the pious philanthropist.

The proper way to recover the rents of London for the people of London is not by charity, which is one of the worst curses of poverty, but by the municipal rate collector, who will no doubt make it sufficiently clear to the monopolists of ground value that he is not merely taking round the hat, and that the State is ready to enforce his demand, if need be. And the money thus obtained must be used by the municipality as the capital of productive industries for the better employment of the poor. I submit that this is at least a less disgusting and immoral method of relieving the East-end than the gust of bazaars and blood money which has suggested itself from the West-end point of view.

Yours, &c.,

G. BERNARD SHAW[22]

A SAFE FOUR PER CENT.
TO THE EDITOR OF *THE DAILY TELEGRAPH*

SIR -

I was much interested in reading the letter signed "Ratepayer," in your impression of to-day, having special reference to the existing sad state of things in common lodging-houses. The excellent scheme of Lord Radstock has been productive of an immense amount of good both morally and physically, and so thoroughly am I impressed with the beneficial results emanating therefrom that I am now preparing an establishment in North-East London upon a similar basis. As a close observer of the London masses for upwards of 30 years I have a strong conviction, amounting to absolute certainty, that a very large per centage of crime and misery is due to the total absence and disregard of the ordinary requirements of domestic life. Although I am perfectly willing to admit - indeed, it should be a *sine qua non*, that the improved establishment should not be treated simply and solely in a commercial point of view, and thereby obtain the somewhat questionable character of "a paying concern," I am equally as firm in insisting that, after all legitimate expenses, there should be a margin of profit of not more than 4 per cent. As stated by "Ratepayer," Lord Radstock's establishment is the only one that I know of where the lodger, be he permanent or casual, can

---

[22] George Bernard Shaw (1856-1950), noted Irish playwright and avowed Socialist. "Blood Money to Whitechapel" is by far the most famous letter to the editor published during the Whitechapel murders, and has been reprinted widely in the Ripper literature.

obtain plain and wholesome refreshment on the premises with all necessary appliances. It is not only surprising but perfectly alarming that the sanitary arrangements of the common lodging houses should be deemed sufficient, with due regard to health and morals, by the authorities whose duty it is to supervise such places. A supply of hot and cold water, together with approved ventilation, should be the rule and not the exception as it is now.

As to the subject which has, through recent deplorable occurrences, invited comment, can nothing be done whereby the model lodging-house may be regarded as an auxiliary in the cause of justice instead of being too often a hindrance? I think it can, and, inter alia, I should require the names, &c., of all persons applying for accommodation, and have the particulars registered in a book kept for the purpose *de nocte per noctem*. Then why could not the police attend daily and inspect this book, from which they might obtain information of paramount importance? These and other precautions of an equally salutary character are universally adopted in France, Italy, Austria, Germany, and other countries. I am well aware that a system of espionage is abhorrent to Englishmen generally; but the time clearly has arrived when false delicacy and puerile sentiment must sink into insignificance where the safety, honour, and welfare of the community at large are concerned.

Yours obediently,

E. BANNISTER
85, Whitecross-street, E.C.,
Sept. 21.

TO THE EDITOR OF *THE DAILY TELEGRAPH*

SIR

Your admirable leader on "Dark Annie"[23] will doubtless draw attention to a subject that has been dormant almost ever since the then Mr. Cross, Home Secretary, brought in a bill for artisans' dwellings in London. I have often wondered how this question has been allowed to slumber. I am sure if the intelligent, industrious artisans and labourers of this great metropolis had made this a burning question these miserable dens in which they dwell would have been demolished years ago, and the vampires and their deputies who fatten on the weekly rents extracted from them would have disappeared along with them. Instead of Trafalgar-square demonstrations and vestry squabbles in which the most blatant and interested parties join to oust the present vestrymen, all hands should concentrate their energies on this most important question, affecting as it does the prosperity, health, and morals of the industrious classes; they should incessantly importune their M.P.'s and the Government and obtain what they want, and thus give tens of thousands employment. This subject is of paramount importance, and I hope that you will not lay down your pen and that

---

[23] Nickname for Annie Chapman.

others will also take the matter up and prosecute it to a successful issue.

Yours, &c.,

A METROPOLITAN REGISTRAR
OF BIRTHS AND DEATHS
London, Sept. 22.

26 September 1888

THE WHITECHAPEL MURDERS
TO THE EDITOR OF *THE TIMES*

Sir,

I have noticed no remark about Dr. Phillips withholding the description of the wounds.

By the Statute de Coronatore, the coroner is bound to inquire the nature, character, and size of every wound on a dead body and to enter the same on the roll.

Originally this was done *super visum corporis*, and the necessity of viewing the corpse thus arises, for it is the coroner's duty to explain the effect of the wounds and any appearances there may be. This is also a reason why the inquest should be commenced as soon as possible before any marks can be effaced, and even before it is moved.

In this case, had Dr. Phillips's evidence been given at once, as it ought to have been, and as I should have insisted, I think "Leather Apron" should not have been arrested. The criminal is probably a person making research from motives of science or curiosity, and not a drunken loafer. If the body had not been washed, and it is a contempt of the coroner's court to do so, there would probably have appeared on the body some finger mark, which would have been very useful.

The object of the inquest is to preserve the evidences of a crime, if any. Until some person is charged, justices of the peace cannot act. Their function is to say whether a prima facie case has been made against the prisoner. A prisoner may not be caught until the evidences of death have disappeared. It is, then, the duty of the coroner to register all the marks which there may be in case of death.

In Perryman's case, which depended upon the marks and bruises, I consider that the coroner did not take down the marks correctly, as proved by medical witnesses afterwards; and though I convinced Mr. Justice Stephen that there was some doubt in the case, causing Perryman to be respited during Her Majesty's pleasure and his execution commuted to imprisonment, I consider that had all the marks been examined soon after death, there must have been found hand marks on the top of the head if his mother were murdered, and none if, as I contended, she committed suicide. At the first inquest these marks would have been visible; at the trial before the Judge they would have been lost in post mortem discoloration. I did not come into the case until after condemnation and judgement. There was no evidence as to the marks on the top of the head.

Yours &c.

Rowland Addams Williams
Late deputy coroner for Crickhowell, Breconshire.
London, Sept. 22.

26 September, 1888

A SAFE FOUR PER CENT.
TO THE EDITOR OF *THE DAILY TELEGRAPH*.

SIR -

I have read with considerable interest the letter of a "Ratepayer" under the above heading, and feel thankful that the subject of the housing of our London poor has been brought forward in so powerful a way in your columns. I can only hope the matter will not be allowed to rest here, but that some *action* will follow, for, indeed, some of us are weary of delay. Five years since I sent a memorial to the District Board of Works touching the "Pearl-street area" referred to by your correspondent, and which forms part of this parish, by way of following up a previous effort to get rid of so foul a spot. But in spite of these attempts and of repeated condemnation on the part of the authorities it exists to-day in all its terrible reality and abounding sin. A large number of so-called "Furnished Rooms" are here let out at 10d a day, introducing into our midst a terrible class, to the annoyance of many who, though poor, desire to be respectable. The sanitary arrangements of the place could not well be worse, no wonder, therefore, that the infant mortality is so great. Some years since a late medical officer of health in the Whitechapel district directed the attention of the Board of Works to the death-rate of this particular area. I quote the following from his report, "In the area known as the Great Pearl-street property, comprising 8,650 square yards, the courts and alleys are of a very unhealthy nature, and here the death-rate per annum is 33 3-10ths per 1,000, while for the whole district the death-rate was only 26 4-10ths per 1,000. The latter rate is serious enough, as will be perceived from the fact that there are parishes in London where the death-rate is only 16 or 17 per 1,000." A medical officer of the Whitechapel Union wrote, as far back as July, 1877: "I think I can assert most positively that diseases of a low type, and especially scrofula and mesenteric disease among children, prevail, and always have prevailed, to a larger extent than in any other part of my medical district in Great and Little Pearl-street."

As a plague spot, therefore, apart from any other consideration, this area should be dealt with. But I venture to hope, for the sake of those who cannot help themselves in the matter, some better house accommodation will here soon be found. That it would be remunerative there can be no question. The poor need to live near their work, and for this end they put up with much inconvenience, but they would gladly exchange their present abodes for more comfortable quarters, especially if these could be had at a less exorbitant rent than that they have now to pay. As public attention has again been called to the state of things in this parish, I cannot but express the hope that something may soon be done to help our present distressed condition.

Yours, &c.

J. S. WHICHELOW,
Vicar of St. Stephen, Spitalfields.
St. Stephen's Vicarage, Sept. 25.

TO THE EDITOR OF *THE DAILY TELEGRAPH*.

SIR -

The lurid light which recent events have cast on the inner life of the great London "residuum" should not be allowed to die down without some good coming, if possible, out of the filthy exposures. We are, probably, all agreed that the very first step necessary to be taken, if we would try to raise some of our humbler fellow-creatures to the level of humanity, is to render it possible for them to live above the level of the brutes. It will be generally admitted, too, that one of the earliest requirements of civilisation, in its most unfledged condition, is a certain degree of privacy in sleeping arrangements. Without this the most elementary decency is out of the question. For its own sake, to put the matter on no higher ground, Society is bound to do its best to place this modicum of respectability within the reach of all, since the degradation bred of hopeless bestiality is a perpetual peril to the State, both physically, socially, and politically. From this point of view, then, since it is of pressing importance to bring as many waifs and strays as possible within the reach of humanising influences, it seems desirable not to aim at too great things at first, but to be content with endeavouring to provide, at a practicable rent, and for all comers (no questions being asked as to how the money is earned which pays for the nightly "doss"), sleeping accommodation such as they have been used to in the common lodging-houses, but differing from it *toto culo* in the fact of each sleeper having a separate compartment, closed by a door locking inside, but openable by a master-key, like the separate chambers at public baths. Very little more space would be required for this arrangement, since the compartments would be open at the top, the partitions (of double match-boarding) being about 8 ft. or 9 ft. high. If desired, the spaces might be roofed over with galvanised wire-netting, to prevent intercommunication. Such an "aviary" would not be very costly to construct, and its superior comfort, as compared with the common dormitory of the lodging-house, might be trusted to attract customers. Moreover, were a "model lodging" started on these lines and proved workable public opinion would not long tolerate the continuance of the present unsatisfactory system, and the existing places would have to be remodelled, with the best results to public decency.

I am, Sir, yours, &c.,

FREDK. J. MONEY, M.D.
10½, Ironmonger-lane, E.C., Sept. 25.

27 September 1888

A SAFE FOUR PER CENT
TO THE EDITOR OF *THE DAILY TELEGRAPH*

SIR -

Should the correspondence now appearing in your columns under the above heading prove the means of initiating a movement for improving the condition of the dwellings of the poorest of the poor in our large cities and towns, by inducing capitalists and investors to turn their attention to the undoubtedly profitable employment of their capital in the direction indicated by your correspondents, you will have inaugurated a great social reform, and have earned the gratitude of countless outcasts by inserting such correspondence and by your able leading article on the subject. Apart from the more speculative aspect of the question, however, a great field of usefulness is now opened out for the County and District Councils to be so soon established, in pursuance of the Local Government Act. Upon this view of the case it may not be out of place to here quote the pathetic (and now prophetic) words of the great master of fiction - Charles Dickens - in "The Old Curiosity Shop," when he says: "Oh, if those who rule the destinies of the nation would but remember this - if they would but think how hard it is for the very poor to have engendered in their hearts that love of home from which all domestic virtues spring, when they live in dense and squalid masses where social decency is lost, or rather never found; if they would but turn aside from the wide thoroughfare and great houses, and strive to improve the wretched dwellings in bye-ways where only poverty may walk - many low roofs would point more truly to the sky than the loftiest steeple that now rears proudly up from the midst of guilt, and crime, and horrible disease, to mock them by its contrast. In hollow voices from workhouse, hospital, and jail this truth is preached from day to day, and has been proclaimed for years. It is no light matter - no outcry from the working vulgar - no mere question of the people's health and comforts, that may be whistled down on Wednesday nights. In love of home the love of country has its rise; and who are the truer patriots or the better in times of need - those who venerate the land, owning its wood and stream and earth, and all that they produce; or those who love their country, boasting not a foot of ground in all its wide domain?"

These stirring words of the great novelist come home to us with startling effect in these present days, when so much needs to be done to stamp out the demons of filth, disease, and crime which rage rampant in our large centres of population.

The adoption of the Labouring Classes Lodging Houses Act, 1851, in many large towns has done great service in the direction of providing clean, respectable, well-regulated lodgings for the poor at a reasonable rate, and in proof of the successful working of this Act in the town from which I write - a manufacturing town in the North, with a population of about 90,000 - a model lodging-house on the most approved principles has been established for many years, and is now under the control of the Town Council.

This house is divided into the following departments, viz., single men's department, single women's ditto, married couples' ditto, and mechanics' home; and the average number of inmates for many years past has been at the rate of 5,000 per month, or 60,000 a year. These pay a small fixed charge per night, and in return get a clean comfortable bed and lodging, whilst every attention is paid to the sanitary conditions and comforts of the establishment. As to the financial aspect of the question, the result has been most satisfactory, and the surplus income, after providing for the necessary sinking fund for the redemption of borrowed capital, goes in reduction of local taxation. Here, then, is a vast field for the enterprise, not only of private speculators, but of the newly constituted local authorities under Mr. Ritchie's Act; and may some of us live to see the day when all the foul dens of pestilence and disease now existing in our towns are swept away from the face of the earth, and cleanliness, health, and comfort reign in their stead.

Yours obediently,

TOWN CLERK.
Yorkshire, Sept. 25.

28 September 1888

TO THE EDITOR OF *THE TIMES*.

Sir, -

The statement made by the coroner to the jury in the inquest on the death of the woman Chapman and your comments thereon induce me, in the interests of humanity as well as of justice, to request your serious attention to the injurious influence which the theory referred to in your article of this morning is calculated to exert on the public mind.

I will, for the sake of argument, assume that the information given to the coroner by the officer of one of the medical schools is correct, and that Dr. Phillips is right in considering that the character of the mutilation in question justifies the assumption that the perpetrator was probably one who possessed some knowledge of anatomy.

But that the inference which has been deduced is warranted, any one who is the least acquainted with medical science and practice will unhesitatingly deny and indignantly repudiate. That a lunatic may have desired to obtain possession of certain organs for some insane purpose is very possible, and the theory of the murdering fiend being a madman only derives confirmation from the information obtained by the coroner. But that the parts of the body carried off were wanted for any quasi-scientific publication or any other more or less legitimate purpose no one having any knowledge of medical science will for a moment believe. To say nothing of the utterly absurd notion of the part, or organ, being preserved in a particular way to accompany each copy of an intended publication, the facilities for obtaining such objects for any purpose of legitimate research, in any number, either here or in America, without having recourse to crime of any kind are such as to render the suggestion made utterly untenable. There can be no analogy whatever with the atrocious crimes of Burke and Hare, the merest insinuation of which is a gross and unjustifiable calumny on the medical profession and is calculated both to exert an injurious influence on the public mind and defeat the ends of justice.

If I have expressed myself strongly you will, I trust, ascribe it to my anxiety that neither you nor the officers of justice should be misled, and not to any mere feeling that discredit has unjustly been thrown on the medical profession.

Your obedient servant,

JAS. RISDON BENNETT.
22, Cavendish-square, Sept 27.

29 September 1888

THE EAST-END.
TO THE EDITOR OF *THE TIMES*.

Sir, -

You admitted a letter in which I suggested among other means for dealing with the lawless life of criminal districts that responsible persons should buy up the property, and as landlords enforce decency.

Various offers have been made by those willing to help in this plan, and the hope is encouraged that a company might be formed which could at once proceed with the purchase of such houses as can be bought.

Will you now permit me to express my willingness to receive the names of those who have money which they are able to invest at low interest, and who are concerned to prevent the present scandal?

I am, truly yours,

SAMUEL A. BARNETT.
St. Jude's Vicarage, Commercial-street
Whitechapel, E., Sept. 24.

TO THE EDITOR OF *THE TIMES*.

Sir, -

With reference to the letter of your correspondent "Gamma" in last Saturday's issue, allow me to state that a company already exists for the purpose of buying up and improving such property as Mr. Barnett describes. It is known as the Tenement Dwellings Company (Limited). Mr. Alfred Hoare, the banker, of 37, Fleet-street, is the chairman, and Mr. Frederick H. Harvey-Samuel, 1, Whittington-avenue, Leadenhall-street, is the solicitor and secretary.

Yours faithfully,

F.G. DEBENHAM.
Cheshunt-park, Herts. Sept. 26.

29 September, 1888

TO THE EDITOR OF *THE TIMES*.

Sir, -

Your correspondent "Gamma" proposes that a number of philanthropic gentlemen should float a company for the purpose of buying up and improving the houses at present dedicated to vice and crime, and suggests that such a company would have every prospect of paying a good dividend.

Permit one who is well acquainted with the East-end slums to point out that the first step needful is the prosecution of the landlords of these rookeries of crime for keeping disorderly houses.

When the houses shall have been closed in consequence of such prosecutions, they will be purchaseable at a fair price that would, after improvement and reletting under conditions compatible with decency, yield a fair return to the philanthropic investor. If bought as "going concerns", the price would be simply prohibitive; for vice pays a higher rent then virtue, and the purchase money would be proportionate to the rental; while the large figure that would be paid by the philanthropist would only encourage the formation of new rookeries of vice to take the place of those suppressed.

The fact remains that the police must act before the philanthropist can step in.

Let an experiment be made in Dorset-street, Flower-and-Dean-street, and Thrawl-street, places made notorious in connexion with the recent Whitechapel murders. In these streets, literally within a stone's-throw of Toynbee-hall and the Rev. S.A. Barnett's Vicarage, are whole rows of so-called "registered" lodging-houses, each of which is practically a brothel and a focus of crime. The police authorities uniformly refuse to prosecute the owners of such places as keepers of disorderly houses, although the fullest evidence is in their possession to insure conviction, and they always throw the odious duty of prosecution on the neighbours who may feel aggrieved. These cannot prosecute in the cases of the Whitechapel rookeries without risking their lives; for such is the lawless nature of the denizens of these places that they would certainly, and probably with impunity, wreak their vengeance on any private individual who would dare to disturb them.

If the Home Secretary would give instructions for the simultaneous prosecution of the keepers of these nests of crime, the houses would be closed within a few weeks, and the owners would then gladly part with their bad bargains at a fair price to the philanthropic investor.

The suppression of these haunts of crime and the dispersion of their lawless population should be the watchword and cry - the *Carthago delenda est*[24] of every social reformer. That such a seething mass of moral filth and corruption should exist in our midst is a disgrace to our much-vaunted

---

[24] Latin for "Carthage must be destroyed!" – famous motto of Marcus Portius Cato (234-149 B.C.). Convinced that the prosperity of Carthage would be the ruin of Rome, he continually urged on what would eventually become the Third Punic War. At the end of nearly every speech he made in the Senate – even on topics completely unrelated to Carthage – he would exclaim "Carthago delenda est!"

civilization, and a danger to the State.

For obvious reasons I suppress my name and prefer to subscribe myself

ONE WHO KNOWS.

The Whitechapel Murders
To the Editor of the *East London Observer*.

SIR,--

One cannot read the horrors of these atrocities without feeling that they disgrace our boasted civilization, and that all should try to some extent to make them impossible in the future. These poor creatures are wandering about seeking the means to provide them with shelter from the night, and a place to sleep and forget for a time the horrors of their every-day life, and meet a fearful death. Think of it you who have daughters whose life must be prolonged long after you have passed away, and subjected to all the vicissitudes of this ever-changing life. I appeal to many who are engaged in missionary efforts, as they are termed, among the heathen abroad, to remember the still worse heathens at home. Such deeds as we read of, that are being committed in our very midst, outshine in horror and brutality anything ever done in savage lands - much of it too bad to print. I want to suggest and help to carry out a remedy, by which the homeless and shelterless may at least have a shelter free of cost.

> "Oh! It was pitiful!
> Near a whole city full,
> Home she had none." [25]

In Paris such shelters are provided at the cost of the municipality. They are large sheds in different parts of the city, open at dark and suitably warmed, with benches, a shelter simply, and a seat of rest. Some friends of mine have offered to subscribe £250 towards building such a shelter in the East End of London, and permanently maintaining it, if four other benevolent individuals will provide an equal sum, or guarantee the balance which may be required to establish it. If you will allow any gentlemen to send their names to you, sir, who are willing to serve on the Committee, or in any way assist, and thus begin the matter, you will be doing a public service.

I am, yours faithfully,

Samuel Hayward, C.E.

---

[25] Extract from the poem "Bridge of Sighs" (1844) by Thomas Hood (1799-1845). The poem mourns the death of an "unfortunate" who threw herself into the Thames. Although Hood was chiefly a humorist, he did pen a number of serious works later in life which were intended to spur social action and reform.

29 September, 1888

THE CORONER AND THE WHITECHAPEL MURDER
To the Editor of the *Pall Mall Gazette*

Sir,

Three weeks have now passed since Annie Chapman was discovered and mutilated in a squalid back court in Hanbury street, and this, the last of a series of terrible outrages that have recently been perpetrated in Whitechapel, within a few hundred yards of each other, already promises to join the majority of undiscovered crimes of cruel London. Mr. Wynne E. Baxter, the coroner before whom the case has been investigated, may certainly be congratulated on the fascinating and astounding theory he propounded on Wednesday in his charge to the jury, though he can scarcely be congratulated on his powers of logical sequence. According to Mr. Baxter, an American gentleman called some months back on the curator of the Pathological Museum, and having explained that he was publishing a medical work, with each copy of which he was desirous of issuing an actual specimen of the part treated therein, he offered the forementioned official £20 for every such specimen he could procure for him. Without wishing to appear frivolous, surely I must ask at what price a work whose "supplement" is to cost £20 is to be published at; and if the cost of production is expected to be covered by the publishing price, where a market is to be found for so costly a work? But the most ingenious part of Mr. Baxter's theory now follows. According to him, a market for such specimens of the human frame having been found to exist, the hour beings forth the man, and a ruffian is found who, tempted by the reward, hastens to procure the object of the American gentleman's desire. Did it not strike the coroner that under the circumstances the murderer left himself no loophole for escape? A work published with so unusual a "supplement" must at once attract considerable notice; and, considering the world wide excitement caused by the late murders, would the author not be immediately called upon to account for every specimen in his possession, the dates on which procured, and every conceivable data relating to each? Had the murderer's object been the one suggested by Mr. Baxter, would he not rather have inveigled his victim or victims into some secluded place, where his crime could have been committed without at once being detected, and therefore not only at once stopping his or her depredations, but beside at once closing his market? Why, again, should he in each case have so arranged the appalling details as specially to intensify the sensationalism of his crimes and so attract the notice of the entire civilized world to them? Again, why within a few weeks commit three different crimes all almost precisely similar in their details, and all in precisely the same neighbourhood, instead, say, of committing one in Whitechapel, another in Bermondsey, and a third in Camberwell? Does this not rather show that the murderer lives in and is acquainted with the locality where the murders were committed? And yet Mr. Wynne E. Baxter remarks: "There is little doubt that the deceased (Annie Chapman) knew the place (the little back court where the murder was committed, one out of hundreds similar to it in the neighbourhood), for it was only three or four hundred yards from where she lodged. If so, it is quite unnecessary to assume that her companion had any such knowledge."

May I ask Mr. Baxter which of the two had most need of security - the woman who entered the court for an immoral purpose, or the man who, according to him, deliberately entered it to commit a terrible murder followed by a long and delicate surgical operation. But, again - which is even more astounding - Mr. Baxter asks us to believe that this human fiend, a comparative stranger, if not a total one, to the locality, at six o'clock on a light September morning, in a neighbourhood where at that hour half the inhabitants are up and hurrying to their work, quietly issues out of No. 29, Hanbury street, "with a brown hat on his head and a dark coat on his back," reeking with blood, with every proof of the crime about his person - a crime which he has not only taken no pains to conceal, but every detail of which he had prepared with almost fiendish ingenuity so as to create excitement, and with the knowledge that within a very few hours ot must be the main topic of conversation throughout the town - and walks carelessly to some distant spot through the now fairly crowded streets, unnoticed and unsuspected, and calmly remits, probably by parcel post, the desire specimen to his American patron.

Yours faithfully,

Charles Ed. Jerningham.

1 October 1888

THE EAST-END.
TO THE EDITOR OF *THE TIMES*.

Sir, -

"One Who Knows" is perfectly right when he tells your readers that the police must act before the philanthropist can step in. But in my humble opinion he might with equal justice go a little further and say that the House of Commons should act besides, and that quickly.

It is an acknowledged fact that wherever overcrowding exists it is the origin of all evil. Crime, misery, filth, and degradation are the outcome, and we well know that the sweating system fattens on this wretched fabric. Why can we not grapple with it successfully? The answer to this is, vested interests forbid it. A lodging-house in a congested district to these house-jobbers is a sure fortune. Shylock has but to send his collector round (and the more hardened is the man's conscience the better business man is he considered), and sums like 5s. 6d. a week for each room in a house, and 3s. 6d. a week for the cellar den in it, are wrung out of England's white slaves. To make the lot of the latter more bitter still, Bismark's destitute Polish Jews have been flung in broadcast to fight the battle of life out with them. It is a positive fact that members of local authorities who have self-interest in this slave trade serve on the local boards, lending no doubt an *otium cum dignitate*[26] to their proceedings. But, I ask, was there ever such a shameless farce played out on those least able to protect themselves? Why should overcrowding be allowed to put a premium on property? But such is the state of the law at present. I maintain that compensation should only be calculated on the base of the capacity of a house and not on the numbers actually living in it. It was to meet this glaring fraud on the public (for it prevents better houses from being built and lower rents charged) that I brought in a Bill at the commencement of this Session to further amend the law relating to the dwellings of the working classes. The Government, I regret to say, still hold their hand, although I have received from all sides of the House of Commons the greatest sympathy and support. I have not withdrawn this Bill, and I do not mean to; but if the public would only come forward and give me their support I feel confident that the best part of my Bill would be on the Statute-book by Christmas. As I plead for a population in our midst as large as Wales and as loyal too, and whose only crime is their poverty, I trust it will not be considered that I have said anything on their behalf one whit too strong.

I remain, Sir, your obedient servant,

HENRY BRUDENELL BRUCE.
September 29.

---

[26] This is roughly translated from Latin to mean "leisure with dignity."

TO THE EDITOR OF *THE TIMES*.

Sir,

Will you allow me to ask a question of your correspondents who want to disperse the vicious inhabitants of Dorset-street and Flower and Dean-street? There are no lower streets in London, and, if they are driven out of these, to what streets are they to go? The horror and excitement caused by the murder of the four Whitechapel outcasts imply a universal belief that they had a right to life. If they had, then they had the further right to hire shelter from the bitterness of the English night. If they had no such right, then it was, on the whole, a good thing that they fell in with unknown surgical genius. He, at all events, has made his contribution towards solving, "the problem of clearing the East-end of its vicious inhabitants." The typical "Annie Chapman" will always find some one in London town to let her have a "doss" for a consideration. If she is systematically "dispersed," two results will follow. She will carry her taint to streets hitherto untainted, and she herself will be mulcted in larger sums than before for the accommodation. The price of a doss will rise from 8d. to 10d. or a shilling, the extra pennies representing an insurance fund against prosecution and disturbance. Are these the sort of results that the Rev. Samuel Barnett is working for?

If vestries seem apathetic in the matter of systematic dispersal, it often is because they know that the demand for action is nothing but an astute manouvre on the part of a house monger, who is anxious (to use the words of one of your correspondents) that the property should become "purchaseable at a fair price."

I am, Sir, your obedient servant,

E. FAIRFIELD.
64, South Eaton-place, S.W.

TO THE EDITOR OF *THE TIMES*.

Sir, -

I beg to suggest the organization of a small force of plain-clothes constables mounted on bicycles for the rapid and noiseless patrolling of streets and roads by night.

Your obedient servant,

FRED WELLESLEY.
Merton Abbey, Merton, Surrey, Sept. 30.

A Word For the Police.
TO THE EDITOR OF *THE STAR*.

SIR, -

There is one thing to be said for the police in defence of their failure to catch the murderer. His victim, it must be remembered, is in a conspiracy to escape the eye of the constable. She, as well as he, watches him out of sight and hearing, and waits to put herself every minute more completely in the power of her destroyer.

Yours, &c.,

FAIR PLAY.
London, 1 Oct.

THE MURDERS IN THE EAST-END
TO THE EDITOR OF *THE DAILY TELEGRAPH*

SIR -

As members of the Whitechapel Vigilance Committee, who communicated without result with the Home Secretary with the view of obtaining, on behalf of the public at large, the offer of a Government reward for the apprehension and conviction of the assassin or assassins in the recent East-end atrocities, we shall be glad if you will allow us to state that the Committee do not for one moment doubt the sincerity of the Home Secretary in refusing the said offer, as he apparently believes that it would not meet with a successful result. If you would, however, consider that in the case of the Phoenix Park murders the man Carey, who was surrounded by, we may say, a whole society steeped in crime, the money tempted him to betray his associates, in our opinion if Mr. Matthews could see his way clear to coincide with our views the Government offer would be successful. The reward should be ample for securing the informer from revenge, which would be a very great inducement in the matter; in addition to which such offer would convince the poor and humble residents of our East-end that the Government authorities are as much anxious to avenge the blood of these unfortunate victims as they were the assassination of Lord Cavendish and Mr. Burke. - Apologising for trespassing on your valuable space, we beg to subscribe ourselves, faithfully yours,

GEORGE LUSK[27]
JOSEPH AARONS.
1, 2, and 3, Alderney-road, Mile-end, E.,
Sept. 29

---

[27] George Lusk (1839-1919), president of the Whitechapel Vigilance Committee, and later recipient of the infamous "Lusk letter" that included a portion of a human kidney, allegedly taken from the body of Catherine Eddowes.

TO THE EDITOR OF *THE FREEMAN'S JOURNAL AND DAILY COMMERCIAL ADVERTISER*
(Dublin, Ireland)

SIR -

The observations of the coroner at the inquest on the body of Annie Chapman, one of the Whitechapel victims, are so peculiar, and I think, so likely to mislead public opinion and create a prejudice against men engaged in the study of tissue changes in unhealthy organs, that I ask your permission to place some facts and deductions from them that will, I think, invalidate the coroner's conclusions.

The fact that the womb was removed from the body of each victim is taken to imply that the organ was the sole object of the murder, and that the crime was committed to obtain it. Every anatomist must know that a large percentage of the dead bodies brought to the anatomy rooms are those of the unfortunate class, and that human wombs are plentiful in the rooms; and, from considerable experience as an anatomy lecturer, I can say I never know of any demand for them as pathological specimens that was not easily met.

To excise the womb in its entirety does require some anatomical knowledge, but not more than any anatomy porter possesses. As for the crime, we find it carried out with a reckless devilry worthy of a monomaniac, but not to be found associated with the cool villainy that characterises the criminal for pecuniary gain.

As any person familiar with the working of the Anatomy Act[28] knows perfectly well that no specimen of any portion of the human body could be offered for sale without the seller being subjected to searching examination into all the details of the case, and he would run the risk, if his statements were not satisfactory, of being handed over to the police.

The Whitechapel murder silenced his victim by a method of choking, or pressing the lower jaw up against the upper one, the method of a bully but not such as a skilful anatomist would adopt, who of necessity should know that a fine cut with a small knife would deprive the person of all power of sound.

The victim's throats were cut, allowing the large vessels of the neck to pour out blood to the risk of besmearing the criminal - a danger which he need not have incurred had he known, as an anatomist would have, how to destroy life; but is not the fact important in pointing out the ruthless determination and (fierce) rage of the deep-dyed ruffian who has thus dared to carry on his crimes

---

[28] Act of Parliament enacted in 1832 which expanded the legal availability of corpses for medical and scientific research. Before this, only the bodies of executed criminals could be used for the purposes of dissection, which led to an illegal and disturbing black-market trade in human corpses (such as Burke and Hare). This act also required anatomists to register and obtain a license for vivisection from the Home Secretary.

with an apparent contempt for all laws human and divine!

I am, sir, yours,

GEORGE FOX

THE HAUNTS OF VICE AND CRIME.
TO THE EDITOR OF *THE ECHO*.

Sir,-

In your article of yesterday you well say, referring to the extinction of dens of infamy, and their replacement by respectable dwelling-houses, "the Home Office must move first." The police possess amply sufficient evidence to shut up every brothel in Dorset-street, Flower and Dean-street, and Thrawl-street, &c. The police have now sufficient evidence to prosecute every notorious brothel in London, it being now incumbent on the constables to report the number of brothels on their beat. At present, however, next to no use is made of the information. It becomes a mass of "statistics." Our Vestries are supposed to be the "guardians of morality." *Quis custodiel custodes?*[29] Many Vestrymen are slum house owners, and brother property holders. The remedy against brothel-keepers is slow and cumbrous by means of the vestries, dangerous if put in force by private individuals, and often even then of little effect. What is a £5 of a £10 fine to a big brothel-keeper? Some Magistrates seldom impose more unless gross disorders or robberies are proved. It seems to me that the police should be instructed (not simply empowered) to keep observation on, and to take action against, all houses of ill-fame, when such houses are reported to Scotland-yard, and, failing redress, to the Home Secretary, or to the Member for the Parliamentary Division. Scandals such as are now gross, open, palpable, would, at least, be greatly reduced. To make men moral by Act of Parliament is undoubtedly impossible, but much can be done to deter from immorality, or laws against theft and murder are a farce. Not to speak of the "Slaughter-ground" (whence comes a rumour of two more horrors), brothels are rife amidst respectable streets, and words, while the comparatively innocent are seduced into those dens of infamy. Our Vestries, where not involved, are usually indifferent, and are practically irresponsible, so far as human law is concerned.

Yours faithfully,

DISGUSTED.
Sept. 30.

---

[29] Latin for "Who watches the watchers?"

2 October 1888

TO THE EDITOR OF *THE TIMES*.

Sir,

Paying my daily visit to my church this afternoon I was surprised to find the caretaker in a semi-stupified state.

Asking her what was the matter, she told me that a man had just entered the church, and finding her all alone inquired whether I was in the vestry. On receiving a reply in the negative he said, "I see you are alone," and immediately took out a pocket-handkerchief and dashed it in her face. The strong smell of whatever liquid it had been steeped in dazed and stupefied her, and she for a moment or two lost her consciousness[30]. The noise of some of the workmen on the roof seemed to have alarmed this scoundrel, and he bolted out of the church.

This incident, Sir, perhaps might afford a clue. At any rate, it will warn solitary women who are in charge of churches.

I am Sir, your obedient servant,

J. M. S. BROOKE.
Vestry of St. Mary Woolnoth and St. Mary Woolchurch
Haw, Lombard-street, E.C.

TO THE EDITOR OF *THE TIMES*.

Sir, -

I cannot help thinking that these Whitechapel murders point to one individual, and that individual insane. Not necessarily an escaped, or even as yet recognised, lunatic. He may be an earnest religionist with a delusion that he has a mission from above to extirpate vice by assassination. And he has selected his victims from a class which contributes pretty largely to the factorship of immorality and sin. I have known men and women actuated by the best and purest motives who have been dominated by an insane passion of this kind, and who honestly believed that by its indulgence they would be doing good service. There are many such in our various asylums. I was myself all but the victim of an assassin who believed that he had a mission to destroy me as the impersonation of all that was evil and hindered the progress of mankind. He was transferred from my asylum in

---

[30] Most likely a reference to the Victorian practice of "chloroforming" a victim into unconsciousness.

Middlesex to that of a county where he had a proved settlement, and subsequently attacked and imperilled the life of its medical superintendent.

A suggestion of this kind may be useful; certainly it can do no harm.

I have, &c.,

EDGAR SHEPPARD, M.D.
42, Gloucester-square, Hyde Park, W., Oct. 1.

TO THE EDITOR OF *THE TIMES*.

Sir,

With regard to the suggestion that bloodhounds might assist in tracking the East-end murderer, as a breeder of bloodhounds, and knowing their power, I have little doubt that, had a hound been put upon the scent of the murderer while fresh, it might have done what the police have failed in. But now, when all trace of the scent has been trodden out, it would be quite useless.

Meanwhile, as no means of detection should be left untried, it would be well if a couple or so of trained bloodhounds - unless trained they would be worthless - were kept for a time at one of the police head-quarters ready for immediate use in case their services should be called for. There are, doubtless, owners of bloodhounds willing to lend them, if any of the police, which, I fear, is improbable, know how to use them.

I am, Sir, your obedient servant,

PERCY LINDLEY
York-hill, Loughton, Essex, Oct. 1.

TO THE EDITOR OF *THE TIMES*.

Sir,

The fearful crimes that have lately stirred up the passions of all point to a more active policy on the part of those who are bound to protect the lives of Her Majesty's subjects (be they rich or poor) from a continuance of crimes that surpass all that have gone before. Far be it from me to blame the action of the Home Secretary, police, or those in authority, but, as a magistrate of more than 30 years' experience among the criminal population of London, as well as much intercourse with the working classes, I have no hesitation in saying that the best way to detect crime of a heinous character is to offer at once a large and substantial reward. Some may say, "Who will protect a murderer?" Let me remind them that an informer is always looked upon as a man to be avoided; so few like to come forward to speak in evidence of knowledge which in the end might prove faulty. A hardworking, respectable man would likewise say, "It will entail a loss of some days' work which I can ill afford to lose," so that silence to him seems the best course to pursue.

I do not know whom to address with authority equal to *The Times*, but venture so suggest that a large reward, say £1,000, should at once be offered, to which, in my humble capacity, I shall be pleased to subscribe £50 (fifty pounds), and, if necessary, to assist in the formation of a fund to be solely devoted to the detection and punishment of crimes of a heinous nature and for the reward of those who may assist in its discovery. If you think this subject worthy of publicity, I have no hesitation in giving my name and address.

I have the honour to remain your obedient servant,

HENRY WHITE,
Magistrate of Middlesex.
30, Queen's-gate,
South Kensington,
Oct. 1.

TO THE EDITOR OF *THE DAILY NEWS*.

SIR,

When will our brave Government have done with the heartbreaking oppression of poor Irishmen, and begin to turn their attention to the awful problems involved in the crimes which are enacted with impunity in England's greatest city? Unquestionable astuteness they discover in hurling from their miserable huts starving families, consigning them to the roadside, reckless of what becomes of them; but precious little capacity do they show in the detection of atrocities which daily are shocking us, or in tracking the criminal to his den and bringing him to justice. Sir, how much longer shall we be governed by these incapables?

Yours truly,

R. JOHNS.
Metropolitan Tabernacle,
Newington,
Oct. 1.

2 October, 1888

TO THE EDITOR OF *THE DAILY NEWS*.

SIR,

As the track of the Whitechapel monster or monsters becomes more and more thickly besprinkled with the blood, and bestrewn with the mutilated remains of successive victims, there is something almost paralysing in the ghastly sameness with which the newspaper reports wind up:- "No clue to the identity of the murderer has yet been found"; "No circumstances specially tending to the discovery of the criminal has been observed"; and "It is understood that although not the remotest clue has been discovered, the police have a theory," and so on ad nauseam. Every reasonable suggestion (and some suggestions which are not reasonable) thrown out by neighbours and bystanders is followed up with praiseworthy energy; promising arrests are made at the instance of lodging-house deputies and others; and the drunken "confession" prompted by the idyllic imagination of an occasional reveler is heard with grave attention, and investigated with patient, if hopeless ability. But "up to the hour of going to press no clue has been discovered." Now, Sir, is not this a matter of grave complaint against our detective system? Is the duty of the sleuth-hound of the law confined to following up the suggestions of outsiders and amateurs? In so such wise have the French and American detectives, whose astuteness excites the wonder and stimulates the imagination of historical as well as fictional writers all the world over, achieved their fame. It is easy to say that without something to work upon the police cannot be expected to smell the murderer out. Is this the language of Vidocq[31] or of Inspector Byrne[32]? Most emphatically I maintain that it is the duty of the detectives to discover and pursue for himself clues suggested by such trifling indications as would escape the attention of the casual or the unskilled observer. We retain a large and expensive body of men; their services are withdrawn from directly productive industry to act as detectives; and we have the right to demand at their hands things which, except to specialists and experts, may rightly be called impossible. Sir Charles Warren, pious disciplinarian and enthusiastic soldier that he is, must feel deeply his responsibility for all this. Doubtless he remembers with a pang that the services of the best detective in the force - certainly of the man in whom the country has the greatest confidence - are lost to the department which owed so much to his genius, and that popular report attributes the loss to friction with the Chief Commissioner. May we not ask whether Sir Charles remembers also that his predecessor's retirement was accelerated by his failure to foresee and prevent certain violence (not violence to life, but only to property), brought about by speeches not more inflammatory than many others delivered under like circumstances in the same place without serious consequence?

Yours obediently,

T.B.B.

---

[31] Eugène François Vidocq (1775-1857) director of Sûreté Nationale and founder of the first private detective agency. Vidocq was himself a reformed criminal and was known to have employed criminals for the detection of crime.

[32] Inspector Thomas Byrnes was Chief of the New York City Detective Bureau (1880-1895).

WOMAN KILLING NO MURDER[33]
TO THE EDITOR OF *THE DAILY NEWS*.

SIR,

The wild beast who is running loose in Whitechapel is apparently a student of psychology. By the ordinary perusal of a newspaper he has become aware that he has only to persevere in his horrible atrocities, and as soon as they have ceased to be sensational by reason of their novelty they will be thought of small consequence. These frightful murders are no isolated events. They are part and parcel of a constant and ever-increasing series of cruelties perpetrated on women, and regarded so lightly by the public, and treated so leniently by judges that it must be a source of genuine surprise to a man when he finds that by chance he is going to be hanged for murdering a woman, or to be sent to a long term of penal servitude for the attempted murder of a woman.

It is surely unfair that a man may not know what he is to expect, if he wants to kill a woman, or if he wished merely to vent upon someone too feeble to return or resist his violence a savage gust of passion, careless whether his blows may kill or may only maim. In perhaps five out of six cases of woman-killing, judges and juries find the crime to be not murder: how unfair it is that a man should not know beforehand whether he is to expect to be one of the fortunate five, to receive a less punishment than he would do if he were driven by want to steal trifling articles and get half-a-dozen convictions for that-or whether he shall be the sixth on the list of woman-slayers, with bad luck enough to be called a murderer, and even, it is just possible by chance, to be hanged as such. How unjust, again, that a man should know that he may ill-use a woman to an unlimited extent for a brief term of imprisonment (less than he would have for picking a pocket), if only she has the strength to live through it; while if the wretched creature completes her career of annoyances by dying there may be considerable fuss made about it. Is it his fault if she have a poor constitution?

The Whitechapel murders, ghastly and terrible though they are in the light of the fact that the murderer is roving at large, are in fact commonplace and even merciful, beside some that judges and juries have within the last twelve months declared not to be murders at all. Is it not worse to hack and mutilate a living woman's sentient body than to kill and cut at the insensible corpse? Is it not a more terrible fate to be slowly beaten to death in instalments [sic] than to be sent from earth by one swift stroke? Yet week by week and month by month women are kicked, beaten, jumped on till they are crushed, chopped, stabbed, seamed with vitriol, bitten, eviscerated with red-hot pokers, and deliberately set on fire-and this sort of outrage, if the woman dies, is called "manslaughter;" if she lives, it is a "common assault." Common indeed! And men who would not themselves lay a hand on a woman except in kindness-men who themselves feel it the greatest satisfaction of their lives that they make some woman's existence happy - are content to know that other men treat other women so, and that demoralised judges and magistrates throw the shield of the law and the authority of their office, not over the victim, but over the crime.

---

[33] See responses to this letter in the *Daily News* of October 3rd, 4th, 6th and 9th 1888, as well as a rebuttal (of sorts) published under "Audi Alteram Partem" in the *Star* of October 9th.

Let us make an end of the pretence that women have full protection against murder and violence from the laws of their country. Let it be recognised and admitted that to kill a woman is not murder - no more in a sensational case than in a more common-place one. Let it be stated that the most brutal assaults on women are of little consequence, and let a limit - such as is now applied in practice - be set on the sentences that are to be given in such cases. It is not fair to leave a man in doubt as to what his sentence is to be when he lets forth his fury on a woman, and it is not well to allow ordinary, decent-minded men to shelter their consciences behind the fact that the law theoretically protects women while the "discretion" of judges and magistrates and the cowardice or indifference of juries makes the law's protection a pretence.

May I briefly justify these hard sayings, that may seem too hard, if the facts are not brought to mind? Before me lies a heap of newspaper cuttings, all taken within the last few months, showing only too sadly that I am not too bitter, not too extreme. Here is Mr. Edlin, the Assistant Judge of the Middlesex Sessions, dealing with a case of burglary, cutting a watch dog's throat, and stabbing the woman of the house in the throat when she resisted an attempted rape, cutting seriously both her throat and the hands put up to protect it-six months' imprisonment! This was something like the Whitechapel cases, except that the throat cutting was not so skilful, and owing to interruption it did not kill; but, on the other hand, the burglary has to be added in the scale. Mr. Edlin again gave a similar sentence in an almost equally outrageous case, a few weeks ago. Nobody appears seriously shocked; for he has just received, as though in recognition of his services, the honour of knighthood, nominally from the hands of the first woman of the realm - the Sovereign who swore at her coronation to protect her people! Mr. Justice Charles a fortnight ago had before him a miscreant who had inflicted months of acute agony and disfigured a poor girl for life by pouring vitriol over her face because she refused to live with him - sentence, eighteen months. The same judge had a man who chopped a woman's head open with an axe - sentence, nine months. Mr. Edlin again had a case of a savage brute biting an old woman's cheek through to her teeth, and "worrying it like a dog" - eighteen months; the next case, settled by the same "officer of justice," being a burglary, with previous conviction proved, eight years. The magistrates are not behindhand in their encouragement to brutality against women. Here, a fortnight ago, is Mr. de Rutzen: a man biting a woman's arm, when her baby was a month old - six months. Mr. Chance: for beating a woman with a ginger-beer bottle, and turning her out of doors in her night-gown - three months. The country magistrates are even worse. The Barnsley magistrates, for a brutal assault with a brick, kicking, and attempted rape, last week gave four months' imprisonment. The Whitehaven magistrates, for breaking a woman's jaw in two places and knocking out six teeth, six months. The Kidderminster magistrates, for a series of violent beatings, fine of 5s.; their next case being against a tradesman for leaving a couch an hour on the footpath, fined 10s. The Wolverhampton magistrates, for cruelly assaulting a woman, two months; for striking a policeman one blow, three months; for cutting one of the Corporation seats, six months. But I must end this catalogue, with which I might fill pages, and I have yet to give instances of woman-killing no murder. Here is Edward Doyle, who, not content with breaking a woman's ribs and scalding her with hot water, next thrust a red hot poker up into her abdomen, and let her lie dying for two days: manslaughter, fifteen years' prison. He will be let out to go on again while still quite in the prime of life; he is no murderer. John Freshfield, tearing off his wife's ear, breaking her breast-bone and also eight of her ribs on one side and nine on the other: manslaughter, (Mr. Justice Hawkins) eighteen months' prison. John Finnemore, stabbing his wife in the abdomen with a knife because his dinner, ordered for three, was not nice when he returned at midnight: manslaughter, twenty years. T. Leyland, setting a woman on fire, with express intention to kill her, by holding a lighted paper to her clothes, and then shutting her out in a high walled yard away from rescue: manslaughter, "recommended to mercy, because he looked a soft sort of man!" James Kelly, Edinburgh, fifty wounds on the head and elsewhere, the end of a long course of brutal usage: culpable homicide, ten years. John Jones, a murder described by the judge as one "for which we might search in vain amongst the records of barbarians to find a case so bad": manslaughter, (Mr. Justice Grantham) twelve months' imprisonment.

I must inflict no more on you. These are only, alas! specimens of a long, long list. What are men going to do? Now, when their consciences and their imaginations are aroused by the stealthiness and barbarous sequels of the Whitechapel murders, I ask them what are they going to do to check the ever-rising flood of brutality to women, of which these murders are only the latest wave?

FLORENCE FENWICK MILLER[34]

LETTERS FROM THE PUBLIC[35]
(From the Daily Telegraph)

We have received a large number of letters, from all parts of the kingdom, indicating the widespread and intense interest which has been aroused by these unparalleled crimes. Our correspondents belong to all sorts and conditions of people. Their suggestions are interesting, if not important. Several gentlemen of the medical profession express regret that in the case of the woman Chapman the coroner should have been led astray, "intentionally or otherwise," as to the object for which the crime was said to have been committed. "The alleged value of £20 in such a case," writes "A Surgeon," "is a gross exaggeration, and it is also a shameful thing that a public officer should have been, I fear purposely, misled upon so serious and painful a subject." "Citizen," "St. John Carr," "A Scotchman," and others advise the police to avail themselves of the aid of bloodhounds, and "Citizen" is convinced that "had a good dog been put on the scent in either case at the moment of the discovery of the bodies, the criminal would have been hunted down." Many correspondents who write from the East-end, including "One More Unfortunate," "A Mariner," and "One Who Knows," believe in a searching and efficient register of strangers, and "in every person

---

[34] Florence Fenwick Miller (1857-1935) was a journalist and vociferous activist for women's suffrage.
[35] *The Daily Telegraph* received so many letters to the editor in the days following the "double event" of September 30th 1888 that they could publish only a small percentage of them. For several days in early October they ran a "Letters from the Public" column which gave a brief overview of the hundreds of letters they'd received but were unable to publish in full.

Florence Fenwick Miller

being compelled to give an account of himself at common and other lodging-houses." Quite a little army of "Special Constables" offer their services in patrolling the East-end and in assisting at a house-to-house investigation of any district at some given moment, "more particularly," says "One of the X Division," "in the event of another murder, which we may surely expect after such successful daring and such an appetite for blood." "A. E. Gower," "W. S." (Derby), and "H. C. W," think the police should patrol their beats silently with the aid of "rubber boots," and "A Surgeon" (T. L.) calls our attention to the fact that "the Sheffield police are supplied with boots not only waterproof, but soft in the sole, which make no noise, and are cheap and durable." Much indignation is expressed against "the action, or want of action" (as "D. C. L." expresses it) of the Home Secretary, "in regard to whose strange apathy" "A Poor Woman" asks, "Does this unpopular but powerful Minister think that because the victims belong to the class termed unfortunate they are of no account? What would he have done if the poor creatures had been rich and titled dames of the West-end"? "Spes" advises the police "to look for the murderer in an empty house where a caretaker is not likely to be suspected of harbouring him." "An Old Detective" says "if the man is taken he will be taken red-handed. The assistance of the class of woman he attacks would be useful, and a clever officer in woman's clothes is an idea which has probably been acted upon." We select from some hundreds of other letters the following for publication:

TO THE EDITOR OF *THE DAILY TELEGRAPH*.

SIR -

With regard to the recent murders, will you kindly allow me a little of your space to urge upon Mr. Matthews the desirability of, even thus late in the day, issuing a Government notification, and for reasons which hitherto I have not seen advanced? Private rewards are all very well so far as they go; but they must be deficient in one particular, which the Crown alone can supply. When rewards were offered for the discovery of a murderer their character was twofold - the money and the promise of a pardon to any accomplice not the actual murderer. The objection to a money reward, that it often went into wrong hands, is tantamount to an assertion that the promise of pardon was in some cases, at least, the inducement to people to give information; and in the present case such a promise might have that effect.

Without attempting to go over the whole of the ground which the promise of pardon to accomplices would cover, I may point out that it is difficult to suppose, even if different hands have committed each of the murders, and taking the case of Annie Chapman alone, that there is not some one who has a well-founded suspicion of the murderer of that ill-fated creature. If he lives in the neighbourhood of the deed he would return home to a waking neighbourhood, if at a distance he would still return to a waking one; and it is almost incredible he should be living such an isolated life that there is not a human being who has some knowledge of his blood-stained hands, and, probably, his blood-stained features and garments, and of the steps he has taken to hide the traces of his guilt. But, if two or more of the murders have been committed by the same person, the supposition of complete ignorance or suspicion of the murderer becomes still more untenable. Why, then, has no information been given? I say simply because, in the first place, there was some one, relying upon the accumulation of horrors, who waited for a Government reward, offered in the usual terms, and who dares not give now the information which three weeks ago his cupidity induced him to withhold. Maybe there is someone who has lodged and fed and clothed the murderer, intending to hand him over to justice as soon as he could do so with profit and impunity to himself. By so harbouring the criminal any such person has rendered himself liable to severe penalties, which no doubt he richly deserves, as an accomplice after the fact; by his own conduct he has placed a seal upon his lips, and unless the Government remove that seal a secret of incalculable value may perhaps be carried to the grave. That such a secret is in existence I submit is very probable.

I therefore urge upon the Home Secretary to notify the promise of pardon to any accomplices in one or more of these murders in the usual terms. Further, there is this to be said in favour of such pardon - if money rewards have a tendency to get into wrong hands, it is possible for a pardon only to reach the right ones.

I am, Sir, your obedient servant.

G. R. H.
London, Sept. 28

TO THE EDITOR OF *THE DAILY TELEGRAPH*.

SIR -

As it is necessary that something out of the ordinary must be done to capture the being who perpetrates these awful deeds, I venture to send the following proposition, in the hope that it may be of some use, or that some more useful suggestion may be gained through it.

For instance, say that a square mile, or any distance that would cover the worst parts of the neighbourhood, where the lowest classes live, and where these crimes have been committed, were divided into so many temporary stations, where an inspector and constable could be, and that every man sleeping in this specified area should be compelled, before going to his bed, to report himself, or not be allowed to enter his lodging until he could show that he had done so. Of course this would mean a great number of police to strictly enforce the regulation.

I am, yours truly,

G. E. K.
Rivermere, Old Windsor, Oct. 1.

TO THE EDITOR OF *THE DAILY TELEGRAPH*.

SIR -

In the face of the half-dozen murders that have recently taken place in our midst without the slightest clue of any importance having been obtained by our detectives or police, it forcibly strikes one there must be a very weak point in our detective department which requires instant remedy. At the present time a man is required to be a certain height and to serve for a definite time as a constable before he is eligible as a detective, during which time he, of course, becomes well known, besides which this arrangement only opens our detective department to one class of men, whereas every class ought to be represented to properly carry out the work.

I should propose that anybody offering himself should be accepted, providing his references were satisfactory and he had a good knowledge of London, trained privately for a certain period, and when efficient he should be entrusted with the class of cases he seemed to show most aptitude for. In this way we should have many men of high education and varied experience only too glad to join the force from a love of the calling, who at the present time are debarred by the useless regulations regarding admission now in force.

I am, Sir, yours obediently,

F. W. DEVEREUX LONG
31, Finsbury-square, and Houndsditch, Oct. 1

TO THE EDITOR OF *THE DAILY TELEGRAPH*.

SIR -

After the awful details of the two murders recorded in the papers, which occurred on Saturday night, surely some stronger measures should be taken to ensure no repetitions of such atrocities which are outrages on civilisation. These horrible mutilating murders may, and probably will go on for some length of time, as there seems to be no possible clue in any of the cases. What I should suggest would be that after dark in certain parts of London every policeman ought to have the right of stopping and searching anyone, to see if he carries a knife such as must have been used in all these hideous crimes. Surely no innocent man would object to this ordeal, and it might have the desired effect of bringing the guilty one to justice, or at any rate checking any further outrage of the kind. I do not know how far the authority of Sir Charles Warren goes, as head of the police, but in such a case surely additional power might be obtained from the Home Office.

Believe me, yours truly,

C. L. M.
Connaught-square, Hyde park, W., Oct. 1.

2 October, 1888

TO THE EDITOR OF *THE DAILY TELEGRAPH*.

SIR -

Reading the account given by Morris the watchman,[36] he remarks, "The strangest part of the whole thing is that I heard no sound. As a rule, I can hear the footsteps of the policeman as he passes by every quarter of an hour." Quite so, and so could any person whose intentions were evil. I have had many years experience in the City at night time, and have often noticed that a policeman's step could be heard a great distance, even from one end of a street to the other. The thought suggested is whether it would not be wise that policemen should be provided with a more noiseless material than iron and leather, especially when on night duty.

Yours truly,

D. EVERETT.
123, St. Paul's-road, Bow, E., Oct. 1.

EAST-END WOMEN.
TO THE EDITOR OF *THE ECHO*.

Sir,

Why do not the woman of the East-end form themselves into a deputation at once and wait upon Mr. Matthews, just in the way that the matchmakers some day visited Mr. Lowe.[37] The result might be equally happy.

Yours respectfully,

A Constant Reader.
Savage Clus
Lancaster House
Savoy, W.c.
Oct. 2

---

[36] George James Morris (b. 1834) was a watchman at the Kearly and Tonge warehouse in Mitre Square on the night of the Catherine Eddowes murder. He saw and heard nothing suspicious until he was alerted by P.C. Edward Watkins that there was "another woman cut to pieces." Morris testified at the inquest.

[37] Reference to the Matchgirls Strike which took place in June and July 1888. After a lecture was given at the Fabian Society concerning the deplorable pay and conditions at the Bryant & May match factory, a group of reformers led by Annie Besant and including George Bernard Shaw helped form a Matchgirls Union which officially went on strike against their employers. After three weeks of conflict (and ample coverage in the press) management conceded and made a number of concessions to improve working conditions at the factory.

BLOODHOUNDS.
TO THE EDITOR OF THE ECHO.

Sir,

I quite agree with your clever contributor "About Town." Bloodhounds are more likely to discover the terribly cunning fiend of Whitechapel than any number of detectives and vigilance committees. I say this from having myself been an eye-witness to the wonderful powers of these keen-scented animals.

Many years ago, when I was sojourning in Dieppe, a little boy was found doubled up in a horse-bin, with his throat cut. Immediately a couple of bloodhounds were put on to the scent, and in less than an hour they had tracked the murderess to a low lodging-house at the other end of the town, where she was found hiding under a bed. As the noble beasts dashed on their way, now to the right, anon to the left, eager-eyed, and nose down, hundreds of people, including the keeper, followed pell-mell in their wake; amongst whom was -

Yours faithfully,

Williams Buchanan, B.A.
11, Burton-street, W.C.
Oct. 1

TO THE EDITOR OF THE ECHO.

Sir,

In reading your very sensible article today in the "Touch-and-Go Papers," it struck me that, instead of finding fault with the heads of departments, would not the better plan be to put the bloodhound idea into practice without waiting for Sir Charles Warren to act? I take it that there is no use to stop either "About Town," or anyone else, doing this, if, as he says, it is not too late. Besides, there is also a splendid reward for the owner of the dog. Let anyone with a practical idea step out and act, and not wait. They can only fail, as the police, so far, seem to have done. Hoping you will find room for this if worth while, yours respectfully,

J. Flynn
42, Moorfields, E.C.
Oct. 1

3 October 1888

TO THE EDITOR OF *THE TIMES*.

Sir,

Will you allow me to recommend that all the police boots should be furnished with a noiseless sole and heel, of indiarubber or other material, to prevent the sound of their measured tread being heard at night, which would enable them to get close to a criminal before he would be aware of their approach?

Yours faithfully,

L.R. THOMSON.
Junior United Service Club, S.W., Oct. 1.

TO THE EDITOR OF THE TIMES.

Sir,

It was estimated in New York that every street electric lamp saved one policeman and was less expensive to maintain.

If every street were well lighted, and every court and alley were brilliantly lighted, deeds of darkness would be diminished and morality promoted.

I am, Sir, your obedient servant,

MORTON LATHAM.
Kingswood, Enfield, Oct. 1.

TO THE EDITOR OF *THE TIMES*.

Sir,

Another remarkable letter has been written by some bad fellow who signs himself "Jack the Ripper." The letter is said to be smeared with blood, and there is on it the print in blood of the corrugated surface of a thumb. This may be that of a man or a woman.

It is inconceivable that a woman has written or smeared such a letter, and therefore it may be accepted as a fact that the impression in blood is that of a man's thumb.

Dr. Hermann Adler

The surface of a thumb so printed is as clearly indicated as are the printed letters from any kind of type. Thus there is a possibility of identifying the blood print on the letter with the thumb that made it, because the surface markings on no two thumbs are alike, and this a low power used in a microscope could reveal.

I would suggest - (1) That it be proved if it is human blood, though this may not be material; (2) that the thumbs of every suspected man be compared by an expert with the blood-print of a thumb on the letter; (3) that it be ascertained whether the print of a thumb is that of a man who works hard and has rough, coarse hands, or whether that of one whose hands have not been roughened by labour; (4) whether the thumb was large or small; (5) whether the thumb print shows signs of any shakiness or tremor in the doing of it.

All this the microscope could reveal. The print of a thumb would give as good evidence as that of a boot or shoe.[38]

I am, yours, &c.,

FRED. W. P. JAGO.
Plymouth

THE MURDER NEAR CRACOW
TO THE EDITOR OF *THE TIMES*.

Sir,

It was with the profoundest concern that I noted a communication in *The Times* of this morning from your Vienna Correspondent, relative to the alleged existence of a superstition that in certain circumstances a Jew might be justified in slaying and mutilating a Christian woman.[39] "Woe unto the ears that hear this; woe unto the eyes that see this!" I may exclaim with an ancient Hebrew sage. I can assert, without hesitation, that in no Jewish book is such a barbarity even hinted at. Nor is there any record in the criminal annals of any country of a Jew having been convicted of such a terrible atrocity. These facts were conclusively proved by Professor Delitzsch, of Leipsic, and Dr.

---

[38] The use of fingerprinting as a legitimate and recognized means of criminal detection was still many years away. Although first proposed by Dr. Henry Faulds in 1880, fingerprinting would not be used in a criminal case until 1892, in Argentina. It would not officially be used in England until 1901.

[39] Reference to the trial of a Galician Jew named "Ritter," who was tried in 1884 for the murder and mutilation of a Christian woman in a village near Krakow. The *Times* of October 2nd 1888 suggested a similarity between this case and the murder of Annie Chapman, and further went on to state that "among certain fanatical Jews there existed a superstition to the effect that if a Jew became intimate with a Christian woman he would atone for his offence by slaying and mutilating the object of his passion. Sundry passages of the Talmud were quoted [at Ritter's trial] which, according to the witnesses, expressly sanctioned this form of atonement." This fed into the rampant anti-Semitism of the day, and caused an uproar in London's Jewish community.

Bloch, a member of the Austrian Imperial Diet, on the occasion of the trial of Ritter, who, living in an atmosphere surcharged with anti-Semitism, had been accused of this crime, but who was ultimately acquitted, there being, as your Correspondent admits, no doubt as to his innocence.

We are, then, surely justified in hoping that, after the experience of many centuries as to the falsehood of such and similar charges, after the concurrent testimony borne by eminent Christian divines and scholars to the horror with which Judaism and Jews have at all times viewed the shedding of blood, this mediaeval spectre has been exorcised forever. And, in sooth, the tragedies enacted in the East-end are sufficiently distressing without the revival of moribund fables and the importation of prejudices abhorrent to the English nation.

I remain, Sir, your obedient servant,

HERMANN ADLER[40]
Office of the Chief Rabbi,
16, Finsbury-square,
London, Oct. 2.

TO THE EDITOR OF *THE TIMES*.

Sir,

It is with utter amazement and stupefaction that I read in your to-day's issue (2nd October) the following passage which your correspondent from Vienna found necessary to convey to you by wire:- "There is no doubt that the man was innocent; but the evidence touching the superstitions prevailing among some of the ignorant and degraded of his co-religionists remains on record, and was never wholly disproved."

Has the writer never seen and never heard that all those depositions and quotations were clumsy fabrications? That the absurd fable - the legend of the blood - has been "wholly disproved" by a host of eminent writers?

Is he going to play the *role* of the "bloodhounds" recommended by various correspondents and, based upon a superstition, place these horrible crimes at the door of my unfortunate coreligionists?

I cannot find expressions strong enough to condemn these atrocious crimes; but it makes man still more despair of the progress of mankind when one sees this revival of absurd legends disposed of long ago.

Some 30 or 40 years ago Professor Theodoras refuted them in the columns of *The Times*, and in

---

[40] Dr. Hermann Adler (1839-1911), Orthodox Chief Rabbi of Britain from 1891 to 1911.

such a conclusive manner, that we thought we had heard for the last time of these legends in England, or in an English paper.

For your correspondent this, however, does not seem to exist; he has probably never heard of the publications of Professor Delitzsch, Chwolson, and a host of others. Nor does he seem to know that these superstitions do not prevail among the Jews even in the most degraded position, but that these are superstitions entertained against the Jews from which the Jews turn with horror and disgust.

Not the slightest shadow of a doubt has been left. This absurd legend has been "wholly disproved." It is forming now only a portion of medieval folk-lore.

Being regularly the outcome of the then *ecclesia militans*, all the religious sects which formed a minority had in turns to suffer from that calumny. Shall I repeat here all those eloquent and vehement protestations of the Fathers of the Church (Tertullian, Minucius Felix, Justinus Martyr, Athenagoras, Origen, Epiphanius, &c.), when the heathen mob accused them of such horrible crimes as the "Feast of Thyestes?" Shall I repeat the denunciations of the Albigenses, Manicheans, Kathars, and after their extirpation, of the Jews during the Middle Ages? or all that has been written against the Schismatics (Raskolinski) in modern times in Russia?

Baseless and without foundation as these legends are, they are dangerous even in normal times; how much more in abnormal? Who can foresee to what terrible consequences such a superstition might lead, when the people frantic with rage and terror, get hold of it and wreak their vengeance on innocent men?

I consider it as a duty imposed upon me by my position to protest most energetically against this and similar calumnies, still more as a duty towards truth, to brand it as a calumny, and not to let it even for a moment pass as having any foundation whatsoever.

Elsewhere we have to look for the perpetrator of these horrible crimes, which cast a gloom over the most civilized town in Europe.

I am, Sir, yours truly,

M. GASTER, Ph.D.,
Chief Rabbi of the Spanish and Portuguese
Jews' Congregations of England.
19, Brondesbury-villas,
Kilburn, N.W.
London. Oct. 2.

LETTERS FROM THE PUBLIC.
(From the Daily Telegraph)

We continue to receive a vast amount of correspondence upon the subject of these appalling crimes. In most cases the writers express deep regret and surprise at "the strange apathy of the Home Office," and all of our correspondents offer suggestions in regard to the motive of the criminal, or criminals, and "methods of capture." "Owen Banford," "S. M.," "G. Standerwick," (Bristol), and a host of others follow up previous proposals to employ women as detectives. A lady writes from "The Boltons," and "A Terrified Woman" from Kensington, mentioning instances of "street ruffians" frightening them at lonely spots. One man followed a young girl shouting, "Stop, stop! I am not Leather Apron," and in another case a man started out of a dark corner "with a loud cry and flashing a knife." Several correspondents imply that "street prowlers" are trying to work up "a sort of reign of terror." "St. Aubin Hamilton," "T. L. Selder," "W. M. R.," "Clergyman," and "Detective" are of opinion that the crimes are committed by an organised gang working singly; that the Armstrong case has driven some "moral purity man" crazy, "and given him a mission to wipe out the social evil, or, at all events, to make such a stir as to arouse the authorities to a sense of their responsibilities"; that "such exciting revivalism as the Salvation Army movement may be responsible in a measure for the condition of mind of the criminal"; and, finally, that "in the event of this scent being wrong, a certain hospital should be visited with a view to obtaining a list of cases discharged incurable." Herbert F. Scott describes the silent boot referred to yesterday. "It is used," he says, "by the police of Leeds. The outer sole and heel, which are of leather, are pierced at intervals by studs or buttons of india-rubber, which are attached to a middle sole of the same material, the inner sole next the foot being of leather. These boots are perfectly silent, and have the additional advantage of being warm and entirely damp-proof, even in the worst weather." "G. C." has a fancy "that the perpetrator is a being whose diseased brain has been inflamed by witnessing the performance of the drama of 'Dr. Jekyll and Mr. Hyde' - which I understand is now wisely withdrawn from the stage. If there is anything in this, let the detectives consider how Mr. Hyde would have acted - for there may be a system in the demonic actions of a madman in following the pattern set before him." "A reform of our police regulations and the management of our streets in the matter of what is called the social evil must follow - and that quickly - these terrible events, however little impression they may make on Mr. Matthews," writes "M. P.," and many other correspondents are of the same opinion. It is impossible to do more than give this general view of our letters from the public and to print the following.

TO THE EDITOR OF *THE DAILY TELEGRAPH*.

SIR -

I wish to assert my mite of protest against what would seem a lack of human feeling on the part of the Home Secretary - were we not cognisant of the fact identified in your admirable description of

"Justice unhappily personified," as being utterly "helpless, heedless, and useless." With such qualifications it would seem that his conclusions must have emanated from another judgement, and if his adviser or advisers be of opinion that rewards are useless, and consequently should be dispensed with, let them call to mind the history of Carey, whose individual villainy at least resulted in the capture of the murderers of Lord Frederick Cavendish and Mr. Burke, the perpetration of which act most probably formed the goal of their ghastly ambitions, and let them judge if they can reasonably withhold a similar provision at the present issue, which, if successful in its object, as we anticipate, would not only rid the world of an incarnate demon - author of six and not two atrocities, if conjectures be correct - but would also prevent the recurrence of fresh victims, whose number bids fair, under the present circumstances, to become "legion"; and if unsuccessful, at all events, the glimmer of credit that may have been reflected on the present Government's home affairs will not be dispelled (as it might otherwise be) by such multitudinous horrors, the continuation of which (many will opine) already owes its origin to the abject weakness of one man, who fears to liberate fellow beings from this awful cloud of terrorism merely because of his timidity of stepping outside the barrier of conventionalism to break the "present rules" - since, perhaps, immediate precedent does not justify such a course.

Rewards are in such cases, as we all know, efficacious, and it is the paramount duty of a Government to protect its own people, to instill into their minds respect for itself, and so consent to the simple petition of all - a petition which is fast becoming more than heartrending.

Yours faithfully,

HOPE.
London, W., Oct. 1.

TO THE EDITOR OF *THE DAILY TELEGRAPH*.

SIR -

In examining the chart representing the locality of the Whitechapel murders, published in your issue of to-day, it is curious to observe that lines drawn through the spots where the murders were committed assume the exact form of a dagger, the hilt and blade of which pass through the scenes of the sixth, second, first, and third murders, the extremities of the guard making the fourth and fifth. Further, the spot where the portion of the apron belonging to the victim of the Mitre-square tragedy was picked up lies in the imaginary line which forms the hilt of the dagger. Can this possibly afford a clue to the position of the next atrocity?

I am, Sir, your obedient servant,

OBSERVER.
London, Oct. 2.

TO THE EDITOR OF *THE DAILY TELEGRAPH*.

SIR -

In the midst of the general horror and indignation inspired by the recent outrages in Whitechapel, it seems to me that one point cannot be overlooked, namely, that in two cases at least (that of Annie Chapman and the latest of the poor victims), their lives might have been saved could they have found a shelter and a bed without being compelled to have recourse to their dreadful trade in order to pay for them. It is surely a most awful responsibility for a professedly Christian country to incur, that any woman, however low and degraded, should be driven to prostitution for want of the shelter which we do not deny to our dogs. If every woman in the kingdom would contribute one penny, such a fund might be raised that refuges might be established in every quarter of London where a homeless woman could obtain a bed by simply asking for it. I am writing in the hope that you may think it worth while to insert this suggestion in your valuable paper, as there are, no doubt, thousands who would be only too thankful to be able, at such infinitesimal cost to themselves, to diminish in any way the dangers and temptations of the unhappy class of "unfortunates." In the case of the "Women's Jubilee Fund" a large sum was collected by dint of a little loyalty and energy. It surely would not be too much to expect from the women of England a warm national response to a call dictated by religion and humanity on behalf of their erring sisters.

Believe me, Sir, your obedient servant,

CARITA.
Clapham, Oct. 2.

TO THE EDITOR OF *THE DAILY TELEGRAPH*.

SIR -

Just about twelve months ago an inmate of the lunatic asylum at Leavesden, near Watford, escaped while out with others in the charge of keepers.[41] He managed to get into the Bricket Woods, and has since evaded capture. The local paper warned females against being out at night in the neighbourhood, as this man was dangerous only to women. The question is, whether the authorities in London have had this lunatic's description, as the fearful crimes of the East-end point to such a person.

Yours obediently,

X.
St. Albans, Oct. 2.

---

[41] See response from Chairman of the Leavesden Asylum Committee in *The Daily Telegraph*, October 5th 1888 (reprinted in this volume).

3 October, 1888

TO THE EDITOR OF *THE DAILY TELEGRAPH*.

SIR -

Referring to your deeply valuable articles on police powerlessness and Home Office incapacity may I not point out what a bitter taunt the brutal callousness of our fossil-like Home Secretary is placing in the hands of the political opponents of the Government?

Should not those who uphold so strenuously and rightly the unity of the Empire be the first to declare in acts, as well as in words, that the same care is given to the protection of the poorest subject, as to the protection of the richest? Does it not make all men of thought blush with shame who listen to the common talk of the inhabitants of the East-end when such inhabitants express their belief that the callousness of the Government arises from the fact of the butcheries being wreaked on the poor and unfortunate. Again, Sir, I gratefully, for one, thank you for your plain speaking and cutting reproaches towards those in lofty official positions, and am, Sir, your obedient servant,

GEO. HY. COMPTON.
The Cottage, Loddiges-road, Hackney, Oct. 2.

THE MOTIVE OF THE MURDERS.
TO THE EDITOR OF *THE DAILY NEWS*.

SIR,

If we hold that the East-end murders are the work of a maniac, or rather of a monomaniac, what profiteth this conclusion, so long as it is a mere abstract one? Of itself it brings us no nearer to the sole desideratum-the detection of the murderer. But if an index-finger be pointed, quite tentatively, toward the elucidation of his particular phase of monomania, may it not be that the utterly barren abstractness of the problem shall be sensibly diminished? May one, at all events make the attempt?

Is the monomania, then, a simple thirst for blood? Clearly not. Else the slayer would kill indiscriminately, and not concentrate his ferocity on women, and on one particular class of women.

Is the monomania of the nature of religious fanaticism; possessing "one who believes that he has a commission from on high to destroy, root out and dishonour the kind of women-sinners whom he so persistently selects?" If so, why should not the slayer content himself with the simple act of life-taking? Why should he proceed to mutilation in which on this hypothesis, there seems no shadow of purpose.

Again, if his monomania urges him simply toward the extermination of loose women, why should he kill only the poor and shabby of the sisterhood? Why should he not occasionally direct his steel against the higher grades of the wretched profession-the "gay women" who flaunt other parts of London? Assuming him to be so mean of attire as to be flouted by these comparative aristocrats of vice, why does he use Whitechapel and its vicinage as his exclusive shambles? If his single aim were prostitute-murder in a seclusion offering an all but certainty of immunity from detection, there are innumerable regions in this metropolis haunted by possible victims offering greater opportunities than does teeming Whitechapel. The parks of nights are fringed by poor creatures plying their sad avocation, whose bosky resorts are out of ken, even of the infrequent policemen. The edges of Hampstead have their sorry night-birds; London Fields are not destitute of nocturnal prowlers; even the lonely lanes about Fulham are not pure from this contamination. But this murderous monomaniac goes afield nowhither; he has restricted himself wholly to the East-end, and to one particular narrow area of that wide-lying region.

We have then a murdering monomaniac who murders only loose women, and these of the poorer grade; who confines his deadly operations to Whitechapel and its environs, and who savagely mutilates as well as slays; who further is not apparently actuated by fanaticism.

Do these limitations and characteristics avail us anything? Suppose his lunacy is the lunacy of revenge, possibly complicated by physical disease. Clearly he is a man familiar with the geography of the Whitechapel purlieus. Clearly he is a man not unaccustomed in the manner of accosting these poor women as they are wont to be accosted. Clearly he is a man to whom the methods of the policeman are not unknown-the measured pace, the regular methodic round, the tendency to woodenness and unalertness of perception which are the characteristics of that well-meaning individual. He knows his crowd, too. How easy-given a certain unostentatious shabbiness of aspect and raiment-to pass and repass among a population strangely self-centered, because of a common and universal poverty. He may have been in every throng that gathered around every victim; he may have been a frequenter of the inquest-rooms; aye, he may have volunteered in identification enterprises.

Probably, a dissolute man, he fell a victim to a specific contagion, and so seriously that in the sequel he lost his career. What shape the deterioration may have taken, yet left him with a strong, steady hand, a brain of devilish coolness, and an active step, is not to be defined. Medical men know how varied, how penetrating, how obstinate are its phases.

It is a curious fact that some men are so constituted as to conceive and foster a bitter hate and furious rancour against the hapless creatures involved. Just as I have heard the British soldier wounded in action rave with oaths for the blood of the individual foe who had unwittingly struck him down from a far-off distance, so I have over and over again heard him denounce the most venomous anathemas on an unfortunate woman. Others I have heard use terms not less strong against the whole class.

The man's physical health ruined and his career broken, he has possibly suffered specific brain damage as well. At this moment-I cannot use exact professional terms-there may be mischief to one of the lobes of the brain. Or he may have become insane simply from anguish of body and dis-

Archibald Forbes, from a cartoon in *Vanity Fair*.

tress of mind. Any how he is mad, and his mania, rising from the particular to the general, takes the fell form of revenge against the class, a member of which has wrought him his blighting hurt, against, too, the persons of that class plying in Whitechapel, since it was from a Whitechapel loose woman that he took his scathe. And so he falls a-killing of them, and of none other of the lieges in Whitechapel or elsewhere. And when he kills, he mutilates, always in the same specific and significant manner, his maniacal impulses of revenge inspiring his semi-scientific butcher work. A wounded wild beast crunches the spear that has stricken him.

Let it be noted, finally, that his work with the knife proves him to possess some knowledge of anatomy. The medical schools of the hospitals have a large attendance, and perhaps it would be futile to inquire whether any one connected with these beneficent institutions may have a vague memory of an excitable, impressionable student whose career had been arrested and whose hopes had been blighted by such a misadventure as I have referred to, whose reason had given way, and in whose mania was the crave that he might have revenge for the mischief that had destroyed him. Between that crave and a monomania stimulating to the acts of the Whitechapel murderer there is no great gulf.

Your obedient servant,

Oct. 2.
ARCHD. FORBES[42]

NO THEORY.
TO THE EDITOR OF *THE DAILY NEWS*.

SIR,

Will you allow me to say that if the detective police wish to come upon the traces of the Whitechapel murderer they should begin by discarding all theories? It is impossible to have followed the particulars which have been published from day to day in the *Daily News* without remarking that the police have hitherto been haunted with the spectre of a dirty, unshaven man of forbidding aspect, who wears a felt hat overshadowing his brows, and slinks away when footsteps are approaching. One other detail has seemed till yesterday to be settled beyond all doubt. That is that this bloodstained miscreant lives in low lodging-houses and moves in the same class of life as his unhappy victims. When it is observed that people of this class would not be likely to possess the anatomical knowledge which the assassin has exhibited, the ready answer is that he was perhaps a broken down slaughterman, or, as some have suggested, a post-mortem room hospital porter. In support of this it is pointed out that the anatomical dissection is rough and clumsy, as if even a

---

[42] Archibald Forbes (1838-1900), British war journalist and member of the Royal Dragoons.

Liston[43] or a Nelaton[44] could perform surgical operations with skill and neatness in a dark corner and in imminent peril of the gallows. Of course it may be that the assassin is a houseless wanderer and a man of very unprepossessing appearance. He may attire himself in a sombrero or even in a leather apron. But what it is desirable that the police should bear in mind is that he may possibly be nothing of the sort. Suppose, for example, he is a medical man whose mania it is to believe himself a chosen instrument for the destruction of a particular class of sinners. Such a maniac might be expected to be dressed like an ordinary citizen; and might be assumed to have a fairly presentable exterior. He could slink out of a night without attracting attention in his own household, and, could certainly get home again and rid himself of traces of his crime with more facility than any chance inmate of a common lodging house. More pertinent still, while a Mr. Hyde slinking about Whitechapel just now in the small hours of the morning would inevitably have the policeman's bullseye turned upon him before he had got far, a gentleman in a black coat and tall hat would pass unchallenged, and hardly noticed. I need hardly say that I am not suggesting that a local surgeon is the criminal. All I wish to point out is that such a notion is at least as sustainable as the wretched outcast, or the prowling black [mauler] theory. The obvious deduction is that the way to find the Whitechapel assassin is to try all clues, exclude no hypothesis, and in brief, have

NO THEORY.

WOMAN-KILLING NO MURDER.
TO THE EDITOR OF *THE DAILY NEWS*.

SIR,

With reference to the eloquent and timely letter on above subject from Mrs. Fenwick Miller, I beg to point out that in your issue of to-day there is what seems to be another instance of the infliction of light sentences for inhuman conduct towards women. I refer to the case of James Henderson, tailor, who violently assaulted an unfortunate woman by striking her three times on the head with a buckthorn stick, causing blood to flow freely, and rendering the poor woman partially insensible, at the same time brutally threatening to "rip her up the same as a few more had been done." Surely a fine of 40s., or a month's imprisonment was an inadequate sentence for such cowardly and ruffianly treatment, yet that was the extent of his punishment. Strange to say Mr. Horace Smith considered the previous good conduct of the prisoner a reason for dealing gently with him. One would think that as he ought to have known better the punishment should have been all the heavier.

Oct. 2.
JUSTICE.

---

[43] Probably a reference to Joseph Lister (1827-1912), a British surgeon who popularized the use of sterilization during medical procedures.
[44] Reference to Auguste Nélaton (1807-1873), noted French physician and surgeon.

TO THE EDITOR OF *THE MORNING ADVERTISER*.

SIR,

I wish to offer a suggestion respecting the recent murders at the East-end of London. Our detectives are principally taken from the police force and adopt the military walk. No matter what clothing they are dressed in, I myself can guess pretty closely as to who is a detective; and the thief, the villain, and the murderer may possibly be sharper in detecting a detective than I am myself. My suggestion is that as those murders occur among women who reside or frequent cheap lodging-houses, all deputies of common lodging-houses should be made detectives; and if they were well paid I think the police might learn something from them which would facilitate the discovery of criminals.

I am, Sir, yours, &c.,

A PUBLICAN

BLOODHOUNDS.
TO THE EDITOR OF *THE ECHO*.

Sir,

I am quite convinced that, had a bloodhound been put upon the track of this diabolical fiend after the perpetration of any of these crimes, that he would not now be at large to the terror of the town. There are several of these noble and exquisite-scented animals in London. Their owners can be ascertained from the secretary of the Kennel Club. I would suggest that one be kept at each of the police-stations in the neighbourhood, and that upon the recurrence of a similar crime - which God forbid - that no one should be permitted to approach the body within a few feet, till the dog has taken up the scent. It requires animal instinct to track this villain. I will wager that once upon his trail, a bloodhound will not leave it till he is found.

Yours faithfully,

J.G. Newfield
173 Strand
Oct. 2

8 August, 1888

METROPOLITAN IMMORALITY.
TO THE EDITOR OF *THE ECHO*.

Sir,

In fairness, I would ask you to permit a reply to "Disgusted." There is a belief that the poor murdered woman were more at the mercy of the slaughterer (if only one) through the very practice which "Disgusted" disgustingly approves of. Surely after these poor virtue-bereft creatures have become vicarious martyrs in place of virtuous and more respectable members of the sex, further persecution of a class of whom it may well be said that "sufferance is the badge of all their tribe" is shameful indeed. Two well-known moral philanthropists, namely, J.B. Wookey and Maurice Gregory, have written thus:-- "I would not join the coward band that think that to drive these unfortunate creatures to prison or to hell is doing God a service." "We have been harrowing the women for centuries without doing any good." I wonder if the elder (and virtuous) brother in the parable of "The Prodigal Son," ever employed any agencies to keep the "disgrace to the family" away from the longing arms of the father at home.

Pro Caritate
Mile-end
Oct. 2

Blood Money to Whitechapel
TO THE EDITOR OF THE STAR.

SIR,

Permit me to comment on Mr. Shaw's letter. I trust it will lead your readers to study the accursed nature of landlordism which preys on our vitals and threatens our national extinction.

I demur to one allusion by Mr. Shaw. We have too good a cause to require such dishonest tactics of statescraft as manufacturing outrages for Ireland, and inventing "Parnellism and Crime."[45] The class Press, that he complains of, perceived that the strike of the Bryant and May girls was a sham. They were paid better than chain-makers or agricultural laborers, and 25 per cent. more than other East-end industries. Some had married and brought up their children in the employ. Socialist leaflets were thrust into their hands when they left work, and grievances were concocted. Such questionable tactics estranged our friends and played into the hands of the enemy. Above all things let us be honest.

Yours, &c.

JOHN WHEELWRIGHT.

---

[45] Charles Stewart Parnell (1846-1891), an Irish political leader who was accused in 1887 of complicity in the Phoenix Park murders of Lord Frederick Cavendish and T.H. Burke. A widely publicized inquiry was held which vindicated him completely. He would later become a member of Parliament.

4 October 1888

LETTERS FROM THE PUBLIC.
(From the Daily Telegraph)

Mary Malcolm's[46] suspicion "that the woman who had been murdered was her sister" because, when she was in bed, she fancied the poor creature came and kissed her three times, has evidently inspired many of our most recent correspondents with suggestions for calling in the aid of Spiritualism and other more or less occult agencies. "A Clairvoyant" is of opinion that "if Ripper's letter were submitted to an efficient medium, the writer might be discovered." "Spiritualist" writes "that there are both male and female practitioners who might be of great service. Of course it is the fashion to scoff at Spiritualistic revelations; but there are on record many authentic cases in which the acute and sensitive medium has been enabled to unravel mysterious occurrences as dark at the outset as is the black and awful mystery that surrounds these current London tragedies." "Inquirer" asks "the Spiritualists of London" to "investigate these murders in their own way, and see what they make of them. If they can, as they unblushingly affirm, call spirits from the vasty deep, why not at once communicate with the unhappy women who have been hurried all untimely to their last account?" "S." writes: "I have read at different times, and also have been told, that when under the influence of mesmerism the medium can described what has taken place on any day and at any locality at the will of the mesmerist. If this is so, cannot mesmerism be applied in tracing the murderer?" "W. H. Bakes," "Fleet-street," and "S. Smithers" refer to the fact that murders similar to those in the East-end have been committed in America and Texas, and that it might be worth while for the police to keep this fact carefully in mind. "X. Y. Z." says: "The Whitechapel fiend is the prototype of the brutal hero of an old Indian story which appeared some time after Cooper's Indian stories gave the romance its title of 'Nick of the Woods.' It recounts the doings of a poor Quaker settler whose farm in the backwoods was burnt, and his wife and children killed, by the Red-Indians, and himself scalped and left for dead. He, however, lived, but with a distorted mind, and, becoming a trapper and hunter, he waged deadly warfare against the Indians. He killed many of them in the woods, and even in their own wigwams, and upon the body of every Indian he cut a deep cross over the region of the chest with a sharp hunter's knife. The Indians thought their race was being destroyed by an evil spirit. This was concerted revenge for wrongs done him by the red race. In all probability the Whitechapel fiend is inspired with the same kind of blind revenge upon all women of the class. Possibly he may have read the story of Nick of the Woods, and has made it his model. If this theory is correct modest women need have no fear." Several correspondents mention strange out-of-the-way places in the metropolis, "dark, unfrequented corners that invite to crime," and "Revenge" describes "a court in Chelsea," attached to a common lodging-house, "where doorless outbuildings in dark places might have been designed purposely for murderous work," and he advises that "the police should have special powers to close these places." "R. Roberts" asks

---

[46] Witness at the Elizabeth Stride inquest. Malcolm identified the body as her sister, Elizabeth Watts. This was disproved when Mrs. Watts made a live appearance at the inquest on a later date.

for "more light - the electric light in particular." "Mentor" says "the worst places are the least lighted." Hundreds of letters refer to "the medical question" in all its phases. They are interesting as indications of the public belief that the murderer is a maniac under the influence of some terrible physical misfortune; as are also an almost equal number which express the belief that the murderer is "mad on religion - thinks himself a divine instrument of vengeance." Edward Dillon Lewis, in a long letter discussing the subject from the point of view of what for a better term he calls "speculative jurisprudence," is convinced, for reasons which we have not space to print, that "the perpetrator of these several outrages is a man of foreign origin. The celerity with which the crimes were committed are inconsistent with the ordinary English phlegmatic nature; but entirely consistent with the evidence given in some more or less similar cases abroad. The mutilation involved a degree of anatomical knowledge and skill which, according to high medical opinion, would not be likely to be possessed by an English slaughterman (to whom, at first, suspicion pointed); whereas, this special skill is possessed, to a not inconsiderable degree, by foreigners engaged in various special trades abroad. The character of the knife used, as suggested by the medical evidence at the inquests, is similar in kind to the instrument known as the French 'Cook's Knife'; or, at least, is, in the circumstances, more consistent with its use by a foreigner than an Englishman."[47] The following letters are selected from among vast numbers which reach us by every post:

TO THE EDITOR OF *THE DAILY TELEGRAPH*.

SIR -

I see that all suggestions that bloodhounds be used in the hunt after the Whitechapel murderer are received with almost ridicule. This appears to me a mistake. Granted that their instinct has greatly deteriorated, and also that under certain atmospheric conditions (which are unknown) scent will not lie on stone, still there are many hounds in England, and many bassets and dachshunds in Germany who would have probably run down the murderer. The errors which have been set forth are, first, that scent is necessarily a foot-scent. The blood on the man's hands would do nearly as well. There are authentic instances in which a sheep's carcase removed in a cart has been tracked for twenty miles. Probably we have now no hounds capable of that, but such scenting power is not needed. Second, the idea was started by Dr. Phillips - admittedly in ignorance - that the body and not the murderer would be hunted. This is also a grave error. It may happen; but two words, "Ware heel!" are ample to correct the mistake. Of this any one may satisfy himself with foxhounds. Third, that scent will not lie on stones. The fact is that no one has the slightest idea where and when scent will lie. I have seen boar-hounds, not remarkable for wonderful hunting powers, carry scent up Regent-street and Portland-place in the early morning, in either '81 or '82. I do not assert for one moment that bloodhounds will be able to do the work, but I know that there is more than a

---

[47] The full contents of this letter by Edward Dillon Lewis were printed in the *Times* that same day, and reprinted in this volume.

possibility of it. It depends more on the will-o'-the-wisp scent than the hounds. Still, it is so possible that scent may lie that they ought to be tried when the probable sequel to these six tragedies happens. I cannot too strongly urge that scent is not necessarily on the ground or a foot-scent.

I am, Sir, yours,

BLOODHOUND.
London, Oct. 2.

TO THE EDITOR OF *THE DAILY TELEGRAPH*.

SIR -

May I suggest that the police should pay close attention to the crews of steamers leaving for the Continent and out-ports on each Sunday morning. Tide served early yesterday morning from the piers in the river. These steamers return during the week, and many of the sailors have only too great a reason to bear animosity to the class of women from which these unfortunate victims come; while the fact that each successive murder has occurred on Saturday night or early on Sunday morning, and that all trace of the murderer has immediately disappeared, would point to the conclusion that his hiding-place, or rather abiding-place, was not far off. Let the night watchmen of the various wharves from which such steamers leave be questioned, as also the watermen at the various "stairs" from which the crews are sculled on board to vessels lying in the tiers.

I remain, Sir, your obedient servant,

WATERSIDE.
London, Oct. 1.

TO THE EDITOR OF *THE DAILY TELEGRAPH*.

SIR -

It is a well-known fact that the Paris police employ disappointed or broken-down gentlemen, who have education, knowledge of life and logic (a rare virtue, and yet invaluable in a detective), and who, having spent their patrimony, are unable to carry out their profession, while the very idea of a situation is nauseous to them. These men are liberally treated in every respect, and are generally very successful.

With regard to the present murders, there is a strong probability that the perpetrators thereof have a home to retire to, and that it is not by merely searching the slums that they will be found, but in better quarters. From Whitechapel he or they have gone to the City, and will, no doubt, if not caught, be soon heard of again in other parts - probably at King's-cross or Pimlico. This, at least, is my idea, based on sound inductive grounds. His modus operandi is, however, so simple that it is a matter of amazement that with nearly all the detective force drafted to Whitechapel (and by the by they are easily enough recognisable) he or they have not yet been caught red-handed by closely watching the movements of "unfortunates" late at night.

Yours obediently,

CANIS
London, Oct. 1.

TO THE EDITOR OF *THE DAILY TELEGRAPH*.

SIR -

It would be interesting to know if the police are keeping a watch on the opium dens in Whitechapel. Excessive indulgence in that drug is known to cause homicidal mania, and the monster who is "wanted" may turn out to be a frequenter of these dens and an excessive indulger.

I enclose my card and remain your obedient servant,

R. H. T.
London, Oct. 2.

TO THE EDITOR OF *THE DAILY TELEGRAPH*.

SIR -

I much deplore the sacrifice of life of my fellow-creatures, and would suggest that all congregations who love Christ will throughout the nation make it a point of special prayer to Almighty God that some truthful information may be forthcoming that will lead to the apprehension and conviction of the wretch who has committed these shocking murders in London.

I am, Sir, your obedient servant,

W. S. PILLING.
Wimpole Lodge, Colchester, Essex, Oct. 1

TO THE EDITOR OF *THE DAILY TELEGRAPH*.

SIR -

There surely can be little doubt that the mysterious demon who has worked such havoc in the East-end is a dangerous maniac. It cannot be that he has just escaped from any lunatic asylum; otherwise he could have been tracked ere now. Is it possible, however, that he may have been some time ago "dismissed" from such an institution as "cured?" If so, could it not be ascertained from the journals of asylums whether any recently dismissed case ever at any time laboured under the appalling delusion with respect to prostitution with which this dangerous madman is possessed. What if not only his delusion, but his insanity, were due to a medical origin, in the first instance? And hence his murderous attacks on this poor and most unfortunate class of women. This clue might prove of some service.

Yours truly,

DAVID SIME, M.D.
Endymion-road,
Finsbury Park, N.,
Oct. 3.

TO THE EDITOR OF *THE DAILY TELEGRAPH*.

SIR -

A remarkable incident in connection with the above is that in no one instance has it been found that the victim made any noise or cry while being done to death. My assistant suggests a theory in reference to this very remarkable fact, which strikes me as having something in it, and as such ought to be made public.

The theory is that the murderer goes about with a vial of rum or brandy in his pocket drugged with an opiate - such as a solution of morphia, which is almost if not quite tasteless - that he offers a swig of it to his victims (which they would all be likely to greedily accept) when he meets them; that in about ten to twenty minutes the poison begins to do its work on constitutions well soaked with alcohol, and that then they are easily dispatched without fear of making any noise or call for assistance.

Having been out of town lately for my holidays, I have not closely followed the evidence at the inquests but there are two questions which would require clearing up, if there is anything in this theory - First, Have the stomachs of most of them been ripped open to do away with the evidence of poisoning in this manner; and, second, has any analysis of the contents of the stomachs been made?

Yours respectfully,

R. MACDONALD[48]
Coroner for North-East Middlesex.
65, West Ferry-road, Millwall, E.
Oct. 3.

TO THE EDITOR OF THE TIMES.

Sir,

In the absence of any definite clue to the perpetrator of the recent dreadful atrocities at the East-end of London, it seems desirable to consider the question from the point of view of what, for want of a better word, I may call speculative jurisprudence.

It will be admitted that if suspicion can be, with even reasonable conclusiveness, focused on a particular and, if possible, small class of persons, there may be a greater probability of the speedy detection of the perpetrator than by a more or less vague inquiry directed over a large and densely populated area. At the same time, assuming my hypothesis to be fallacious, there is no reason why, while investigating it within its own narrow limits, the wider inquiries now being pursued should be diminished.

There is, I think, a reasonably general consensus of educated opinion that the late several murders, with their exceptionally concomitant horrors, are the work of one and the same person.

Inquiry has also fairly established that the theory suggested that the murders and mutilation where to secure a particular organ of the victim's body is untenable.

Robbery, or the gratification of animal passion, or revenge in its ordinary personal acceptation being beyond the question, the solution of motive may have to be sought in some form of mania arising from one or other, possibly, of the following causes - viz., some wrong, real or imaginary, sustained at the hands of the class to which the poor murdered women belonged; or an insane belief as to the good to result to society by their extermination.

It is to be observed that homicidal mania, in the sense of an unrestrainable desire to kill merely, is not here present, the tendency being directed against a particular class exclusively.

---

[48] Dr. Roderick Macdonald (1841-1894) would later serve as coroner for the Mary Kelly inquest on November 12th 1888.

These questions are, however, for the moment comparatively unimportant beside the more pressing one as to the direction in which the murderer or homicidal maniac is to be sought.

For reasons which I shall state concisely, I venture to suggest that the perpetrator of these several outrages is a man of foreign character.

The grounds for this conclusion are:-

(a) That in the whole record of criminal trials there is, I believe, no instance of a series of crimes of murder and mutilation of the particular character here involved committed by a person of English origin; whereas there are instances in some foreign countries of crimes of this peculiarly horrible character.

(b) The celerity with which the crimes were committed is inconsistent with the ordinary English phlegmatic nature; but entirely consistent with the evidence given in some more or less similar cases abroad.

(c) The mutilation and removal of certain organs involved a degree of anatomical knowledge and skill which, according to high medical opinion, would not be likely to be possessed by an English slaughterman (to whom at first suspicion pointed); whereas this special skill is possessed, to a not inconsiderable degree, by foreigners engaged in the charcuterie and other kindred trades abroad.

(d) The character of the knife used, as suggested by the medical evidence at the inquests, is similar in kind to the instrument known as a French "cook's knife," or at least is, in the circumstances, most consistent with its use by a foreigner than an Englishman. In offering these opinions I do not desire to suggest what indeed my experience negatives, that a foreigner, as such, has any monopoly of brutality over an Englishman. There are forms of brutality which are committed by Englishmen which a Frenchman or an Italian, for instance, would never dream of. But there are also idiosyncrasies of crime which are, as it were, peculiar to particular countries, both in their conception and mode of execution.

I am, Sir, your obedient servant,

EDWARD DILLON LEWIS
8, Bow-street, Covent-garden, W.C., Oct. 3.

TO THE EDITOR OF *THE TIMES*.

Sir,

Having been long in India and, therefore, acquainted with the methods of Eastern criminals, it has struck me in reading the accounts of these Whitechapel murders that they have probably been committed by a Malay, or other low-class Asiatic coming under the general term of Lascar, of whom, I believe, there are large numbers in that part of London. The mutilations, cutting off the nose and ears, ripping up the body, and cutting out certain organs - the heart, &c. - are all peculiarly Eastern methods and universally recognized, and intended by the criminal classes to express insult, hatred, and contempt; whereas, here the public and police are quite at a loss to attach any meaning to them, and so they are described as the mere senseless fury of a maniac.

My theory would be that some man of this class has been hocussed and then robbed of his savings (often large), or, as he considers, been in some way greatly injured by a prostitute - perhaps one of the earlier victims; and then has been led by fury and revenge to take the lives of as many of the same class as he can. This also is entirely in consonance with Eastern ideas and the practices of the criminal classes.

Hundreds of these men have resided long in that part of London, speak English well - although when necessary they cannot understand a word - and dress in ordinary English clothes.

The victims have been the poorest and most miserable, and probably only such would consort with the class of man I speak of.

Such a man would be quite safe in the haunts occupied by his fellow-countrymen, or, should he wish to escape, he could join a crew of Lascars on the first steamer leaving London.

Unless caught red-handed, such a man in ordinary life would be harmless enough, polite, not to say obsequious, in his manners, and about the last a British policeman would suspect.

But when the villain is primed with his opium, or bang, or gin, and inspired with his lust for slaughter and blood, he would destroy his defenceless victim with the ferocity and cunning of the tiger; and past impunity and success would only have rendered him the more daring and reckless.

Your obedient servant,

NEMO.
October 2.

MR. FORBES'S THEORY.
TO THE EDITOR OF *THE DAILY NEWS*.

SIR,

Mr. Forbes, in the letter you publish to-day, suggests that the Whitechapel murderer cannot be a religious monomaniac, believing himself to be the appointed instrument for ridding the earth of a certain class of sinners, because he confines his operations to Whitechapel and "mutilates as well as slays." This seems to me to afford another example of the perils of theorizing. Such a maniac as he is here contemplating would naturally desire to deter as well as to destroy; to strike terror-and so far he has unquestionably been very successful-into the hearts of the wicked as well as to rid the earth of their presence. If so, would not this explain the mutilations quite as satisfactorily as the suggestion of a medical student blindly avenging personal sufferings? As to confining himself to Whitechapel, the murderer, whoever he may be, would probably feel the need of a basis of operations not far removed from the scene of his outrages - a place whence he could conveniently sally forth and whither he could as easily return to divest himself in private of those traces of his crime which can hardly have been entirely absent in any one instance. We have only to suppose that this retreat is in Whitechapel and we have at once a plausible answer to the question why-for the present at least-Whitechapel is the locality he selects. I have not as yet met with a single suggestion which is not open to some such obvious alternative suggestion. This is why I continue, and would advise others to continue, to have

NO THEORY.
Oct. 3.

WOMAN KILLING NO MURDER.
TO THE EDITOR OF THE DAILY NEWS.

SIR,

It is impossible of course to deny the force of the satire in Mrs. Fenwick Miller's letter under this heading in Tuesday's Daily News. She has a right to be angry at savage treatment of her sex. She has a right to think that the barbarians who assault women but stop short of murder are too lightly punished. It is not quite so clear that she is right in railing at the judges and the magistrates. It is never quite safe to conclude that a necessarily short report of a police-court case or of a trial at sessions or assizes contains all the facts essential to a fair judgment of the fitness of the sentence. Let Mrs. Miller reflect on the position of the prosecutors in such cases as she cites. They are not Shylocks insisting on their pound of flesh. On the contrary they are in too many cases unwilling witnesses of their own hurt. Often they plead with the magistrate so earnestly not to send their brutal husbands or "protectors" to trial, and not even to punish them, that he is sorely puzzled how to decide betwixt conflicting claims of justice and of mercy. He is told, and he knows, that if the man goes to gaol the woman and her children must go to the workhouse. Tears are often added to entreaties for mercy. What, in such circumstances, would Mrs. Fenwick Miller do? Insist on aggravating the misery of the woman in order to increase the severity of the man's punishment? From the cases Mrs. Miller mentions I would rather draw the conclusion that more must be done to make women independent, to open markets for their labour, and generally to enable them to protect themselves by means far more efficacious than punishments.

Yours, &c.,
Oct. 3.
A.P.

THE WHITECHAPEL MURDERS.
TO THE EDITOR OF *THE ECHO*.

Sir,

It would be unwise to pin one's self entirely to one theory; but the presumption that the four last Whitechapel crimes have been the work of one individual is very strong, almost overwhelmingly so, because, although you might get two or more to combine to do such things for profit, you could hardly get them to do so for the sheer love of murder or mutilation. The ruffianism that prevails all over London, and especially in the East-end, also in some of our manufacturing towns, is due partly to the want of stringency in the law, but more to the utter callousness exhibited by Judges and Magistrates in its administration. The sentences inflicted for violence against the person are utterly ridiculous. For violent assaults on three persons, the other day, a Magistrate inflicted a sentence of £15s., or fourteen days; comment on such leniency is unnecessary. Had the man stole a watch worth ten shillings perhaps he would have had three months. The lash for aggravated assaults, when totally unprovoked, would almost entirely suppress them. Minimum sentences should be fixed, for both Judges and Magistrates have shown themselves unworthy of discretionary power. Prosecutors, as well as prisoners, should have a right of appeal.

Yours truly,

COCKNEY.

TWO PRACTICAL SUGGESTIONS.
TO THE EDITOR OF *THE ECHO*.

Sir,

May I suggest through your columns the desirability of our police being provided at night time with indiarubber "clumps" to the soles of their boots, whereby their tread would be as noiseless as the wheels of a bicycle similarly shod? The tread of the policeman may now be heard at dead of night a quarter of a mile off, and is as useful a warning to the burglar as was the voice of the night watchman of old, when calling the hour. It is to be hoped that our rowdy M.P.'s will take warning by the horrible atrocities lately committed, and discontinue their abominable avocation of inciting the ignorant - directly or indirectly - towards lawlessness and crime, and resistence to the police in their arduous efforts to preserve order.

I am, &c.,

W.E. Corner
Oct. 3.

THE EAST END TRAGEDIES.
TO THE EDITOR OF THE ECHO.

Sir,

Will you allow me to support your suggestions of the advisability of the authorities to supply policemen on night duty with noiseless boots? I have frequently seen people meet after dark under suspicious-looking circumstances, disperse immediately on hearing the heavy measured tramp of an advancing policeman - whereas, if he had been wearing silent boots he probably would have been in time to have seen what their little business really was. I firmly believe the noiseless booted policeman would greatly tend to diminish street lawlessness.

Yours faithfully,

Henry Bax.
16, Lincoln's-inn-fields, W.C.

TO THE EDITOR OF THE TIMES

Sir,

In reply to a letter of the 2nd inst. from the Clerk of the Board of Works for the Whitechapel District transmitting a resolution of the Board with regard to the recent atrocious murders perpetrated in and about Whitechapel, I have to point out that the carrying out of your proposals as to regulating and strengthening the police force in your district cannot possibly do more than guard or take precautions against any repetition of such atrocities so long as the victims actually, but unwittingly, connive at their own destruction.

Statistics show that London, in comparison to its population, is the safest city in the world to live in. The prevention of murder directly cannot be effected by any strength of the police force; but it is reduced and brought to a *minimum* by rendering it most difficult to escape detection. In the particular class of murder now confronting us, however, the unfortunate victims appear to take the murderer to some retired spot and to place themselves in such a position that they can be slaughtered without a sound being heard; the murder, therefore, takes place without any clue to the criminal being left

I have to request and call upon your Board, as popular representatives, to do all in your power to dissuade the unfortunate women about Whitechapel from going into lonely places in the dark with any persons - whether acquaintances or strangers.

I have also to point out that the purlieus about Whitechapel are most imperfectly lighted, and that darkness is an important assistant to crime.

I can assure you, for the information of your Board, that every nerve has been strained to detect the criminal or criminals, and to render more difficult further atrocities.

You will agree with me that it not desirable that I should enter into particulars as to what the police are doing in the matter. It is most important for good results that our proceedings should not be published, and the very fact you may be unaware of what the Detective Department is doing is only the stronger proof that it is doing its work with secrecy and efficiency.

A large force of police has been drafted into the Whitechapel district to assist those already there to the full extent necessary to meet the requirements; but I have to observe that the Metropolitan police have not large reserves doing nothing and ready to meet emergencies, but every man has his duty assigned to him; and I can only strengthen the Whitechapel district by drawing men from duty in other parts of the metropolis.

You will be aware that the whole of the police work of the metropolis has to be done as usual while this extra work is going on, and that at such a time as this extra precautions have to be taken to prevent the commission of other classes of crime being facilitated through the attention of the police being diverted to one special place or object.

I trust your Board will assist the police by persuading the inhabitants to give them every information in their power concerning any suspicious characters in the various dwellings, for which object 10,000 handbills, a copy of which I enclose, have been distributed.

I have read the reported proceedings of your meeting, and I regret to see that the greatest misconceptions appear to have arisen in the public mind as to the recent action in the administration of the police. I beg you will dismiss from your minds, as utterly fallacious, the numerous anonymous statements as to the recent changes stated to have been made in the police force, of a character not conducive to efficiency.

It is stated that the Rev. Daniel Greatorex announced to you that one great cause of police inefficiency was a new system of police whereby constables were constantly changed from one district to another, keeping the ignorant of their beats.

I have seen this statement made frequently in the newspapers lately, but it entirely without foundation. The system at present in use has existed for the last 20 years, and constables are seldom or never drafted from their districts except for promotion or from some particular cause.

Notwithstanding the many good reasons why constables should be changed on their beats, I have considered the reasons on the other side to be more cogent, and have felt that they should be thoroughly acquainted with the districts in which they serve.

And with regard to the Detective Department - a department relative to which reticence is always most desirable - I may say that a short time ago I made arrangements which still further reduced the necessity for transferring officers from districts which they knew thoroughly.

I have to call attention to the statement of one of your members that in consequence of the change in the condition of Whitechapel in recent years a thorough revision of the police arrangements is necessary, and I shall be very glad to ascertain from you what changes your Board consider advisable; and I may assure you that your proposals will receive from me every consideration.

I am, Sir, your obedient servant,

CHARLES WARREN.

5 October 1888

LETTERS FROM THE PUBLIC.
(From the Daily Telegraph)

The state of panic under which many of the letters addressed to us have been written has passed into what may be called the sympathetic phase of the subject. In addition to the correspondence which follows these notes we have received numerous other suggestions that charitable action should be taken in the interest of "the wretched women of the East-end." "A Mother" would at once "help in providing refuges for houseless wanderers." "Matron" says "such refuges should be altogether distinct from casual wards, and be conducted with a view to save miserable creatures from the stony wretchedness of the streets." "An Englishwoman" points out that "there was last season a good deal of that social craze called 'slumming,' but it was only a fad; it did not go down into the gutter, or if it did, not with practical grip and intention; it ought to be impossible in a great Christian and powerful city such as ours that a woman should wander about homeless and penniless." "T. W. S.," following up this train of comment, dwells upon "the failure of our Poor-law system, and the utter inadequacy of the police relief that is given through the means of casual wards, &c.," and proposes that the "Primrose League should form out of its own ranks 'a League of Mercy,' to aid the City missionaries, clergy, relieving-officers, and police in ameliorating the lot of the unfortunate women upon whose dreadful lives recent investigations have shed a red and realistic light." The detective system of the London police is discussed by "Vindex," T. Jones, M. Williams (Liverpool), and many others rather in a spirit of suggestion than criticism. J. Morris (Manchester) believes that "the detectives of the great cities of the North are a better trained body of men than the London force." "A. W." says: "We must have detective officers with whom the criminal cannot make himself familiar. We must have a body of men who are unknown, and are able to make their way unsuspected and, in fact, trusted by the very criminals themselves. It is worth while to remind the public of what has occurred several times in France, where, perhaps, the secret police is the most efficient in the world. It has not unfrequently happened that members of the secret police there, even women, have become trusted members of bands of ruffians, and have taken a leading part in the planning and preparation of a crime. At the right moment they have, of course, arranged for the capture of the whole gang, and stood side by side in the dock with the criminals unsuspected and believed to be virtually of their class, and have received at the hands of the judges sentences as if they had actually participated in the crime. They have subsequently, of course, been removed to a place of safety, and rewarded as their valuable services deserved." Several correspondents refer to the caligraphy of the "Ripper." "F. C." says "the writing is a decided Civil Service hand." "M. S." has no doubt "the writer is an American." H. E. Bell sets forth many reasons for thinking that "the man is a fish-cleaner in one of the markets or elsewhere." Henry Harrison, on the other hand, thinks the expression "squealed" points to a pig-sticker, and "Amateur Detective" emphasises the fact that "there are slaughterhouses near the scene of the tragedies, and one is a place where decayed and 'played-out' horses are butchered." Among the various "hints to the police" are many which have already been acted upon. "F. T.," however, thinks "that the empty warehouses and factories of the district have not been sufficiently searched"; and Alfred C. Calmour (Arundel Club) "ventures to suggest that the sewers in the neighbourhood of the late murders should be searched, as there is just the possibility of the murderer having escaped by them." "M. H." says: "A man could escape through the sewers to more than one place of safety, and could hide his changes of clothing on his way to and from the scenes of his dreadful 'work,' as the 'Ripper' calls it." "Bloodhound," combating the idea that the murderer is a madman, says: "I have had a larger practical acquaintance with homicidal maniacs than Dr. Forbes Winslow ever had, for I have lived with them, and I emphatically assert that this series of crimes is the work of no lunatic, homicidal or otherwise. There is too much coherence of idea, too much fixity of purpose, too much self-control displayed. Insanity has its saving clauses, and this is one of them. These atrocities are the handiwork of no individual, but of a confederacy. This explains everything: the amazing audacity, the ease with which detection has been evaded, and the commission of two consecutive murders in one night, obviously by the same agency, but not, possibly, by the same hand." "W. H.," "Citizen," and "Ellerford" express satisfaction with Sir Charles Warren's letter; but "Wideawake" is of opinion that the police will never unravel the mystery unless the Government supplements the rewards now offered by the promise of "a free pardon to any confederate who may confess to a guilty knowledge of the assassinations."

TO THE EDITOR OF *THE DAILY TELEGRAPH*.

SIR -

In your report of the proceedings at the Worship-street Police-court on Tuesday last, and which appeared in your columns of yesterday, I am stated to have made an observation to the magistrate, Mr. Montagu Williams, which - in consequence perhaps of addressing the magistrate, and not the reporter - has been somewhat misrepresented. The magistrate denounced in strong language the tendency to immorality and crime which the common lodging-houses of the East-end fostered, and the facilities they afforded for the concealment of the criminals and outcasts of society.

The inspector of police present made a remark to the magistrate, and I, as *amicus curia*, said, not as reported, that there was only one section in the Criminal Law Amendment Act[49] which could deal with these cases, but that such cases - indiscriminate letting of beds to strangers of both sexes - could not be dealt with under the Criminal Law Amendment Act, unless it could be proved that the premises were used for habitual prostitution. The magistrate suggested that further legislation was required. That may be desirable, but does it not suggest to any ordinary observer that the same law which would prevent a travelling tinker and his wife, or companion, from staying in a

---

[49] The Criminal Law Amendment Act of 1885 was a direct result of the "Modern Babylon" child-prostitution scandal. It raised the age of consent from thirteen to sixteen and strengthened laws against prostitution and homosexual activities.

common lodging-house in a "double" would also apply to Lord Boldash and Lady Nocash staying at the Grand or any other hotel? I agree with the magistrate that these houses are the haunts of, to a large extent, the criminal class, but these houses are inspected by and are under the eyes of the police.

Suppress the houses, and what becomes of the *habitué*? They are not suppressed. So long as the class exists they will have their haunts and resorts. You do not destroy the vermin by simply destroying their nests. Neither can you suppress wickedness and crime by driving them into holes and corners. Mr. Montagu Williams professes to have had large experience with this class of people. Suggestions from an authority such as Mr. Williams for the amelioration of the criminal class and for the prevention of criminal practices are what society is now anxiously waiting for.

I am, &c.,

G. WALKER,
Vestry Clerk, St. Leonard, Shoreditch.
London, Oct. 4.

TO THE EDITOR OF *THE DAILY TELEGRAPH*.

SIR -

Permit me to suggest, in reference to the tragedies that are at present occupying the mind of everyone -

1. That the idea that the letters attributed to the murderer could have been a "practical joke" or "hoax" is quite untenable. It is inconceivable that any human being, even the most degraded, could joke on such a subject. Rather, the more degraded the class, the more sympathy there would be with these unfortunate women. Besides, the letters breathe the very spirit of such a murderer.

2. It is unlikely that the man's dress or exterior is at all in keeping with his crimes. Probably he is well dressed, and his entire appearance is such as to totally disarm suspicion, otherwise women would not trust themselves in his company in the way they seem to do.

3. His letters favour far more of American slang than of home. They are the exact reprint of the Texas rough's style, and probably the Texas solution of the mystery is the true one.

I am, &c.,

OBSERVER.
Edinburgh, Oct. 3.

TO THE EDITOR OF *THE DAILY TELEGRAPH*.

SIR -

I am anxious to make one suggestion in the matter of the late horrible murders which, to my mind, is a most important one, and has evidently been overlooked.

Supposing this "living monster" has an accomplice (which I cannot but think he must have in some shape or form), would the said accomplice be tempted, even by the offer of a large money reward, to give information respecting the actual murderer until he was assured that a "free pardon" would be granted him (the accomplice), seeing that the very moment he gave information he might be charged with being an "accessory" both before and after the fact?

The Home Secretary has stated that he does not see his way clear to offer on the part of the Government a money reward, but I question whether he would not be prepared to concede this point if his attention were drawn to it.

I am, Sir, yours obediently,

H. R.
London, Oct. 4.

TO THE EDITOR OF *THE DAILY TELEGRAPH*.

SIR -

A letter in your columns to-day has expressed thoughts which have been for some days in my mind. Your correspondent points out the ease with which an immense sum was contributed by the Women of England for a Jubilee offering. Also the urgent need of a night shelter for those unfortunate ones in the East-end, who cannot afford the price of a night's lodging, and are therefore forced to buy a few hours rest with the wages of sin.

I feel sure most Englishwomen's hearts burn with shame for these poor unfortunates; but they would gladly stretch out a hand to raise and help them, if they only saw a way of doing so. Were the women of London appealed to they would eagerly contribute towards a scheme for helping their fallen sisters. What is wanted is someone to set the ball a-rolling, and the women of London will not let it stop until sufficient means have been raised for building and placing on a working basis this much-needed refuge.

Is there no one in London capable of starting such a scheme and of bringing the matter to a successful issue?

I am, Sir, yours obediently,

E. R. L.
Kensington, Oct. 3.

TO THE EDITOR OF *THE DAILY TELEGRAPH.*

SIR -

I am requested by the committee of the Leavesden Asylum to advert to the letter signed "X" in your issue of this date, respecting the escape of a patient from this asylum some twelve months ago, and to forward you the following certificate respecting the condition of the patient prior to and at the time of his escape from the asylum.

Oct. 3, 1888.

"The patient who escaped from this institution whilst out with a walking party on Sept. 16, 1887, was, during his residence here, perfectly quiet and harmless, and certainly had no homicidal tendency. - H. CASE, Medical Superintendent."

I am, Sir, your obedient servant,

JOHN BELL SEDGWICK,
Chairman of the Leavesden Asylum Committee.
Leavesden Asylum, near Watford, Herts, Oct. 3.

TO THE EDITOR OF *THE DAILY TELEGRAPH.*

SIR -

What we really need in the detective service, is a staff of men selected more for their brain power and ability to meet cunning with cunning, than for their height and chest measurement. We want a detective force whose members shall be unknown except to a few superiors, and shall be trained to patiently investigate and follow up criminals, something after the manner of Lecoeqs and Pinkertons, and who shall be selected without reference to their physical development; the only qualification needed being brains and ability to use them. A body of men such as this, unhampered by red tape, would do more to rid the metropolis of crime than double our present automaton militarised police force.

I am, Sir, yours faithfully,

JO. PERROTT.
London, Oct. 3.

TO THE EDITOR OF *THE DAILY TELEGRAPH*.

SIR -

According to the account of the Mitre-square murder in your paper of yesterday's date I understand this poor woman, who was so brutally mutilated in the early hours of Sunday morning last, was arrested for drunkenness on the previous evening, taken to Bishopsgate Police-station, and retained there until one o'clock in the morning, and then sent out into the streets. What for, but to be driven to and fro by the police?

Such treatment as this is inhuman to the very extreme. Here is a poor woman, with no friends and no home, sent adrift at an early hour in the morning, and barely twenty minutes after is led to the slaughter by a fiend.

If it had been a respectable person, who had taken an extra glass, she would have been retained until about eight or nine o'clock, and fined for being drunk and incapable. But in this case it is a poor creature without a cent in her pocket towards payment of a fine, and she must suffer, being sent away immediately she is sober.

If she had been retained like a respectable person would have been, she could not have met with her death.

Would to God these poor creatures were treated kindly on every hand, and pointed to Christ, which is the only way to check them in their downward walk in life.

Yours, &c.,

E. A. HARVEY.
Leyton, Oct. 4.

TO THE EDITOR OF *THE DAILY TELEGRAPH*.

SIR -

The recent dreadful crimes in London must have filled every heart with pity and sorrow for the poor forlorn outcasts of the East-end of our beloved city. Poor creatures, whose history shows them to have been at one time in quite respectable positions, but have most surely sunk to the lowest depths through that great curse - drink. Here in the North one hears nothing but pity and indignation that such a state should exist, while subscriptions are being continually raised for foreigners in distress. Is it not time something was done to help the poor creatures in our cities, and let them know they are not so utterly God-forsaken as one of your correspondents feelingly remarks? It was while seeking a shelter that these poor lost sheep have met their deaths. I am sure if a fund were opened every woman in England would gladly and thankfully offer their mite to help our poor and fallen sisters to feel that while there is life there is hope. If you will kindly insert this, believe me, yours,

L. K.
Birkdale, Oct. 3.

TO THE EDITOR OF *THE TIMES*.

Sir,

Perhaps you will allow me to suggest that the murderer's object may be - first, by his crimes to cause a reward to be offered, and then by the accusation of an innocent man, and by the manufacture of apparent tokens of guilt against him (as by staining his clothes with blood), to win that reward. A second Titus Oates[50] is not impossible.

I remain, Sir, your obedient servant,

H.P.B.
40, Mostyn-road, Brixton, S.W., Oct. 3.

POLICEMEN'S BOOTS.
TO THE EDITOR OF *THE ECHO*.

Sir,

The proposition of your Correspondents, "W.E. Corner" and "Henry Bax," that the police should be supplied with noiseless boots is simply absurd. They seem to forget that the desired "noiseless boots" would lead to no end of serious frights, and possibly fatalities. What is more fatal to a nervous person than to become suddenly aware of the presence of an unknown person behind one. Even a strong-nerved man would be very apt to be "frightened out of his wits" by the "sudden feeling" that someone were behind him. The idea is ridiculous.

Yours truly,

Ernest Fisher.
Harley-street, W.

---

[50] Titus Oates (1649-1705) was infamous for being responsible for the execution of more than a dozen innocent Catholics after he spread rumors of a non-existent Catholic plot to execute King Charles II. In a 2006 poll by *BBC History Magazine* Oates was ranked the sixth worst Briton of all time. Jack the Ripper was voted #1.

Whitechapel.
TO THE EDITOR OF THE STAR.

SIR. -

The Star suggests watch societies as aids to the police. A helpful suggestion; but should we do the work of the police and pay them for their inefficiency - so leaving them more at leisure to break our heads? Is this a fair way of taking money from the taxpayer? No wonder the police are inefficient when members of the detective force, in order to make their work thorough, are expected to pay necessary expenses out of their own pockets. We are too busy paying pensions, or wishing to do so, to the already overfed and over-wealthy. The Home Secretary can't offer rewards now for the detection of crime. It's only half a dozen poor women who have been butchered. We forget that the poor Prince of Wales's eldest son must have an establishment, for which when Parliament meets a demand will be made. What does it matter about the poor? We must not forget the practical service done for us by these crimes; they create a diversion. Truly Mr. Jesse Collings says, "What do we care for the civilised world?" Our civilisation, indeed! What a mockery! Practical Christians like Mr. Balfour want to make of Ireland another Whitechapel; but Ireland, who is crucified for us, declines to be made criminal by Coercion. All these frightful butcheries are being continued with an appalling regularity, and Endacotts and Bloys swarm in our police force; and why? Ireland blocks the way. How terribly fulfilled are the words of our great leader. We can't afford to do justice. We must even promote our criminal constables for bludgeoning unprotected women in our streets "for fear Home Rule should be given to Ireland."

Cannot Mr. Matthews and Sir Charles be proclaimed from our house-tops. Is all decent humanity and mercy so dead within us that we must keep silence? Our evil deeds are coming home to roost with a vengeance, and I call on all honest men and women to see to it that our rulers shall be made to listen to us.

Yours, &c.,

C. H.

6 October 1888

TO THE EDITOR OF *THE DAILY TELEGRAPH*.

SIR -

In reading your report on Monday of the murder in Whitechapel I notice that the unfortunate woman[51], when seen by Constable Lamb, 252 H Division, was clutching some grapes in her right hand and sweets in her left. Is it not probable that the murderer bought the grapes for his victim? Supposing that to be so, is it not also probable that the grapes were purchased only a few minutes before the murder, and in the immediate neighbourhood? I would suggest a strict inquiry among the vendors of fruit in that locality.

Yours truly,

R. E. LAWFORD WEBB
Bedford Hotel, Bognor, SussexOct. 4.

TO THE EDITOR OF *THE DAILY TELEGRAPH*.

DEAR SIR -

Would you kindly give room in your columns for a few remarks in reference to a paragraph in your paper of Tuesday last, respecting a statement made by cabmen. They are reported to have said that a very suspicious-looking man called at one of the cabmen's shelters on Sunday afternoon, and asked if they would cook him a chop, which they did. While it was being prepared they conversed with the stranger about the Whitechapel murders. Then the stranger remarked, "Don't you know who did it? I am the man," and so on. He produced a brandy-bottle, asking them to drink with him. The cabmen said they were all teetotalers. According to their report, they asked him to sign the pledge, which he did. I should like to know through your columns if the writing on the letter and post-card has been compared with the pledge-paper. If it in any way corresponds, the cabmen would be useful instruments in identifying the man, supposing him to be the murderer.

Yours obediently.

E. R. B. C.
Brockley, Oct. 4.

---

[51] Reference to Elizabeth Stride.

TO THE EDITOR OF *THE DAILY TELEGRAPH*.

SIR -

I trust you will allow me space in your columns to make a protest against the unjust and preposterous statement made by your correspondent "Observer" in to-day's issue. He declares that the letter supposed to have been written by the Whitechapel murderer is "an exact reprint of the Texas rough's style." Now I take the liberty of doubting whether "Observer" has had better opportunities of studying the genus "Texas rough" than I have. I have ridden up the "trail" (any Western man will know what that means), and have spent the last three years in railway camps, where the "Texas rough" pure and simple abounds, and I venture to say that the ghastly "sang froid" which the perpetrator of these murders has proved himself to possess is utterly contrary to the character of the "Texas rough." Beyond being addicted to an over-indulgence in bad whisky and an unpleasant readiness with his six-shooter, the Texan has none of the qualifications which are indispensable to the stealthy assassin.

With regard to the series of murders which occurred in Austin, Texas[52], some three years ago, the motive was without doubt "outrage and robbery"" the victims being invariably killed afterwards with an axe, hammer, or some other weighty weapon, mutilation in the Whitechapel sense being completely absent.

Yours obediently,

ANGLO-TEXAN.
London, Oct. 5.

TO THE EDITOR OF *THE DAILY TELEGRAPH*.

SIR -

As certain of your correspondents think it would be useless to put the bloodhounds on the murderer's track some time after, as the scent would be destroyed by the number of people crossing in the streets, I would suggest that a bloodhound should be kept at some of the police stations in Whitechapel, and if another murder is committed the animal should be sent for immediately, and it would soon find the murderer's whereabouts, as the scent would be fresh and strong. The hound should be sent for as urgent as a fire engine. - Hoping something will be done to unearth the monster, I remain, yours obediently,

H. J. CUSHING.
London, Oct. 5.

---

[52] A series of eight grisly axe-murders were committed between December 1884 and December 1885 in Austin, Texas. The perpetrator was never discovered.

6 October, 1888

TO THE EDITOR OF *THE DAILY TELEGRAPH.*

SIR -

The horrible revelations in connection with the Whitechapel murders have cast a lurid light upon some of the sadder aspects of the East-end life of our great city. Are these to fade into oblivion so soon as the momentary excitement shall have subsided, or is there to be any practical outcome? "Sweating" and "slumming" have been but evanescent crazes. Is there not here and now a distinct and definite opportunity to hurl back the charges of want of sympathy and "touch" on the part of the pulpit with these darker shadows of the sin and suffering with which we are encompassed and confronted? Many suggestions have been made, none more practical than that of a great central night shelter for the penniless and the abandoned, a friendly aisle which will preclude the possibility of the dread alternative between an all-night wandering over the stony streets or a brief rest in the horrid den of a common lodging-house procured by the wretched "wages of sin."

I shall be happy to hear from any London ministers who may be willing to co-operate in the institution of such a plan.

I am, Sir, faithfully yours,

GEORGE H. GIDDINE.
Syivan Villa, Woodford.

TO THE EDITOR OF *THE DAILY TELEGRAPH.*

SIR -

I would suggest a system of patrol by police in plain clothes, say, from eleven at night till five in the morning. This system was introduced during the time I was in the Montreal Police Force. I can assure you the patrol was a terror to evil doers, and also a great assistance to constables on their beat, coming to their assistance in many cases unexpectedly. The law-breakers were always in dread, never knowing when the patrol would drop on them.

I am, Sir, yours respectfully,

EX-CONSTABLE C. BADDELBY.
Pimlico, S. W.,
Oct. 5.

TO THE EDITOR OF *THE DAILY TELEGRAPH*.

SIR -

The letter and post-card of the murderer are thought by many to be merely the ill-timed and senseless act of some low caste man bent on a stupid hoax; but I am inclined to consider they come from the murderer himself. There is much character in them, several American expressions, the handwriting of a firm and determined man, still young. Then the threat on Sept. 25 of the "double event," which was fatally carried out on the 30th, and which no one in London could foresee but himself. Drunk with success he could not help issuing some boasts of his hideous and unnatural skill. The idea of publishing fac-similes of his handwriting in *The Daily Telegraph* was a most excellent one, and may yet lead to important results. We may suppose his vocation requires writing more or less often, and surely there must be several persons in London who know his penmanship. Will nobody come forward to announce his knowledge or suspicions? By degrees it is to be hoped the "Ripper" may be traced before further crimes are committed. I do not think it at all likely there are accomplices. The motive is either revenge or monomania. No one would join in a course of crime, dangerous, barbarous to the last degree, and with scarce a prospect of pecuniary or any other advantage.

Your obedient servant,

H. Y. P.
Bayswater,
Oct. 5.

TO THE EDITOR OF *THE DAILY TELEGRAPH*.

SIR -

Just a line to point out that the two letters signed "Jack the Ripper" could only have been written by an American, or by one who had resided "across the herring pond" long enough to have thoroughly mastered the Yankee language. Surely this fact, taken in conjunction with the coroner's remarks, and that nothing has been heard from the American said to have offered £20 for the parts taken, would point to American agency in the matter.

I am, Sir, your obedient servant,

F. SCHAFFTER.
Hague,
Oct. 4.

TO THE EDITOR OF *THE DAILY TELEGRAPH*.

SIR -

Your correspondent "E. R. L." will be pleased to hear that such a movement as he speaks of has been started to provide shelters for those poor creatures wandering about our streets. In Paris shelters are provided and maintained at the cost of the municipality, and have answered the purpose in every respect. No one need to be shelterless there during the night. I hope to have one of these shelters opened in the East-end of London during the present month; the difficulty is to provide a fund to permanently maintain them. Be it remembered that in London alone there are upwards of 15,000 homeless and shelterless wanderers through its streets every night in the year. It is a cruel fact.

Yours, &c.,

SAML. HAYWARD, C. E.
212, Devonshire-road, Forest-hill, S. E.
Oct. 5.

THE PERSONAL APPEARANCE OF THE EAST-END MURDERER.
To the Editor of *the Pall Mall Gazette*.

SIR,-

If, as seems highly probable, the four last East-end murders are the work of the same individual, he has involuntarily supplied those who have studied the connection between character and appearance with certain indicia respecting himself which may prove useful in the search which is now being made after him. To give in full the reasons for every statement made below would need several columns of your paper. Suffice it to say, that a careful study of all the circumstances of the case have led me to the conclusion that the following description represents roughly the appearance of the murderer:-- He is a man of about the middle height, or not much above it, with broad shoulders and powerful muscular development. The hands are muscular, the fingers short, the thumbs thick and stunted. The feet are broad in proportion to their length. He is of dark complexion, with dark hair, but, in all probability, stone-grey or steel-grey eyes, as these are the only absolutely relentless eyes. These eyes at times open in such a way as to show some of the white above the pupils, but, as a rule, the lids are half-closed, the lower lids rising more than is usual. The jaw is square and firm, and the ears are situated low down in the head. He is probably about forty years of age, and is certainly not under thirty. He is dressed in dark clothes and wears a flannel shirt, and a dark silk handkerchief round the neck. He also wears dark gloves and thin side-spring boots. His hat is probably a dark stiff "bowler." He is a man of education and some means, and his appearance is entirely respectable. His manner is quiet and composed, and there is nothing to betray the monomaniac except a certain mingled restlessness and some cunning in the expression of the eyes. Such a description may seem somewhat fanciful, but there is a reason more or less valid for every item; in fact, it would be strange if coincident and convergent circumstances gave no clue to personal appearance as well as character.

Faithfully yours,

October 4.
A. EUBULE EVANS.

BLOODHOUNDS IN LONDON.
To the Editor of the Pall Mall Gazette.

SIR,-

Much nonsense is being written just now about the bloodhound and its use in the detection of crime. Credited with a morbid, insatiable craving for blood, it is said to have a savage and ferocious nature, which makes it as dangerous to friend as to felon. The plain fact is that the average bloodhound of to-day is a docile, gentle, faithful creature of high, nervous temperament, but singularly free from "vice," and particularly suitable as a reliable playmate for children. The bloodhound does not crave for blood. He is content with such Spartan fare as Spratt's biscuits and the water-trough afford. The keen scent, quick intelligence, patience, and power of concentration found in a well-bred, highly-trained bloodhound -- to say nothing of his good looks -- have made him the hero of much harmless romance. The bloodhound, for instance, is credited with having tracked down Fish, the Blackburn murderer, goodness knows how long after the deed. The dog which did assist, in the remotest way, in Fish's capture was not a bloodhound, but a dog of some mixed breed. In old Border work -- sheep-stealing, slave-hunting, and in all cases where the conditions of place and time have given the bloodhound a fair chance of following up the scent -- he has done good, and sometimes astonishing, service. But the presence of blood is not essential to the successful tracking down of the quarry. If a hound is to track men he must be trained specially for this class of work, as the harrier for the hare, the foxhound for the fox, and the deerhound for the hart. Indeed, in old times the bloodhound was trained for all these purposes. The first Lord Wolverton's pack hunted either the red or fallow deer, I forget which.

A well-known Northern breeder of bloodhounds to-day treats his hounds to an occasional outing by giving some needy and obliging tramp sixpence, half-an-hour's start, and an assurance that the hounds "won't hurt him." The tramp starts off at the top of his speed, the hounds are cast off in half an hour or so, and they find the tramp either up a tree or in the sanctuary of a wayside inn imbibing beer and emitting maledictions. That the exquisite scent and splendid powers of the bloodhound could be directed to the detection of crime in cities, after long, patient, and intelligent training, I have little doubt. But is there a hound living that has had this training? If a country-trained hound were allowed to make casts in, say High-street, Whitechapel, I should expect to find it next minute in some innocent butterman's shop, intent not upon the murderer but on the margarine it scented from afar. The butterman might fall a sacrifice to an infuriated crowd, and the day of the bloodhound would be done. He deserves a better fate than this. The London police will find a good friend in the bloodhound, given patience to train him in the way he should go.

I am, Sir, your obedient servant,

PERCY LINDLEY.
York-hill, Loughton, Oct. 3.

"UNFORTUNATES."
TO THE EDITOR OF *THE TIMES*.

Sir, -

Now twice again are we confronted with the atrocious work of this assassin who chooses his poor victims from a class whose lives at the best are, of all known classes, every way the most pitiable - a struggle for daily sustenance only to be purchased by the basest physical abasement.

There will be, nay, there is already, a panic on the pavement; those who have to tread it in their sad midnight calling, one to which they had served an early apprenticeship, must be content to starve; or seeking foul lodgings - trade - as sought, not seeking, and this with scarce the chance of earning the cost of lodging, much less that of the food to sustain life in it.

It has been no writing on the wall which has thus warned the "unfortunates;" the order to depart is writ in crimson on that pavement, in those secluded spots, to which the wearied feet of the midnight seeker of the harlot's hire, by force of necessity, are but too willingly led.

When all the coroner's work is done, the sickening detail published for our whole Christian nation's perusal, then come the texts from which so many sermons will be preached, and now in ordinary pauper form these mangled remains will be committed to the earth, the fully ripened, but decayed fruit of "unfortunate" humanity; packed in the parish shells, scant covering of the shells which but lately clothed immortal souls. Then will be heard the voice of the cemetery chaplain - "It is sown in corruption; it is sown in dishonour." Had such graves echo power, how fitting would here be its effect! "God has taken to Himself the souls of our dear sisters here departed." Yes, ye of society, its upper class, ye, the dwellers in all attainable luxury, the fortunate of the earth, let your rank be what it may, your wealth a tale of millions, the Godward life of many of you ever in evidence, or the Godless life not less so; the Established Church of your nation proclaims in that solemn hour in which your own graves will be open, that these - the society labelled "unfortunates" - are before the God to whom you have been taken - your sisters. You may seek to ignore their existence. To speak of them at all is in bad taste; if forced to do so, it is as if they were a sort of human vermin, unclean parasites, a humanity affliction admitted in its existence, but so existent to be held as a matter of course; fortunately scattered where their presence does not intrude on that of those, the made of the same Creator, who dwell in all that the "fortunate" of this life can obtain of this life's enjoyment.

We seem to be on the verge of a creed that, as this state of things has so long existed, it is to be viewed as preordained, and therefore beyond human power to alleviate; it lies in our road of life, but we systematically pass by on the other side, and yet as Christians we affect to be taught of Christ.

The question, to me, seems now to be forced upon us. Is the arm of the Lord shortened, or are the hands which assume to be those by whom He would have his deeds of mercy done paralyzed? Is the axe to strike at the root of evil double-bladed, one edge fitted and sharp to deal with it in heathen lands, the other blunt and ill-adapted for home use? Are we to believe that tens of thousands of those our National Church proclaims to be our brothers and sisters, when dead, are living disgospelized, so born and reared as to be of a race the Gospel tidings and teachings cannot touch?

There is one crumb of comfort in the method by which these poor outcasts were done to death. There can have been little bodily suffering, yet who can say what that one instant feeling may have been, when the clutch of the murderer's hand on the throat of his victim flashed on her sense? This is he whose fell work had formed the theme of the "unfortunates" talk for many an hour. How many hundreds of this class reach their graves, on the other hand, by a path of utter torment to mind and body, under all the suffering of the loathsome disease, the result of their foul lives? The "pavement" is a thing of the past, changed for the filthy bed from which they will never rise; no wages can now be earned. Those who still earn such, in compassion may help to stave off actual famine; may find the lodging-money. These can feel for a sister; every surrounding of these last days just such as that on which the life of sin has been spent. The end comes, scant preparation for removal to the contracting undertaker's premises, to wait a sufficient supply of such dead to remove to the cemetery - mere waste material of lodging-house life.

After all, some will say, is there anything novel in all this? Is it not just an everyday tale of the termination of the life of such sinners? Why force it on our attention? Why not confine all reading of this foul page of humanity to those whose official duty may force them to study it, or to those who have taken voluntarily on themselves the unsavoury task of trying to purify it; it is insulting to society that it should be written where society reads? I answer it is in society's own interest that I write. I wish to open eyes wilfully closed to dangers not less dangerous because thus shut out from sight.

It is well that the fact should be pressed that all rank, wealth, high position is held in trust, has its duties as well as its privileges. The deeds may not be engrossed, the breach penalty may not be open to the eye, the day of its enforcement may be delayed; but come it will, and that often when least expected. Long sufferance may seem to have indicated impunity, but such sufferance has its limits. Wealth and station in its embodiment may at one moment be inclined to cry "Ah, ha, I am warm." It may be the moment in which the warmth only precedes an eruption volcanic which brings destruction. In my poor opinion these are just the days when apathy to the condition of the lowest classes is most fraught with danger to all other classes.

Lewes.
S.G.O.

WHITECHAPEL.
TO THE EDITOR OF *THE TIMES*.

Sir,

It seems desirable, although it ought to be unnecessary, to point out, amid the general demand for further police action, that the citizens themselves of any city are the ultimate constabulary force of that city; that with them rests the final responsibility for the maintenance of order and decency in its streets; that without their support, readily and freely given under all circumstances, but specially organized in times of special danger, the Executive alone cannot fulfil its duties.

After some experience of what may be done in the back streets of Whitechapel and Spitalfields by a few citizens who are prepared to guard the privileges they enjoy, we would urge Londoners to resume for a time their share of those functions which they have in part intrusted to the police, to lend their active and persistent support to that body, and to use the opportunity thus given for studying how our police force may be better fitted for its difficult task.

Members of the Streets Committee established in this neighbourhood for the maintenance of these principles are about in the streets every night under a systematic plan. They report every week in writing on the disturbances that have occurred, the action they or the police have taken, the state of the neighbourhood, &c. The materials thus accumulating will one day form the substance of a report which will be submitted to the public; but in the meantime the committee make representations, where it appears desirable, to the local and police authorities.

When the lovers of order have asserted their right to possess highway and byway alike in the face of those who brawl, when the owners of the houses that disgrace our byways have been obliged by the force of public opinion to perform their duties as landlords, when our local authorities have been roused by their masters, the people, to suppress disorderly houses, to cleanse and widen the streets, to pave and light the courts and alleys, the chief external conditions that favour murder will have been removed. But these things will never be accomplished so long as it is thought that the service of the State can be finally commuted by the payment of policemen, or that a public disaster like this series of murders is to be met by the offer of £1,000 reward.

Those of us who know Whitechapel know that the impulse that makes for murder is abroad in our streets every night; we are aware that these symptoms of unrighteousness can be made to disappear only by the salvation of individual character; but we feel that for this the action of the community must prepare the way. "Only the collected strength of the whole people, organized and (morally) armed to take the initiative - only it, is in a position to cope effectually with social misery. Well for us if we succeed in organizing our people in this sense."

We are, Sir, your obedient servants,

THOMAS HANCOCK NUNN.
THOMAS G. GARDINER.
Toynbee-hall. Whitechapel, Oct. 3.

THE EAST-END.
TO THE EDITOR OF *THE TIMES*.

Sir,

You were good enough to insert a letter from Mr. F. Debenham in your issue of Sept. 29 calling attention to the Tenement Dwellings Company, and I should be glad if you would allow me to state more fully the aims of the company and some of the difficulties incident to its operations.

Our object is to buy at a fair price houses occupied in tenements by respectable people, to keep them in good repair and sanitary condition, and, when practicable, to reduce their rents; to act, in short, the part of a liberal landlord. It is a somewhat long step from this to the position proposed by Mr. Barnett in his recent letter to you. He asks that philanthropic persons should combine to buy up some of the property in the worst districts of Whitechapel, and manage it in such a way as to reform it. This is very easy to say; but there are few who know so well as Mr. Barnett how difficult it would be to carry out. There is, however, one difficulty of his own creating, which consists in the publicity he has given to his proposal, thereby inviting the owners of such property to raise their terms, as their houses are going to be bought by philanthropists, of course at a fancy price. I do not for a moment suppose that this view of the matter has escaped Mr. Barnett's notice, and I should be glad if he would state the reasons which have led him to set it aside. Whatever these may be, in the particular instance of Whitechapel, I cannot conceive that any material improvement in the dwellings and surroundings of the labouring classes can be effected so long as the execution of the sanitary laws is in the hands of authorities elected like the present local authorities, upon a franchise limited to the rate-paying class - the class many of whom are directly interested in high rents and absence of repairs. No doubt something may be done by the pressure of public opinion upon the local authority even as at present constituted, and particularly by such organized effort as the Mansion-house Council on the Dwellings of the Poor are able to apply; and I would urge upon all who have been moved to ask themselves if there is nothing they can do towards remedying the state of affairs depicted in connexion with the recent horrible murders to subscribe to the funds of the Council, the office of which is at 31, Imperial-buildings, Ludgate-circus. As things now stand, under what circumstances are owners of ill-built and worse repaired houses likely to offer them for sale? Will it not be when the question of executing repairs cannot be much longer delayed, or when the fear of dilapidations at the end of a lease begins to be felt? Then, if the owner can find a philanthropist foolish enough to buy his property upon the basis of the existing rents, he will drive a bargain in which there is likely to be a less of 20 or 30 per cent to the purchaser - a bargain which, if generally known, will tend to increase the value of dilapidated house property and raise rents of tenements. If, on the contrary, intending purchasers steadily decline to give more for houses than is consistent with moderate rents while keeping up repairs, laying by for rebuilding, and earning a safe 4 per cent upon the capital invested, while no stone is left unturned to make the ownership of bad property a losing game, we may then hope by degrees to remove much of the squalor of the poorer quarters of London.

I am your obedient servant,

ALFRED HOARE,
Chairman Tenement Dwellings Company (Limited).
37, Fleet-street, London, Oct. 3.

A FRENCH CHAPTER OF WHITECHAPEL HORRORS.
TO THE EDITOR OF *THE TIMES*.

Sir,

The terror which has naturally been so widespread among the masses in the districts where the recent shocking murders were committed was intense enough without its being aggravated by the gratuitous theory of the Coroner, that these horrible outrages were not the act of a maniac, but had been coolly committed by a sane person, who wished to earn a few pounds by gratifying the whims of an eccentric American anatomist. It will, no doubt, be found that the idea that Yankee enterprise gave a stimulus to these terrible atrocities is utterly baseless.

For weeks I have been expecting that some one would draw attention to the fact that precisely the same crimes were many years ago committed in Paris, and were ultimately found to have been the acts of a monomaniac.

Last summer, while travelling in France, I picked up and glanced over a French work resembling "Hone's Every Day Book," which gave an account of a remarkable criminal who must have strongly resembled the fiend who has created such consternation in the East-end of London. For months women of the lowest class of "unfortunates" were found murdered and mutilated in a shocking manner. In the poorest districts of the city a "reign of terror" prevailed. The police seemed powerless to afford any help or protection, and in spite of all their watchfulness fresh cases were from time to time reported, all the victims belonging to the same class, and all having been mutilated in the same fiendish way.

At last a girl one night was accosted in the street by a workman, who asked her to take a walk with him. When, by the light of a lamp, she saw his face, it inspired her with a strange feeling of fear and aversion; and it instantly flashed upon her that he must be the murderer. She therefore gave him in charge of the police, who, on inquiry, found that her woman's instinct had accomplished what had baffled the skill and the exertions of all their detectives. The long-sought criminal had been at last found.

It subsequently came to light that he had been impelled to commit these crimes by a brutal form of homicidal monomania. He had sense enough to know that from this class of women being out late at night, and being friendless and unprotected, he could indulge his horrible craze on them with comparative safety and impunity, and he therefore avoided selecting his victims from a more respectable class.

He was convicted and executed, to the great relief of the public; and if any persons were afterwards tempted to imitate him, his prompt punishment effectually deterred them.

This notorious case must be well known to the Parisian police and to thousands of persons in France, and if inquiry is made its history can be easily procured.

No doubt a ruffian like him has turned up in East London, and will be also detected. When he is, we must trust that he will meet with the same stern justice that was meted out to his French prototype.

Yours obediently,

MICHAEL MACK

FRIENDLESS AND FALLEN IN WHITECHAPEL.
TO THE EDITOR OF *THE TIMES*.

Sir,

While the public are aghast at the atrocities against women of a certain class at the East-end of London is it not possible that out of this appalling evil some good may come if only suitable and prompt action be taken?

Great fear has come upon these unfortunate women, and for a time they avoid their accustomed haunts, though to many of them the loss of the wages of shame brings instantly the want of the barest necessities of life. Now is the opportunity to offer to these poor people, who at all times deserve our sympathy and help, a specially open invitation to forsake their evil lives and to return to the paths of virtue. The various societies which are constantly at work in this direction could not bear the strain of a sudden and large influx of refugees from the streets without large additional funds, and if the panic continues it might be needful to strengthen the organization as well as the finances of these societies. Among these who thus fly from the horrors of the streets, some no doubt would return to their old life when the panic was past, but if only a small proportion of the tens of thousands of London street walkers were rescued this crisis would not have occurred in vain.

If such a fund can be raised, I shall be willing to contribute £50 towards it, and many others will doubtless do much more than this.

Yours truly,

WALTER HAZELL.
15, Russell-square, Oct 2.

THE HOMES OF THE CRIMINAL CLASS.
TO THE EDITOR OF *THE TIMES*.

Sir,

In the *Fortnightly* of last January I ventured to recommend certain remedies for "distress in London." It was impossible in writing on that subject to omit reference to the lowest class of our population; and at this moment, when the veil that hung over the lives of that class has been rudely torn away, I beg that you will kindly allow me to repeat what I then suggested. My words were:-

"That some agency, official and voluntary, be formed to explore the haunts and lairs of the criminals and dangerous refuse of the population. It would need local authorities, detectives, laymen, and ministers of religion acting together. Such a raid might be tried on one district at first. We need knowledge in order to cope with the evil. Police facilities granted by Government to a volunteer committee would help in any organized effort to discover how deep the disease may penetrate. We must make a determined effort to deal with paupers and criminals, instead of, as at present, winking at their existence in our midst."

We have it on the authority of the Rev. S. Barnett, who, at all events, knows Whitechapel thoroughly, that the infected area there is not large. This may also be the case in other parts of London; but this will make the matter easier to deal with.

If the above suggestion is not considered feasible, I hope that the member for Whitechapel will, when Parliament meets, move for a Select Committee to inquire into the number of plague-spots, into the "dossing," or lodging-house system, and into the amount of supervision exercised by our police.

Faithfully yours,

COMPTON.
Oct. 4.

WOMAN KILLING NO MURDER
TO THE EDITOR OF *THE DAILY NEWS*.

Sir,

All women must be grateful to Mrs. Fenwick Miller for her timely and courageous letter in your issue of Tuesday last. The callous indifference with which the English people at large view the wholly inadequate sentences meted out to ruffians who are daily and hourly committing the most dastardly assaults upon defenceless women is a crying shame upon our nineteenth century Christian civilization. It would almost seem as if magistrates and jury alike were in league with the prisoners against the protection of the assaulted women. And yet these men must have hearts and feelings, for we see the universal indignation aroused in their breasts by the present horrible succession of murders. The same men who have been settling a case of wife beating, almost amounting to murder, by three months' imprisonment in the morning, are throwing themselves heart and soul into vigilance committees in the evening, to unearth the greater monster. The only conclusion we can draw from Mrs. Fenwick Miller's able letter is, that the protection of women and children by law is a sham and a failure; and it can scarcely be otherwise because women are ciphers in the country as far as their own interests are concerned. In illustration of utterly inadequate sentences I would draw the attention of all thoughtful men and women to but one of two or three similar cases recorded in your issue of Tuesday. It occurred in the Police court at Dalston, before Mr. Horace Smith. A man, or rather a brute, James Henderson, 22 years of age, not only threatened to "rip up" an unfortunate woman who refused to accompany him, but actually struck her several heavy blows on the head with the buckthorn handle of his stick, causing blood to flow freely, and producing partial insensibility. Her screams attracted notice, and prevented further harm being done. The man pleaded drunkenness, and was let off with a fine of forty shillings, or one month's imprisonment. The man only just escaped being a brutal murderer such as the Whitechapel monster, and yet he was discharged with a fine only. Had he succeeded in achieving his evident intention, manslaughter would have been the verdict on account of his drunkenness. A crime appears to be less a crime when committed under the influence of drink. In my opinion - and that, I believe, of all total abstainers - it is doubly a crime, because we would make drunkenness a crime and not a venial offence to be lightly dealt with and even joked about. A man seems to think that he has only to plead drunkenness in cases of common or criminal assault, and that will be sufficient justification for his brutality, and will exonerate him. Evidently men of this class have studied the law according to the police courts. But, Sir, Mrs. Fenwick Miller asks in her concluding paragraph, "What are men going to do.... what are they going to do to check the ever rising flood of brutality to women, of which these murders are only the latest wave?" I think that all women who take any interest whatever in social questions, and who see and welcome the dawn of their emancipation rising before them - be it ever so faintly - will have but one answer, and that is, that the time has fully come when women must take a part, however indirectly it may be at first, in making the laws which govern their country. Also women ought to be called upon to serve on juries in such cases as the one I have quoted, and certainly many more women ought to be elected to serve as Poor Law Guardians, on the School Boards, and in fact in every capacity where the interests of women and children are at stake. I venture to state in conclusion, for I firmly believe it, that the extension of the franchise to women will do more to regenerate society and to solve all social problems than another hundred years of masculine legislation. The time and the necessity have come for women to be recognised as an active and integral part of this great nation, if England is to keep her place in the van of civilization.

Kate Mitchell
Licentiate of the King's and Queen's
College of Physicians, &c.
Sloane street, S.W.

WOMAN KILLING NO MURDER
TO THE EDITOR OF *THE DAILY NEWS*.

Sir,

May I offer a few remarks in endorsement of Mrs. Miller's splendid letter "Woman Killing No Murder," but principally to notice the absurd and ludicrous inequality of sentences? Your correspondent confines her remarks to lenient sentences, to use a very charitable expression, but haven't we almost as many the other side, disproportionately severe sentences, for often almost trivial offences. I contend that magistrates should have no power to deal with severe cases of assaults, as their sentences are restricted to six months' imprisonment, but let them go for trial, the verdict there may be most inadequate to the offence, but at any rate, they are more likely to meet with their deserts. I know of no society that especially interests itself in such matters, but I should be most happy to see one formed, their principal object being the consideration of disproportionate sentences, with the view of forwarding brief particulars and comments to the morning and evening papers with the name of the presiding judge or magistrate who was responsible for such mockery of justice. Such accounts from time to time would draw public opinion forcibly to such shameful legal farces; and our dispensers of justice (query) might be induced to think twice before making a public exhibition of themselves, and temper their judgements with common fairness and good practical common sense.

Obediently yours,

D.H.

WOMAN KILLING NO MURDER
TO THE EDITOR OF *THE DAILY NEWS*.

Sir,

I trust Mrs. Fenwick Miller's letter may be productive of great good, the worn our arguments of "A.P." in answer thereto notwithstanding. The conduct of the judicial and magisterial bench is absolutely defenceless. First, as to wives pleading for mercy to their brutal husbands (and here let me say "A.P." should have taken notice Mrs. Fenwick Miller did not confine herself to cases alone of husband and wife), the wife's pleas are the result of sheer terror as to future consequences, and should always be interpreted in a contrary sense. Then as to the wife and family going to the workhouse when the husband is in prison; Suppose a brute for sheer amusement kicked "A.P." within an inch of his life, and the magistrate excused himself for giving a term of imprisonment long enough to be deterrent on the ground that the prisoner's family would have to go to the workhouse meanwhile. How would "A.P." appreciate his own arguments? Besides "A.P." ought to know the ruffians who knock their wives about do not usually work for them. And then there is the case in which men kill their wives, not mercifully - like the Whitechapel murderer - but by slow degrees. Extending the sphere of female labour to render them more independent of husbands is likely to influence Mrs. Fenwick Miller more than myself, for I clearly see, from practical experience, that it simply means extending the system of men living on the labour of their womenkind. In conclusion, I will give one example of judicial callousness in addition to those quoted by Mrs. Miller. Some roughs set upon a woman in the street, who took refuge in a small dairy, the woman in charge of which came forward with a poker to assist the one in distress. The poker was wrenched from her, and used about her with the result that she died. One of the miscreants was convicted of manslaughter; sentence - ten months with hard labour!

> Oh Lord, our gentry care as little
> For delvers, ditchers, and sic cattle,
> They gang as saucy by poor folk
> As I wade by a stinking brook.

A.J.M.

POLICEMEN'S BOOTS.
TO THE EDITOR OF *THE ECHO*.

Sir,

Your Correspondent "Ernest Fisher" is quite mistaken in thinking noiseless boots for policemen on night duty ridiculous. Let him try a few nights at detective work. Others more competent than myself have seen the necessity of it. When a policeman suspects a burglary is going on at a particular house, why does he approach it on tiptoe?

Yours faithfully,

H. Bax.
16, Lincoln's-inn-fields, W.C.
Oct. 5.

LONDON POLICE - A SUGGESTION.
TO THE EDITOR OF THE ECHO.

Sir,

The numerical weakness of the London police being apparently an established fact, it behoves us to seize upon any "resource of civilisation" that will tend to reduce the admitted weakness. My suggestion may not be new, but that it is worthy of consideration I am convinced. It is simply the establishment of a police-cyclist patrol. A few years back the idea would, doubtless, have been laughed to scorn. It may be to-day, but whatever treatment the suggestion receives, the fact will remain, that for rapid, silent, and economical patrol duty, the cycle stands pre-eminent. Indeed, its many advantages are so obvious, that it would be wasting your valuable space to specify them.

I beg to subscribe myself,

Progress.

A STRANGE OMISSION.
TO THE EDITOR OF *THE ECHO*.

Sir,

I think, in common with all the female inhabitants of the Metropolis, I have a right to complain of a sensational morning paper. Why, while its artistic young man was sketching the Whitechapel murderer, did they not send for a constable or two, and give him into custody. I assume, of course,

The sketches (from *The Daily Telegraph*) referred to in the letter from "A Frightened Woman".

that the "likenesses" are real, for otherwise they would be a gross insult to an intelligent public. It is true that the "likeness" published by the same paper very nearly enabled Lefroy[53] to escape, so completely unlike him was it in every respect. But I take it that this time the murderer has really been to Peterborough Court.

Now, Sir, could it have been part of the compact with the gentleman that if he would allow himself to be sketched he should not be given up? Or did he leave - with that horrified look which is depicted on his face in one of the drawings - on finding he was to be paid by cheque instead of cash, before a policeman could be sent for?

I certainly think that it was a strange omission on the part of the proprietors of the sheet in question to have no policeman ready to meet the murderer, and I hope that they have at any rate arranged that, now he is scot-free once more, he will commit no fresh outrages.

Yours respectfully,

A Frightened Woman.

---

[53] Percy Mapleton Lefroy was convicted and hanged for the murder of William Gold, committed on the train between London and Brighton in June 1881. The case was notable because *The Daily Telegraph* published, for the first time in newspaper history, a sketch of the wanted man which was widely distributed throughout England. No less than twenty-nine men were arrested as a result. Fortunately for the police, Lefroy was one of them.

8 October 1888

THE OLD ENGLISH BLOODHOUND OR SLEUTHHOUND
AND HIS CAPABILITIES AS A MAN-HUNTER.
TO THE EDITOR OF *THE TIMES*.

Sir,

Since the bloodhound ceased to be used in the pursuit of sheep stealers, the breed has become scarce, and he is now chiefly regarded as an ornament to our dog shows and a good model for the artist.

I hope that you will allow me a little space to advocate the restoration of this noble hound to his old position in the detection of crime. I may say that I have been a breeder of bloodhounds for nearly 20 years, have had some experience in training to hunt "the clean boot," and take great interest in the history of the breed and its great possibilities of usefulness.

Barnaby and Burgho being trained for use by police, as depicted in *The Penny Illustrated Paper*.

I find that most people have the impression that the bloodhound is a savage treacherous brute. I think that this idea is the result of recollections of "Uncle Tom's Cabin," "Dred," and books of that kind. The Cuban bloodhound, which was used for slave-hunting, was a savage animal, and would pull his man down when he came up to him, but this is quite a different breed to our bloodhound, and does not resemble him at all either in appearance or disposition. I often run men that my hounds have never seen, and when the hounds come up and have smelt them over they take no further interest in them. The bloodhound may be of great use in tracking criminals, but will be of little service in capturing them.

In moss-trooping times it was no uncommon thing to run the scent of a man who had 10 or 15 hours' start, and to do so successfully, although the hounds of that time were so slow that when the pursuers came to soft ground where the track was plain they took up the hound and carried him on the saddle-bow to save time and laid him on again when they came to hard ground.

I have letters from two men who have the charge of hounds which are attached to penitentiaries in Texas. They give most wonderful accounts of the capture of convicts with hounds, although the men had in some instances 24 to 36 hours' start, and in one case they ran their man over 40 miles. These hounds are a cross between the Cuban bloodhound and foxhound, splendidly trained and kept constantly at the work.

Our English bloodhound is infinitely superior to this or to any other breed in natural scenting power, for, luckily, our breeders have developed the long, narrow, peaked head and immense flews, always associated with this faculty, to an extent never known before.

The misfortune is that scarcely any owners of bloodhounds take the trouble to train them, and although the latent power is there and the hounds are very easily entered to man-hunting, it will take some years of careful training to attain the best results. If a few intelligent men who have had some experience in working hounds or in breaking dogs to the gun would take the matter up the capabilities of the bloodhound would be made so manifest that he would be constantly used by the police, and the deterrent effect would be incalculable.

The bloodhound can hunt a lighter scent than any other hound, and when properly trained will stick to the line of the hunted man, although it may have been crossed by others.

I doubt whether there any bloodhounds in England sufficiently trained to have a good chance of tracking a man in crowded thoroughfares such as Whitechapel, and unless laid on at once the chances are that the hound might hit off the wrong trail, but if a well-trained bloodhound had been tried at Gateshead[54] before the scene of the murder had been much trampled over he would have been very likely to run the man down.

---

[54] Reference to the murder of Jane Beadmore (a.k.a. Savage). Her body was discovered in Birtley, south of Gateshead, on September 23rd 1888. A few press reports suggested a possible link between this murder and those of Nichols and Chapman, but generally the Gateshead event was recognized as an isolated tragedy. William Waddell, a spurned lover, was convicted and hanged for Beadmore's murder.

Some years since a so-called bloodhound caused great excitement in connexion with the Blackburn murder. The animal was a mongrel with little, or no trace of bloodhound about it, but it led to the discovery of the murderer by finding some bones concealed in a chimney. Of course any other cur would have done as much.

The great value of the pure bloodhound is that he can be trained to hunt the scent of a man through his boots and without any artificial aid such as blood. It is scarcely likely that a murderer would be so obliging as to smear his boots with the blood of his victim.

I shall be pleased to give any further information to any one interested in the training of bloodhounds, or to answer any queries that might suggest themselves to your readers.

EDWIN BROUGH[55]
Wyndyate, near Scarborough, Oct. 5

THE WHITECHAPEL MURDER MYSTERY.
To the Editor of *the Pall Mall Gazette*.

Sir,

I have had several years intercourse with the most desperate of London criminals, and you may, possibly, on that account consent to add the following to the many suggested theories put forward in your admirable paper to explain the motive of, and thereby start a clue to, the Whitechapel murders. It appears to me that the murderer must have the three following qualifications for the successful perpetration of his crimes:-- (1) Cause for deadly vengeance against the unfortunates of the streets; (2) an intimate knowledge of Whitechapel, and equal familiarity with the snail-like alacrity of the London police; with (3) some experience of a dissecting-room. I would suggest to Sir Charles Warren that he should obtain from Sir Edmund Du Cane[56] the names of such convicts as have been liberated, saw, during the last six months, who have been employed as infirmary orderlies in the respective prisons from whence discharged. Also the additional information, where such ex-prisoners hailed from before sentence, and whether prostitutes were associated with the police in their original detection or conviction. I believe the murderer to be a man who has suffered a long term of penal servitude for some crime that was brought home to him through the betrayal of one of those casual unfortunates who "pal in" with burglars and other such criminals while spending the "swag" on a successful "bust." I have worked and conversed with hundreds of such men in more than one convict prison, and I cannot help remembering the ferocity with which they invariably spoke of "the moll who put them away," and how they would "do" for her

---

[55] Edwin Brough was the owner of Barnaby and Burgho, the two bloodhounds which were put on trial in Hyde Park in October 1888 to gauge their effectiveness in tracking criminals. They were never used in the actual Whitechapel murders investigation.

[56] Sir Edmund Du Cane (1830-1903) served as the Director of Convict Prisons from 1869 to 1887.

whenever they were "chucked up." Desperate as these men are when outside of prison, many of them -- especially the "old fakes" -- are models of good behaviour while undergoing penal servitude, as they seek thereby to qualify for the most coveted of prison "billets" -- infirmary orderly. In this position they acquire a good deal of knowledge about the use of dissecting-knives, &c., as they are employed to clean up the place where the prison doctors carry out their post-mortem examinations of dead convicts.

My theory, therefore, such as it is, is this:--

1. The murderer is of the "old-fake" criminal type.

2. He belongs to or is very familiar with Whitechapel.

3. He has served a long term, perhaps many terms, of imprisonment, some or all of which punishment he attributes to the class to which the murdered women belong.

4. His previous criminal career makes him familiar with the beat-system of the London police.

5. He has been an infirmary orderly in some convict prison, and he has recently terminated his last sentence.

Yours, &c.

"EX-CONVICT."

THE REPRESSION OF IMMORALITY
To the Editor of *The Morning Advertiser*.

Sir,

The period of the year at which most of the elections to municipal offices take place appears to be a fitting one for asking your attention to the open provocation of immorality with which so many of our cities and towns abound. It is to the electors we must look for the use they make of the franchise in selecting those only who will manfully strive for the protection of their property and the security of their own families and the public morals. In the metropolis and many other centres of population certain streets swarm at night with those whose life is one of shame, and the boldness with which they ply their trade is greatly on the increase. The places in which they reside, or to which they resort, are rapidly multiplying. The knowledge of evil is thus spread out before the young of both sexes, and the downward path rendered both easy and attractive. Public decency is outraged, and proceedings tolerated which are a disgrace to our moral character and our Christian profession. Much, of not all, this display of profligacy it is in the power of civic, municipal, and parochial bodies to prevent. The law may and does require strengthening; but it is useless to cry out for more power whilst that which we have is not used; and it is in vain to expect that it will be used unless those having authority or influence are alive to the necessity. The purpose of this society is not to usurp the functions of those in whom the power resides, but to so raise the tone of public opinion as to encourage and enforce its exercise. It is ready, however, to aid in preventing, repressing, and rescuing through the instrumentality of local associations; and if necessary, by direct appeals to the law as circumstances may dictate. It would also point out that any two ratepayers may insist upon proceedings being taken, and under provisions of the law expressly devised for that purpose, to prosecute to conviction at the expense of the locality in which the mischief exists. The suppression of houses of ill fame, and the restraint of street solicitation, properly fall within the province of town councillors, overseers of the poor,. &c. The police authorities come in to aid the local officers. Proceedings in the first instance ought to be taken by those who suffer inconvenience from the presence of persons and places devoted to immorality, and the overseers, municipal authorities, and police should be ready to respond most vigorously to the calls of the public, and ought themselves to search out and proceed against this vice. Prostitutes, brothel keepers, and owners of premises rented for their purposes are alike subject to prosecution. Hitherto there has not been any general effort for repression and prevention, and interference has often been limited to the abatement of the nuisance, where it had become too open, by simply driving the perpetrators out of the district, rather than extended to such a punishment as may deter them from a repetition of the offence elsewhere. Thus, by leaving them to renew their misconduct in other localities, the authorities have incurred a tedious repetition of the process, oftentimes ending in the return of the offenders to their original haunts. Our desire on the present occasion is to gain your attention to the serious nature of the evil which prevails in our midst, and to express our hope that, in seeking election to positions of local power, you will bring this matter prominently to the notice of those whom you are preparing to represent, and in so doing receive their mandate that it shall not continue. The records of our courts of justice, the diaries of our clergymen and district visitors, the facts to which none can shut their eyes, all unite in testifying that immorality is so rife as to be eating out the nation's life, sapping the sources of our greatness, and provoking the indignation of that Power which may either preserve our prosperity or pronounce our destruction, according as we are found honouring the purity in which He delights, or practising the profligacy which He abhors.

We have the honour to be yours faithfully,

Westminster.
Meath.
R.N. Fowler.
Central Vigilance Committee for the Repression of Immorality,
15 York Buildings, Adelphi.
Oct. 6, 1888.

9 October 1888

WOMAN KILLING NO MURDER.
TO THE EDITOR OF *THE DAILY NEWS*.

Sir,

Will you allow me to point out to Mrs. Fenwick Miller that the penalties inflicted on men for assaulting women depend upon the social position of the individual man and woman? There are cases in which the magistrate not only protects the woman, but savagely revenges her. A week or two ago a labourer was convicted of having kissed against her will the daughter of a major; for taking this liberty he was sentenced to six months' imprisonment with hard labour! If the labourer had kissed a labouring woman against her will, would he have been punished in the same way? Or if a gentleman were to kiss a working woman against her will, would the same sentence be passed on him? Or if a gentleman were to kiss a lady against her will in the public street, would he be sent to prison for six months with hard labour? There can be but one answer to these questions. Our laws are by no means the same for the rich and the poor, as any one who reads the daily papers can see. Mrs. F. Miller seems to think that, in the various cases of brutal assault which she cites, the magistrate – being a man – thought to himself "It does not matter much; the victim is only a woman." But it is more probable that – being a middle-class man – his thought was "It does not matter much; she is only a working woman." Class legislation and class administration must always mean injustice.

Yours faithfully,

Oct. 8.
CONSTANCE HOWELL.

THE RECENT MURDERS IN LONDON
TO THE EDITOR OF *THE IRISH TIMES*

SIR –

I read with very great interest your leading article in a late issue touching on the recent murders in London. One would think that the London police had lost all ingenuity and tact. In my book published in 1884 I made the following remarks about their supineness:-

"Undetected crime in London has assumed a very formidable and disappointing shape. Note the Great Coram street murder, the Waterloo road murder, the Euston Square murder, the Burton Crescent murder, the Stoke Newington murder, and various minor atrocities. It seems that the Stoke Newington murder, having baffled the ingenuity of the detectives, has been ascribed by them to a case of suicide. This is a very adroit subterfuge, but it is rather hackneyed. The surroundings in the Stoke Newington tragedy were too palpable to admit of any other conclusion but that of foul murder. The knotted handkerchief, the earrings found on the scene of the scuffle, the various footmarks on the bank, all these point to a bloody deed."

Again is London startled with most appalling murders, committed with impunity in its most crowded thoroughfares. We in Ireland even stand aghast at the enormities of the crimes; although, God knows, we have bloodshed enough to answer for.

I have always been a strenuous advocate for rewards in cases of serious crimes. The police should certainly share in these rewards - i.e. taking into account extra duty, &c. The Government do not hesitate to give substantial sums of money to the inventors of destructive weapons, or to officers after a successful campaign. Why, then, should they hesitate to reward any person for the detection of a crime?

Yours, &c.,

EDWARD WILSON.
Author of "Reminiscences of a Frontier Armed
and Mounted Police Officer in South Africa."

THE CHILDREN OF THE COMMON LODGING-HOUSES.
TO THE EDITOR OF *THE TIMES*.

Sir,

Stimulated by the recently revealed Whitechapel horrors many voices are daily heard suggesting as many different schemes to remedy degraded social conditions, all of which doubtless contain some practical elements. I trust you will allow one other voice to be raised on behalf of the children. For the saddest feature of the common lodging-houses in Whitechapel and other parts ofvLondon is that so many of their inmates are children. Indeed, it is impossible to describe the state in which myriads of young people live who were brought up in these abodes of poverty and of crime.

I and others are at work almost day and night rescuing boys and girls from the foul contamination of these human sewers; but while the law permits children to herd in these places, there is little that can be done except to snatch a few here and there from ruin and await patiently those slower changes which many have advocated. Meanwhile, a new generation is actually growing up in them. We want to make it illegal for the keepers of licensed lodging-houses to which adults resort to admit young children upon any pretext whatever. It is also desirable that the existing laws relating to the custody and companionship of the children should be more rigidly enforced. At the same time some provision is urgently required for the shelter of young children of the casual or tramp class, something between the casual wards of the workhouse and the lodging-house itself, places where only young people under 16 would be admitted, where they would be free to enter and as free to depart, and which could be made self-supporting, or nearly so. A few enterprising efforts to

Thomas J. Barnardo

open lodging-houses of this class for the young only would do immense good.

Only four days before the recent murders I visited No. 32, Flower and Dean-street, the house in which the unhappy woman Stride occasionally lodged. I had been examining many of the common lodging-houses in Bethnal-green that night, endeavouring to elicit from the inmates their opinions upon a certain aspect of the subject. In the kitchen of No. 32 there were many persons, some of them being girls and women of the same unhappy class as that to which poor Elizabeth Stride belonged. The company soon recognized me, and the conversation turned upon the previous murders. The female inmates of the kitchen seemed thoroughly frightened at the dangers to which they were presumably exposed. In an explanatory fashion I put before them the scheme which had suggested itself to my mind, by which children at all events could be saved from the contamination of the common lodging-houses and the streets, and so to some extent the supply cut off which feeds the vast ocean of misery in this great city.

The pathetic part of my story is that my remarks were manifestly followed with deep interest by all the women. Not a single scoffing voice was raised in ridicule or opposition. One poor creature, who had evidently been drinking, exclaimed somewhat bitterly to the following effect:- "We're all up to no good, and no one cares what becomes of us. Perhaps some of us will be killed next!" And then she added, "If anybody had helped the likes of us long ago we would never have come to this!"

Impressed by the unusual manner of the people, I could not help noticing their appearance somewhat closely, and I saw how evidently some of them were moved. I have since visited the mortuary in which were lying the remains of the poor woman Stride, and I at once recognized her as one of those who stood around me in the kitchen of the common lodging-house on the occasion of my visit last Wednesday week.

In all the wretched dens where such unhappy creatures live are to be found hundreds, if not thousands, of poor children who breathe from their very birth an atmosphere fatal to all goodness. They are so heavily handicapped at the start in the race of life that the future is to most of them absolutely hopeless. They are continually surrounded by influences so vile that decency is outraged and virtue becomes impossible.

Surely the awful revelations consequent upon the recent tragedies should stir the whole community up to action and to the resolve to deliver the children of to-day who will be the men and women of to-morrow from so evil an environment.

I am, Sir, your obedient servant,

THOS. J. BARNARDO[57]
18 to 26, Stepney-causeway, E., Oct. 6.

---

[57] Thomas Barnardo (1845-1905) was an English philanthropist and founder of The National Association for the Reclamation of Destitute Waif Children – commonly known as "Dr. Barnardo's Homes." He may have come under some suspicion during the autumn of 1888 because of his medical background and his association with "fallen women" whilst performing philanthropic work in the East End.

WHITECHAPEL.
TO THE EDITOR OF *THE TIMES*.

Sir,

Will you kindly allow me in your columns to reply to many correspondents who have desired to be informed of the best way to befriend the poor women in Whitechapel, Spitalfields, and the neighbourhood, whose miserable condition has been brought before the public so prominently by the late murders?

I was for ten years rector of Spitalfields, and I know full well the circumstances of these poor creatures, and have been constantly among them by day and by night. A night refuge has been proposed, and it was but natural it should suggest itself as a means of benefiting the class. In my judgement it would serve no good end, and I earnestly hope nothing of the kind wil be attempted. I am sure it would but aggravate the evil. It is not the fact that many of these women are to be found in the street at night because doors are closed against them. Another night refuge is not required. It would attract more of these miserable women into the neighbourhood and increase the difficulties of the situation. But what is needed is a home where washing and other work could be done, and where poor women who are really anxious to lead a better life could find employment. There are penitentiaries and there are mission houses into which younger women can be received. The public generally are little aware of how much good work has been done of late among these. But for the older women, many of whom have only taken to their miserable mode of earning a living in sheer despair and who would gladly renounce it, we have not the home, and it is of the utmost importance one should be provided. It would in its management differ from the ordinary penitentiary.

If intrusted with means to provide such a home I would gladly undertake the responsibility of conducting it, in conjunction with the clergy and others, who are only too anxious to see it established.

It has oftentimes saddened my heart to be unable to assist the older women and to save those who were hopelessly falling into a life of sin. Such a home would be a fitting addition to the "Court House", the home for younger penitents at Walthamstow, which bears the name of Mrs. Walsham How, and was founded by her in the time of my predecessor, the present Bishop of Wakefield. If anything is to be done it should be done at once. Two thousand pounds would enable the experiment to be tried, and I have no doubt at all of its being a success.

Pray allow me space to say to ladies who have been moved to devote themselves for work in these parts that I shall be delighted to hear from such and to advise them where their services are most required and how they can best give effect to their charitable intentions. It is my bounden duty to use my position and experience to turn to the best account the painful interest that has been excited by late events in the East-end.

I am, your obedient servant,

R. C. BEDFORD, Bishop Suffragan for East London,
Stainforth-house, Upper Clapton, E., Oct. 8.

THE DUTIES OF THE POLICE.
TO THE EDITOR OF *THE TIMES*.

Sir,

The following incident in some way illustrates the manifold duties of the police.

On Sunday afternoon, close to the Albert-gate, a little girl was run over by a hansom cab. The wheel passed over her body, and I think over her head. She got up and staggered a few paces, moaning pitifully. A policeman dashed at her and caught her up in his arms. He then jumped into the hansom, summarily ejecting the passenger, and was driven to St. George's Hospital.

I should think that the whole occurrence took only a quarter of a minute. The amazing promptitude of the constable and the tender way in which he laid the poor child's bleeding head on his breast seemed a strange commentary on the abuse which some people are pleased to levy at the police for their supposed "brutal conduct" on other occasions.

I am, Sir, your obedient servant,

T. WENTWORTH GRANT.
6, Westbourne-crescent, Hyde Park, W., Oct. 8.

Audi Alteram Partem[58]
TO THE EDITOR OF *THE STAR*

SIR,

The "East-end atrocities" have certainly been an ill-wind that has blown grist to the mill of the votaries of the modern woman-cultus. To the unsophisticated mind it would be difficult to see how the murder of a few women by an obviously unique kind of maniac could possibly raise any general point respecting the "woman question" any more than the murder of, say, two or three City clerks by an ex-principal whose mind was affected by losses occasioned through the negligence of penmen he had employed should raise the general question of the social position of City clerks. But there is no one like your woman's rights advocate for making capital out of everything that comes to hand, and nothing like the modern English Press for giving him or her a one-sided hearing.

Accordingly we find Mrs. Fenwick Miller and her allies in the *Daily News*[59] all athirst for the blood of men, seeking to raise the wind in favor of barbarous judicial sentences. The truly bestial howl for the torture of the lash which comes with the regularity of an intermittent fever, is again heard in our midst. The Rev. Mr. Burnett moralises in *The Star*, the general drift of his remarks being that

---

[58] Latin for: "Hear both sides."
[59] Reference to the "Woman Killing No Murder" letter published by the *Daily News*, October 1st 1888.

the working man is a kind of semi-monster and his wife a wingless angel let loose from Paradise. Mr. Barnett has, of course, never come across women whom have wrecked the lives of working men - oh, dear, no! If there is one thing that might make a working-man hesitate before contracting a legal marriage, it is that nowadays law and middle-class public opinion place him entirely at the mercy of his wife. As a recent correspondent (a barrister) of the *Daily Telegraph* observed, the whole legislation of the past quarter of a century has been entirely in favor of women at the expense of men.

And now as to these sentences so much talked about. No one who reads his newspaper can deny the extreme reluctance of juries to convict women of any serious offence and the excessive leniency of sentences passed upon them. Only the other day (on the north-west circuit, I think) a big powerful woman was convicted of the murder of her husband, a poor, feeble, paralytic old man, by battering his head in, a continued course of ill-usage having been proved, and was recommended to mercy! Imagine the howl that would have arisen had the cases been reversed. Again, every one must have noticed the growing tendency to twist what would formerly have been regarded as manslaughter cases into murder cases where women are the victims. Then as to mere brutality, who shall deny that in many of the worst instances of cruelty to children women are the culprits? Only a short time ago a woman tortured her stepson, a little boy of three years old, by burning him with a red-hot iron. Does anyone propose that a brute like this should have the lash? Oh, no; divine woman must not be subjected to degrading punishments!

I write, sir, as an advocate of equality between the sexes. At the present time, apart from mere political rights, which are, after all, only a means to an end, women constitute a privileged class, and the aims of their advocates is to give them a still more privileged position. They are virtually freed from the criminal punishments to which men are liable, and they can compel men to support them on pain of imprisonment. It is all very well to talk about women being economically dependent on men. The feudal lord was also economically dependent on his serfs; that is to say, he would have been in a sorry plight if his vassals and serfs had suddenly deserted him, and would then probably have had to have taken to what used to be euphemistically known as the "road;" much as "deserted" women now sometimes take to the streets. Yet the feudal lord is none the less usually deemed to have belonged to a privileged class.

The desperate and glorious inconsistency of your woman advocate is aptly shown in his criticism of seduction cases, where the man is always painted as the malignant scoundrel and the woman as the innocent young person who does not know her right hand from her left, and yet we are told in the same breath this simple young innocent, unable to protect herself against the wiles of wicked man, is the equal of man in all respects, and fit to be entrusted with every political and social function.

Mr. Barnett admonishes the working-man to regard his wife as his equal. Now do let us put aside cant on this subject for once. How can the working-man regard a woman as his equal when she is obviously not his equal. Apart from mere intellectual inequality, most working men know that the greatest obstacle in the way of their political work for the emancipation of their class is precisely the "drab" at home who is perpetually nagging and browbeating him.

Yours, &c.,

JUSTICE AND EQUALITY

The Poverty of the East-end of London
TO THE EDITOR OF *THE STAR*.

SIR,

In a leading article commenting on the Rev. Mr. Barnett's letter in your issue of 5 Oct., you say truly that "it is poverty which lies at the root of what we, perhaps rightly, call the social evil, and it is by aiming at the abolition of poverty that we shall cure a variety of woes which we usually set down to an entirely different set of causes." I entirely concur with you in this statement; and, as I have had a very long practical acquaintance with the poorer classes of the East-end of London in my capacity as physician to the Metropolitan Free Hospital, which was once situated close to Whitechapel Church, I claim to speak with some experience. To me, then, the extreme squalor and hopelessness of Whitechapel, St. George's-in-the-East, and Bethnal-green are due to the two causes so well pointed out by the Archbishop of Canterbury, in a lecture in Bethnal-green this year, viz., to over-population and drink. The birth-rate of Bethnal-green last year, 1887, was nearly 40 per 1,000 as compared with that of Kensington, which was only 19.5; and as a consequence of this poor families are compelled to crowd together in these sad haunts of the poor about which we have heard so much during the last few weeks. I found on inquiry from out-patients attending at the Metropolitan Free Hospital a few years back, that the average number of children to a family was 7.2 - i.e., 100 married women over 45 had had 720 children on an average of many hundreds I questioned. The average of children to a family in prudent France is now 3.2, and although naturally we, with our colonies, could afford to support more children than the French, yet the average of 7.2 is utterly beyond the powers of the poor of the East-end. Alcohol, too, is another of the causes of misery in the East-end; and these two causes combined are quite enough to account for the terrible misery of Bethnal-green, Whitechapel, and St. George's-in-the-East. So that it is not so much of importance that the West-end should give alms to the East-end. What is wanted is that West-end people should teach East-end people to have smaller families, and thus escape from early death and lifelong destitution.

Yours, &c.,

C. R. DRYSDALE, M.D.
23, Sackville-street, London, W., 6 Oct.

11 October 1888

TO THE EDITOR OF *THE TIMES*.

Sir,

There is one statement in your otherwise very exact account of the trials of bloodhounds in Hyde Park which I shall be glad to be allowed to correct.

My hounds Barnaby and Burgho have not been purchased by Sir Charles Warren for the use of the police.

Yours truly,

EDWIN BROUGH
October 10.

THE DETECTION OF CRIME
TO THE EDITOR OF *THE TIMES*.

Sir,

It is to be hoped that the excellent letter of Sir Charles Warren[60], which was given to your readers on the 4th, will have had the effect of somewhat allaying the misgivings as to the efficiency of the police force which recent events in the east of London appear to have roused among Londoners. To my mind there is not, and never has been, any substantial cause for apprehension on that score. It is always easy to jump from a minor premise to a foregone conclusion, provided that the major premise be dispensed with and by this process of reasoning, the fact that the perpetrator of the Whitechapel murders has hitherto escaped detection may be held to prove that the police force is, as regards its detective element, inefficient, but by this process only. Those who thus hastily form their judgement of course assume that the police have opportunities which they are not turning to the best account. But where is the evidence of this? A detective, be it remembered, can no more get on the track of a criminal without a clue than a hound can hunt a fox without a scent; but - and here we come to the gist of the matter - while a fox cannot travel without leaving a scent behind him, a criminal may, although he seldom does, succeed in escaping from the scene of his crime without leaving the slightest trace of his route or indication of his personality. As a rule, either from want of education, from natural dullness, from carelessness or forgetfulness, some small thing is done or left undone which starts as the starting point of pursuit - it may be a bit of gravel

---

[60] Reprinted in this volume, see October 4th 1888.

in a horse's foot, a smear of brown paint on a lady's dress, or even a single straw. The slip of the tongue by which Houseman, the confederate of Eugene Aram, proclaimed his guilt will occur to many, "That is no more Dan Clark's bone than it is mine." Something, I say, there generally is, and something there must be for guidance if a crime is to be detected, so long as detectives are but human, whatever may be their skill and experience. But there is no reason why a particular criminal should not combine in himself the various qualifications requisite for eluding discovery. That these six murders have been the work of the same hand we are all, I think, pretty well agreed; and on this hypothesis the accumulated experience of the criminal tells in his favour and against detection on the very ratio of iteration. Now Sir Charles Warren has forcibly pointed out that the Whitechapel murders were so arranged as to leave no clue whatever; and it appears to be beyond question that in the present instance we are concerned with one who is a consummate master of his art and as wide awake to contingencies as any detective.

Sir Charles Warren has hit the right nail on the head in telling the Whitechapel District Board of Works that "the very fact that you (they) be unaware of what the Detective Department is doing is only the stronger proof that it is doing its work with secrecy and efficiency." There are apparently some wiseacres who cannot be satisfied unless they see everything, detectives included, with their own eyes, and hear everything with their own ears. If we all really knew exactly what detectives are doing and where they are working, then woe betide us. The detective for our wise friends would be the gentleman in the "House in the Marsh," who solemnly reports himself to another gentleman who proves to be the very man "wanted", and who forthwith proceeds to drug his interviewer in the most effective manner. Readers of Gaborian may remember by way of contrast the interview between the Mayor of Corbeil and M. Lecoq. A terrible murder has been committed, and as a matter of course the great detective is summoned from Paris. The civic dignitary, who is much scandalized by Lecoq's very ordinary dress, instead of the tightly buttoned frock coat with military stock collar, that he had expected, and by his somewhat late arrival in court, offers to explain what has occurred. "Oh, that's quite useless," retorted Lecoq... "I've been here the last two hours." In fact, he had been quietly poking about among the crowd, and had learned all that there was to know. It would be with some sense of humiliation that we should read the exciting tales of Gaboriac, of A.K. Green, and of Laurence Lynch (E. Murdoch), if we were obliged to believe that, whatever may be the case in France and America, we have at home no match for M. Lecoq, Dick Stanhope, Van Vernet and Mr. Gryce. I have little or no knowledge personally of our present detective staff; but if the history of the dynamite outrages is to be taken as a criterion I do not think that we have much cause for misgivings.

I remain, Sir, your obedient servant,

D.

DETECTIVES
TO THE EDITOR OF *THE TIMES*.

Sir,

Allow me to ask a question a propos of Sir Charles Warren's announcement published in your issue of this morning. Why should such a thing as a female detective be unheard of in the land? A clever woman of unobtrusive dress and appearance (she need not be 5ft 7in) would possess over her masculine rivals not a few advantages. She would pass unsuspected where a man would be instantly noticed; she could extract gossip from other women much more freely; she would move through the streets and courts without waking the echoes of the pavement by a sonorous military tread; and, lastly, she would be in a position to employ for whatsoever it may be worth that gift of intuitive quickness and "mother wit" with which her sex is commonly credited. Your readers who may be familiar with the "History of the Crimean War" will remember the splendid chapter wherein Mr. Kinglake sets forth how the masculine minds of all the generals and War Office dignitaries together failed to grapple with the problem of the hospitals, and how the feminine mind, impersonated in Miss Nightingale and her little band of nurses, came to the rescue and out of chaos and indescribable misery brought order and relief. Is it not worth trying now in another public difficulty whether womanly faculties may not again be useful? A keen eyed woman might do as well in her way as those keen nosed bloodhounds (of whose official engagement I rejoice to hear) may, we hope, do in their peculiar line. Should it so fall out that the demon of Whitechapel prove really to be, as Mr. Baxter seems to suspect, a physiologist delirious with cruelty, and should the hounds be the means of his capture, poetic justice will be complete.

I am, Sir, &c.,

Frances Power Cobbe.
No 1, Victoria street, S.W., Oct. 10.

RATCLIFF HIGHWAY REFUGE
TO THE EDITOR OF *THE TIMES*.

Sir,

My attention has just been called to Mr. Walter Hazell's letter in Saturday's issue of *The Times*.

Nine years ago I came to live in Ratcliff Highway with the simple determination to find out how best to help that class of poor, miserable women whose mode of living has been so prominently brought forward by the horrible events of the past few weeks. During all this time I have been able to keep an open door for them, and with my fellow helpers have been learning, as we could only learn by experience, how most wisely and effectively to help those who come to us. The work has been very quietly carried on, but our houses have always been full to overflowing, and while hundreds of young girls and children have been rescued from the most dangerous surroundings, trained as little servants, emigrated to the colonies, and in other ways given a fair start in life, still many more from among the fallen have found our home a "bridge of hope" by which they have passed on to better things.

The revelation of existence in Whitechapel lodging houses and in the streets of our great city must not simply evoke words of commiseration or be allowed to die out as a nine days' wonder, but must surely result in very practical measures being adopted for permanently benefitting those at least who are willing to be helped. Hundreds of women in this sad East end lead their degraded lives of sin for daily bread, or to secure a night's shelter in a fourpenny lodging house, a fact of which none can now plead ignorance, for the horrors of a few weeks (to our shame as a nation be it said) have brought out in awful relief the conditions under which so many of our fellow creatures exist, and which, though told persistently and without exaggeration by East end workers, have made but little impression.

Finding that the missing link in the work in Ratcliff Highway was a night shelter, we have, during the past year, built one as a wing to our new refuge, and this will be opened on the 30th inst. by the Bishop of Bedford, although circumstances have compelled us already to give shelter in it to many who needed immediate help. Night shelters, answering only the purposes of a casual ward, may be the means of as much harm as good, but, managed with judicious discrimination and constant personal supervision, I believe that our "bridge of hope" night shelter will be an effectual means of helping not only those who have fallen but of saving very many friendless young girls from utter despair, when they come to their last resources. At this moment the strain of the work is very great. While people are devising, and very rightly so, how best to organise new methods and larger schemes, it sometimes appears that those who have been plodding on in the midst of the misery, and who have to bear the brunt of sudden emergencies, are apt to be forgotten, and however unwillingly we do so, it seems right to call attention to our present need of financial help. We are always thankful to see visitors, or to send reports if desired.

    Apologising for taking up so much of your valuable space, I am, Sir, yours faithfully,

Mary H. Steer,
Hon. Supt.
Ratcliff Highway Refuge
St. George's in the East,
London, E.
October 8.

THE JEWS AND ANIMAL KILLING.
TO THE EDITOR OF THE ECHO.

Sir,

In your yesterday's issue there appeared a letter signed "S.," accusing the Jews of an "atrocious" mode of killing animals. As President of the Slaughtering Board for the Jewish community, permit me to assure your readers that the Jewish mode of killing animals has been pronounced by Christian experts to be far more humane than the method of killing sheep, calves, and pigs adopted by Gentiles.

Yours obediently,

Samuel Montagu.
12, Kensington Palace-gardens
Oct. 10

11 October, 1888 163

Samuel Montagu, from a *Vanity Fair* cartoon.

12 October 1888

THE EAST END.
TO THE EDITOR OF THE JEWISH CHRONICLE.

Sir,

The time has now arrived when something should be done to ameliorate the condition of the distressed foreign Jews in the East End of London. The amount of immorality daily growing among the women is a blot on our community at large.

This matter ought at once be taken up and thoroughly investigated by the Council of the United Synagogue.

I should suggest that a committee be formed equally of ladies and gentlemen to carry out an enquiry upon the same principle and procedure as in the House of Commons, to make a report and advise the best ways and means to remedy the existing evil. The expense of this Committee to obtain necessary information would, I am sure, be willingly defrayed (if not by the Council) by many city men as anxious as I am to be able to pass though Liverpool Street and other parts of London without witnessing the degradation of their sisters. I would willingly act as Honorary Secretary to such a Committee and give the services of a clerk free of expense.

Yours obediently,

MICHAEL ZEFFERTT.
12, Clifton Gardens, Maida Vale, W.
October 7th, 1888.

THE SLEUTHHOUND AS A TRACKER
TO THE EDITOR OF THE MORNING ADVERTISER

Sir,

Allow me to contribute my little experience to the discussion now current as to the value of the bloodhound (or sleuthhound as I prefer to call it) in tracking. I had some years ago a dog of the best strain, a son of Mr. Holford's famous "Regent." I took great interest in training "Reveller" to follow the slightest scent, which he did admirably. One instance will suffice. A few days only after I took him in hand I showed him a dry bone, and then started a lad with it, giving him instructions to conceal it a few miles away, the route and hiding place being both unknown to me. An hour after I started with the dog, and with unfaltering and unerring scent he led me from Upper

Norwood, over Streatham common, to Tooting Bec common, and to a bush at the latter place, wherein the bone, which I had previously marked, was found. The distance was considerably over three miles.

But the sleuthhound scent is merely the high development of a faculty common to all dogs. As a humorist recently pointed out, when two dogs converse in the street, they do not say "Where have you been?" or "What have you seen?" but "What have you smelt?" I am constantly reminded of this by the actions of a Newfoundland dog which is used as a yard dog at the firework factory of Messrs. C.T. Brock and Co., where I am engaged. At the present time, owing to the immense pressure of the November business, many fresh hands are temporarily employed. These are always introduced to and smelt by the dog. After the first introduction, he invariably recognises them by the scent as they enter the gate, until his sight is as accustomed to them as is his nose; and they can go to their work unmolested as soon as the latter organ is satisfied as to their bona fides. Apologising for the length of this letter,

I am, Sir, yours &c.,

W GRIST
South Norwood, London, S.E.
Oct. 10, 1888

AN APPEAL FROM THE EAST-END.
TO THE EDITOR OF *THE DAILY TELEGRAPH*.

SIR -

While the public mind is stirred to its depths with horror at the awful revelations of sin and misery which accompany some women's lives in the East-end, it may not come amiss to record also the efforts made for their assistance and for the attainment of a truer ideal of womanhood. Only those who are well acquainted with the existence of the very poor, the sordid details, the unending struggle to make both ends meet and just keep body and soul together, know their dread of sickness, how it cripples their resources and puts the whole machinery of the family out of gear. Especially is this the case at the time of a woman's confinement, when she has worked many hours a day up to the very last, when little or no preparation can be made or extra comfort given in a small garret occupied by a husband and children. Decency, health, or well-being are under such circumstances impossible. To alleviate some of the suffering and supply some of the wants felt, a small lying-in home for respectable married women was established, nearly four years ago, in Shadwell, in the heart of a poverty-stricken and populous neighbourhood, close to the scene of the Whitechapel murders. In all East London there is no lying-in hospital except this little home, which is immensely appreciated by the people. It has already done incalculable good, in refining, helping, and restoring poor women to health. Not one life out of the 327 nursed has been lost, in spite of want of space, many critical cases, and slender means. Assisted by no palatial buildings or expensive staff of officials, the little institution offers what it aims at - a real home, clean, orderly, decent, where privacy (each woman has her own room), food, and medicine, together with skilled attendance and good care may be obtained. If such houses of refuge were multiplied all over East London, and well supported, they would prove most beneficial to the health and morals of the population. Our funds are at the lowest ebb, however, and winter coming on; we therefore appeal confidently to your readers for their generous help and sympathy. Donations thankfully received by Mrs. Ashton Warner, the Mothers' Home, Glamis-road, Shadwell, E., who is the lady superintendent; or by the London and Westminster Bank, St. James's-square.

I am, Sir, yours obediently,

VIOLET GREVILLE.
No. 7, Chesterfield-gardens, Mayfair, Oct. 11.

"WHITECHAPEL MURDERS"
TO THE EDITOR OF *THE IRISH TIMES*

SIR,

From time to time I have read in your journal of the manner in which the police authorities have and are being troubled and deceived by persons coming forward and making voluntary confessions that they are the persons guilty of these horrible butcheries.

On investigation these self-accusations turn out either to be the ravings of a drunken person or a deliberate attempt to hoax the authorities, ending in the discharge of the self-incriminated.

Is there no law, sir, to grapple with such persons and under which they could be committed to prison until their heads would cool, and thus give them ample time for recovering their judgement? A few lashes of the cat would be very effective in teaching such troublesome ness a lesson.

The authorities, in my opinion, are liable to enough public odium in their tracing of crime without having to undergo the perplexity and annoyance entailed by the idle and groundless accusations which, especially in connection with the above murders, they have been troubled with.

A READER
Cookstown, County Tyrone,
Oct. 10th, 1888.

12 October, 1888

The Sensationalism of Our Day
TO THE EDITOR OF *THE STAR*.

SIR. -

We seem to be breathing nothing but the odor of the slaughterhouse. Is it necessary? The murders are horrible enough, and we must hunt, but we are getting too familiar with "ghastly details." What good end is to be served by that? Talking of this a few days ago, I took up a Leicester paper, with no special selection, and just as a test. Here is the result. The following headings appear in this one copy alone: - "Shocking affair at Chorley," "A priest's dead body burned to cinders in church," "Cut to pieces on the railway" (this was so relished that it was repeated in another part of the paper), "Cut to pieces at a railway station," "Sudden death of a child," "The Blackfriars mystery," "A cruel case," "A child worried by a pig," "Another suicide with carbolic acid," "The wife murder at Huddersfield," "The Whitechapel murder," "Attack on a Mormon agent in Wales," "A clergyman fined for drunkenness," "Another Thames mystery," "A human arm found in a timber yard," "Another railway accident in America - serious loss of life."

Why rake so much in one direction? It is becoming a serious question whether a decent and well-ordered household should go on admitting such buckets of slush.

Yours, &c.,

J. P. H.

Leicester, 6 Oct.

[We insert "J.P.H's" letter, but we confess we do not quite see his point. How can newspapers avoid telling their readers about these things. We admit that they should record them in a non-vulgar and truthful way, but it is useless to shut one's eyes to what daily happens. For instance, if clergymen get drunk why should they not be fined, and why should not their fine be recorded as an example to other clergymen. If terrible murders occur in the East, why should not the West be told of it, and why should not the public be instructed in the worst as well as the best facts? Truthful realism is good; it is only lying realism which should be avoided. - ED. *Star*.]

Shelters for the Homeless
TO THE EDITOR OF *THE STAR*.

SIR. -

The Bishop of Bedford, or anyone having an anxious desire to raise the condition of the East-end population, be they so-called fallen or otherwise, need not fear that Mr. Hayward or his friends will trespass upon their ten years' preserved land or cash with their efforts. By all means let it be a long pull and a strong pull and a pull together. We do not wish to glorify ourselves, but to attempt to glorify God by doing or assisting in a good work. Mr. Hayward only wishes to take out of the streets those who are sleeping on doorstep or wandering about without a shelter from the inclemency of the night, be they men or women, upright or fallen: the same God is over all. Bishop of Bedford, go to work and raise the fallen women; it is Christian work. Meantime, they shall not be shelterless, nor the men, in this Christian land of ours if we can give them shelter.

Yours, &c.,

DOBRA.
9 Oct.

13 October 1888

"The Moral of the Murders."
TO THE EDITOR OF *THE STAR*.

SIR. -

Kindly forgive any seeming presumption in adding to your correspondence on this subject, but it appears to me a fair case for the criticism of those who have dedicated their lives to the service of the poor. I will try to make my remarks at once trenchant and tender.

The difficulties suggested range themselves under two heads - social and moral. Socially, the whole affair points unmistakably to the regulation and comparative suppression of vice by the State, unflinching and absolute equality being dealt out to both sexes. So-called "degraded" women are the result of equally degraded men, and vice versa, but there is not an atom of difference in the guilt of either.

The men who morally assert the contrary are not men, whoever they may be and whatever the position they may occupy. The drink traffic is at the bottom of half this misery and vice. Let it be dealt with as it deserves, and let the blow be struck at the fountain-heads, on whom will fall the curse when justice is meted out. The poverty is in the end traceable to the most despicable and common sin, "love of money" on the part of landlords and "sweaters," who ought to be heartily ashamed of thus grinding the faces of their poorer brethren.

The dismal, unhealthy, overcrowded, and underlighted streets with cul de sacs inviting to evil, should be dealt with by each Vestry separately, and drastic measures, however expensive or apparently stern, should be taken for the eventual good of the community, by means of a rate levied on ground-rents throughout the metropolis generally. The burden would thus fall on the proper shoulders. Nothing is more instructive than the difference between the East and the newer parts of South London in this respect. In the latter locality such events as the recent murders could never have occurred without discovery. It is an absurd thing, however, to throw the blame on the police, who, as known to us clergy, are amongst the most hardworking and hardly tried of the population, and it shows a still grosser lack both of taste and reason to cast the slightest innuendos against Sir Charles Warren or the Home Secretary in this particular. The fault is with the State, and the cause must be looked for at St. Stephen's where such a question should absorb our legislation in place of this eternal wrangling about Ireland.

Morally the keynote is "piecework of individual sacrifice," which is repellent to theorists, of whom the majority is composed. One "Home" is a drop in the ocean. One "parish" is a cipher, though it gain a spurious notoriety for the moment. So long as men and women are selfish, and so long as they live in luxury or break the law of purity, they have not the slightest right to cast a stone at a single incident throughout the transaction.

In plain language, it means that the rich must confine themselves to necessities, or some day there will be a revolution, which is only a matter of time, and which will have the best hearts in the country on its side. It means that ladies should personally befriend and raise their downtrodden because fallen sisters, if not by actual contact, at least by money and sympathy. Above all, it means that the young men of the present day should themselves abstain from vice, and that our would-be statesmen should learn a little more of what they intend to talk about by living for a time on the spot, or else that they should be decently silent.

No man can be a saviour without being crucified. This is the whole business in a nutshell, and we must set our faces like flints to live out this truth if we would not be ashamed. "The remedy of all blunders," says Emerson, "the cure of blindness, the cure of crime, is love."

Yours, &c.,

HUGH B. CHAPMAN
Vicar of S. Luke's, Camberwell.
11 Oct.

WHITECHAPEL.
TO THE EDITOR OF *THE TIMES*.

Sir,

Will you allow me space to thank those who have responded to my appeal in *The Times* of Tuesday last and to say that a list of contributions will appear early next week. I am advised that the sum required will be larger than my first estimate of the probable cost of the home and the necessary plant; but the response is so encouraging that I have no doubt of success. Contributions and promises of support should for the present be sent to me.

I am, Sir, your obedient servant,

R. C. BEDFORD,
Bishop Suffragant for East London.
Stainforth-house, Upper Clapton, E.

TO THE EDITOR OF *THE TIMES*.

Sir,

Will you allow space to an invalid East London clergyman to allude to the subject-matter of the Bishop of Bedford's appeal? To strike while the iron is hot is good. But it is also most desirable not to do anything in a panic, lest matters are made worse instead of better. The importance of care and mature consideration comes out from a public notice that the manager of the Lyceum Theatre is going to assist in raising funds for more night refuges.

What could be more foolish, and more likely to accentuate the evils of middle-life prostitution? The Bishop of Bedford has most wisely deprecated any increase of night refuges. My experience of nearly 20 years in East London corroborates the caution of the Bishop that if there is any remedy at all it must be otherwise than by the increase of night refuges. I believe that the police will substantiate this view.

What, then, is the remedy? This will depend upon the nature and causes of the evil. I agree with the Bishop of Bedford that sheer necessity has to do with middle-life prostitution. But I regret to differ from him as to the share which that cause has. We can only speak from personal knowledge; and I have found one thing far more conducive to the production of this evil than any other - viz., strong drink. In the vast majority of such cases drink has been the originating and continues the stimulating cause. The appalling facilities for drinking in East London explain much.

Will, then, a "laundry" such as the Bishop of Bedford proposes be of any benefit? I say that it will, but not, in my judgement, to the extent which the Bishop so sanguinely anticipates. It will no doubt save a few; and that is something for which to be thankful. But far more will have to be done than can possibly be achieved by the laundry system now suggested. The drink traffic of East London will have to be grappled with. Legislative restrictions of a drastic character will have to be introduced to lessen the temptations and to reduce the facilities for drinking.

The whole publichouse system demands reform, not merely in regard to the hours, but also as to harbouring or encouraging prostitution in and from them. The police should be freed from the supervision of the publichouse system, and a separate force of detectives in plain-clothes constituted to supervise and to prosecute, both for drinking offences and acts of prostitution. This is important. Steps must also be taken to punish the men as well as the women. The male sex have far too much licence allowed them by the law. At present the law is unfair and oppressive to one sex. Let the balance be adjusted, and considerable improvement will appear in the morals of the masses.

One thing is worthy of notice. These middle-life women, who are said to be driven by downright starvation to vice, can find a home in the unions. Why do they not? Some few dislike the unions from a feeling of shame, and so choose a greater shame. But clergy, guardians, and union officials know that most refuse the home thus offered because of the discipline maintained within and the difficulty of obtaining drink. Many loathe the honest existence within unions because they love licence (or, as they term it, liberty) and strong drink. It is better to face facts than to ignore them.

How is this to be grappled with? I have long thought that there should be two grades of unions; one for the lazy, vicious, and criminal, and the other for the honest, distressed, and industrious. They should not be required to herd together under one stigma of reproach. This would remedy many evils raging today, and it would do something to save a few women from starving and then sinking into prostitution. But the magnitude and aggravated character of the evil cannot be reached to any appreciable extent by any one or more of the proposals, or by any hasty, spasmodic, and temporary effort of sentiment. The whole community must rise to the emergency, and, putting their shoulders to the wheel, take no rest until by combination of remedies, an arrest has been put to a great extent upon the vicious traffic in our midst.

The £2,000 asked by the Bishop of Bedford and the laundry suggested ought to be at once forthcoming to save a few. But what are these compared with the many who must be reached, if at all, by vaster and more thorough efforts?

W. M. ADAMSON,
Vicar of Old Ford
The Vicarage, Old Ford,
London, E.,
Oct., 10.

BLOODHOUNDS AS DETECTIVES.
TO THE EDITOR OF *THE TIMES*.

Sir,

With reference to the trials made with bloodhounds (mentioned in *The Times* of yesterday) in some of the London parks with a view of determining the probability of tracking murderers by the aid of canine instinct, I think it will be readily admitted by any one who has the least knowledge of the scenting power of dogs that the experiments instituted by Sir Charles Warren, or whoever is responsible for such silly proceedings, are practically of no value whatever in deciding as to whether the splendid animals in question would be likely to track to his hiding place a murderer who committed a crime similar in character to those which have lately horrified the whole country. Instead of wasting time in these foolish experiments (we may hear of another murder at any hour), I would suggest that a practical test as to the power of the bloodhounds might be made by endeavouring to track a person under conditions which it may be supposed the murderer of the Whitechapel victims got free. Several tests as to the capabilities of the animals might be made. For instance, a man should be given 15 or 20 minutes' start, and should make his way out of some side street across some great thoroughfare, intersected by tramcar rails, and on to some low lodging-house. Again, a trail should be laid on a man who makes his way along both frequented and unfrequented streets and on to some railway station, where he should take his ticket and travel to the next station. Various other variations in tracking should also be made.

Should it be considered unadvisable to try the experiments in Whitechapel, there are surely other places in and around London very similar in their surroundings where the hounds, hunted on the leash, might get a trail at a time of night and morning when the general public would not be attracted. If these trials were properly carried out I think we might get at some practical knowledge as to the manner in which the hounds should be worked when required.

I think too much faith should not be placed on the use of bloodhounds as detectives. But, in the name of common sense, let us not waste precious time in testing their tracking powers under conditions totally dissimilar to those which accompanied the murders at Whitechapel.

I am Sir, &c.,

HENRY FENNELL.
11 October.

POLICE SUPERVISION.
TO THE EDITOR OF *THE TIMES*.

Sir,

It seems to me that Mr. Dover, like many other persons, expects too much of the police. If a London householder goes away and shuts up his house, leaving no one in charge, he certainly runs the risk that somebody acquainted with the circumstances may carefully remove his household goods in broad daylight, leaving the front door wide open during the process. How is a policeman, seeing men who in appearance may be respectable upholsterers' men openly removing furniture from a house in broad daylight, to know that a robbery is being effected?

The shoulders of the police are broad, but it is unreasonable that every householder should seek to place upon them the consequences of his own imprudence.

Mr. Dover mentions that his house is 300 yards from a police fixed point, as if this were an aggravation of what he complains of. But I have always understood the object of the "fixed point" to be that a constable shall always be at a known place and at call in case of need, not that he shall take in and form an accurate judgement of everything that happens within a radius of 300 yards from his point.

Your obedient servant,

H. DELAHOOKE.
33, Union-grove, Clapham, Oct. 11.

A SHELTER FOR FEMALES.
TO THE EDITOR OF *THE MORNING ADVERTISER*.

SIR,

A shelter for outcast females will be opened in a few days at Harlow House, 34, Mile-end-road. Such poor creatures who are without home, food, friends, or money will be given a warm shelter, with a supper of a pint of coffee and bread, but the same applicants will not be admitted more than three nights in any week. Conveniences will be provided for washing, &c. Applicants will be received from ten p.m. until two a.m. every night, and those admitted can leave from five to eight o'clock in the morning, to enable them to obtain the casual employment that requires early application. The shelter will be cleansed each day, and, every means taken to make the poor creatures feel that it is not a casual ward, but a temporary shelter provided by those who sympathise with them in their sufferings. The only conditions will be-abject poverty and decorous conduct while in the shelter. Applicants will be able to obtain an order form the police-stations or any constable in the district.

We have secured on easy terms a site in Whitechapel, and if a little assistance is given us we will soon erect a large iron or other building on the site, which is close to the scene of one of the late brutal murders. We are negotiating for other sites, and will extend our operations if the necessary help is forthcoming. Members of the Vigilance Committee have offered their help, as they have found in the courts, alleys, passages, carts, vans, &c., countless poor creatures crouching away and in abject fear. Any donation, however small, will be thankfully received and duly accounted for. We shall also be glad of the assistance of ladies and gentlemen. With the exception of the attendant at the shelter there will be no paid officer, all services being rendered gratuitously. We ask for assistance, believing that if the movement is fully carried out it will not only be a great service to the destitute poor, but will also remove a stigma at present cast over a district peopled by honest, industrious artisans and labourers.

R.H. WINTER, J.L. DALE, Hon. Secs.
Office, 94, Mile-end-road, E.

15 October 1888

THE WHITECHAPEL MURDERS
To the Editor of *The Times*

Sir,

I have been a good deal about England of late, and have been a witness of the strong interest and widespread excitement which the Whitechapel murders have caused and are causing. Everywhere I have been asked about them; especially by working folk, and more especially by working women. Last week, for instance, in an agricultural county I shared my umbrella during heavy rain with a maid servant, who was going home. "Is it true, Sir," said she, "that they're a-cutting down the feminine seck in London?" And she explained herself to mean that "they was a'murdering of 'em by ones and twos." This is but one of many examples, and my own main interest in the matter is, that I myself have been taken for the murderer. And if I, why not any other elderly gentleman of quiet habits? It may therefore be well to record the fact by way of warning.

Two days ago I was in one of the mining districts, I had just called on my friend the parson of the parish, and was walking back in the twilight, alone, across certain lonely, grimy fields among the pits and forges. Suddenly I was approached from behind by a party of seven stout collier lads, each of them about 18 years old, except their leader, who was a stalwart young fellow of 23 or so, more than 6ft high. He rudely demanded my name, which, of course, I refused to give. "Then," said he, "You are Jack the Ripper, and you will come along wi'us to the police at ____;" naming the nearest town, two miles off. I inquired what authority he had for proposing this arrangement. He hesitated a moment, and then replied that he was himself a constable, and had a warrant (against me, I suppose), but had left it at home. "And," he added fiercely, "if you don't come quietly at once, I'll draw my revolver and blow your brains out." "Draw it, then," I said, feeling pretty sure that he had no revolver. He did not draw it; and I told him that I should certainly not go with him. All this time I noticed that, though the whole seven stood around me, gesticulating and threatening, not one of them attempted to touch me. And, while I was considering how to accomplish my negative purpose, I saw a forgeman coming across the field from his work. Him I hailed; and, when he came up, I explained that these fellows were insulting me, and that, as the odds were seven to one, he ought to stand by me. He was a dull, quiet man, elderly like myself, and (as he justly remarked) quite ready for his tea. But, being an honest workman, he agreed to stand by me; and he and I moved away in spite of the leader of the gang, who vowed that he would take my ally in charge as well as me. The enemy, however, were not yet routed. They consulted together, and very soon pursued and overtook us; for we took care not to seem as fugitives. But, meanwhile, I had decided what to do, and had told my friend that I would walk with him as far as our ways lay together, and then I would trouble him to turn aside with me up to the cottage of a certain stout and worthy pitman whom I knew. Thus, then, we walked on over barren fields and slag heaps for half a mile, surrounded by the seven colliers, who pressed in upon me, but still never touched me, though their leader continued his threats, and freely observed that, whatever I might do, I should certainly go with him to the town. At last we came into the road at a lonesome and murderous looking spot, commanded on all sides by the mountainous shale hills of disused pits. Up among these ran the path that led to the pitman's dwellings which I was making for. When we reached it, I said to my friend the forgeman, "This is our way," and turned towards the path. "That's not your way," shouted the tall man, "you'll come along the road with us," and he laid his hand on my collar. I shook him off, and informed him that he had now committed an assault, for which I could myself give him in charge. Perhaps it was only post hoc ergo propter hoc, but, an any rate, he made no further attempt to prevent me and my friend from ascending the byway. He stuck to us, however, he and his mates; swearing that he would follow me all the night, if need were. We were soon on the top of the col, if I may so call it, from which the pitmen's cottages, lighted within, were visible in the darkness against a starry sky. "That is where I am going," I said aloud. To my surprise, the tall man answered in a somewhat altered tone, "How long shall you be?" "That depends," I replied, "'you had better come to the house with me." "No," said he, "I shall wait for you here;" and the forgeman and I walked up to the cottage together. At its door I dismissed my ally with thanks and a grateful coin; and, entering in, I told my tale to my friend the stout pitman and his hearty wife, who heard it with indignation. In less than a minute, he and I sallied from his dwelling in search of the fellows who had dogged me. But they had vanished. Seeing me received and welcomed by people whom they knew, they doubtless felt that pursuit was futile and suspicion vain.

Now, I do not object to adventures, even in the decline of life; nor do I much blame my antagonists, whether their motive were righteous indignation, or, as is more likely, the hope of reward. But I think them guilty of a serious and even dangerous error of judgement in not distinguishing between the appearance of Jack the Ripper and that of your obedient servant,

An Elderly Gentleman.

Whitechapel
TO THE EDITOR OF *THE STAR*.

SIR,

The terrible crimes perpetrated within these last months must fill every true woman's heart with pity for her poor fallen sisters, and surely their own sex will be willing to show them some practical sympathy. It was suggested in one of the daily papers that every woman in London should give one penny for the sake of these poor outcasts, and the amount would be sufficient to provide clean and good lodgings for them. Surely no one would grudge so small a sum.

But that is not all that is requisite: a refining influence must be shed over these low London slums, and who could do it better than the ladies of England "who dwell at home at ease"? Surely there are some who have leisure and money to befriend these poor, homeless women. One can but feel indignant at the conduct of Mr. Matthews in this case. Even the poor blind Tories must condemn it.

Excuse the liberty I have taken, and believe me, yours, &c.,

A GIRL RADICAL.

16 October 1888

"THE MORAL OF THE MURDERS."
TO THE EDITOR OF *THE STAR*.

SIR,

The Vicar of St. Luke's, Camberwell, in your issue of the 13th inst., declares that the moral of the Whitechapel murders is that "the rich must confine themselves to necessities." But may I ask what, in that case, is to become of the millions of workers now employed in producing luxuries? The Vicar may reply, "Let them cease producing luxuries, begin to produce necessities" but as they have no control whatever over production, they have no power under present conditions to do this. Where, then, is the magician who will turn tapestry looms into ploughs, court dressmakers' workrooms into bakeries, and jewellers' shops into kitchen gardens; and who will teach weavers to make straight furrows, milliners to bake, and lapidaries to raise peas and beans? Does Mr. Chapman think the rich will do it? Not they: if, when they have filled their stomachs, they agree to desire nothing further, it will simply mean that their demand for wage-labor will be so much the slacker that wages will fall and land go out of cultivation, filling the streets with starving crowds of those who are now employed to produce luxuries. The people live at present not by supplying their own needs, but by waiting on their masters, the landholders, who only allow a few of them to produce necessities enough to keep the whole proletariat squalidly alive, whilst it is waiting on them. The result is that their is neither machinery nor trained skill to produce more necessities than are at present in the market. The mere abstention of the rich cannot do anything but bring to a standstill the machinery and the skilled labor which now produces what they would abstain from. In a community where slavery prevails - in other words, wherever land is private property and the country fully populated - the whims of the rich are the opportunities of the poor. The demand for luxuries benefits them; and all the assertions of political economists to the contrary are based on the perfectly irrelevant truth that if the people were free the demand for luxuries would not benefit them (which is indisputable, as it would not even exist). But of what concern is that to people who are not free? If a voluptuary has six footmen, and a vicar persuades him that he ought to be content with one, the result is that five men are deprived of their means of subsistence - nay, their fellow-slaves who were only employed to make their cockades, their plush stockings, and the beef and bread to stuff their calves, are thrown out too, the voluptuary simply leaving his land fallow by exactly so much as his wants are diminished. Why, the very fundamental assumption on which the individualist economists used to prove that private property would employ the whole population, was that the proprietors would be practically insatiable.

The fact is, Mr. *Star* Editor, these philanthropic and right-hearted clergymen who talk about the rich abstaining, sharing, giving "money, sympathy, and personal contact," and so on, have no idea what an uncommonly tight place we have got into. If they mean to uphold the present system it is their duty to preach extravagance to the idlers and slowness and shirking to the workers - to resist machinery with all their might, and to encourage everything that tends to depopulate the country.

In the presence of such a mortal gangrene in society as the open subjection of industry to idleness, a clergyman must either clamor for the extirpation of the gangrene or say - as he virtually does say in 999 churches out of a thousand to-day - "Evil, be thou my good." The only abstention that the landlord can beneficially practise is compulsory abstention from the land. Once that is achieved, his habits will no longer concern the people. Let him be as extravagant then as he likes - or as he can.

Yours, &c.,

A FABIAN.

BLOODHOUNDS AS DETECTIVES.
TO THE EDITOR OF *THE TIMES*.

Sir,

I am glad to see that the views I was permitted first to offer in *The Times* upon the use of bloodhounds in cities are endorsed by Mr. Henry Ffennell.

But I would venture a little further than Mr. Ffennell, and say that no country-trained hound should be allowed even to be tried in the streets of London. For town use a bloodhound must be trained in town, and from puppyhood. And if it is to be trained to assist in the detection of murder it must be trained for that one purpose only. Such work would form the supreme test, under the most favourable conditions of time and place, of the finest qualities in the keenest hound.

Any trials such as have been suggested could bring only ridicule on the breed generally, while for the particular hounds tried it would be most unfair.

Bloodhounds, from their extreme nervous temperament, are acutely sensitive to new or strange conditions. To instance this, a few weeks ago I had a bloodhound out, on leash, at an Epping Forest deer-hunt. The shouts and wild noises of the labourers driving the deer from cover to cover so unnerved the hound that, when I tried to work the scent of a deer which had got away after one of the "sportsmen," though he had hit it, the hound proved quite useless. Some mornings later I put her on the scent of a deer which had been seen "running on three legs." The hound worked on leash from the spot where the deer had lodged and took up the stale trail over some rather trying ground without a fault to a point at which, in deference to the Forest bylaws which make no provision for wounded deer being followed up, I deemed it prudent to stop.

While writing on this subject may I instance the precocious powers of well-bred bloodhound puppies. Yesterday morning I took into the woods a 13 weeks' old puppy for the first time, and for its first outdoor lesson. Smearing my boots with a little blood, and letting the puppy scent them, I walked away through thick cover. When I was well out of sight the puppy was unslipped and encouraged forward on my trail, which it took up at a trot, and "set" me without a fault. I continued the lessons with rests and rewards between, and without the blood. The last trial I made was from the centre of a wood, over ground partly covered with dry leaves, partly with heather and bracken. I took a quarter of an hour's start, placing a small brook and a broad, well-trodden green ride between me and the puppy. Neither brook nor ride bothered the hound, and I was tracked down in rather less time than it had taken me to cover the ground.

I dare say that known breeders like Mr. Brough, Mr. Hood Wright or Mr. Collingham Tinker can give similar instances of the precocious power of the bloodhound from six months old and upwards, but in a puppy of 13 weeks such neat working on a scent is interesting, if it is not altogether strange.

I am, Sir, your obedient servant,

PERCY LINDLEY.
York-hill, Loughton, Essex, Oct. 16.

THE LONDON POLICE
TO THE EDITOR OF *THE DAILY NEWS:*

Sir,

All friends of good government in London must welcome the excellent article in your issue of today on the London Police. The lines which you advocate for putting them under the control of the London County Council and for reorganizing them are practically those which were urged in the House of Commons by the London Liberal members during the late debate on the County Government Bill on my police amendment. Recent events and recent disclosures have shown the truth of our contention at that time, that the military character which the London police was rapidly assuming was unfitting it for its ordinary and natural duties. You may rest assured that the London Liberal members will raise the matter in the House of Commons at the earliest opportunity during the sitting of Parliament next month, and that we shall not be content with a scapegoat only, but shall be satisfied with nothing less than the complete change of the system in the direction you indicate, so that the effectual control of the police of London may be placed in the hands of the ratepayers of London.

I am, yours faithfully,

James Stuart.
Cambridge, Oct. 15.

17 October 1888

"CAN ANYTHING GOOD COME OUT OF WHITECHAPEL?"
To the Editor of *the Pall Mall Gazette*

Sir,

At the present moment, when the heart of London is thrilled with the realization of the ghastly truth that there are large districts in our midst where violence and outrage are so common that murder itself stalk unnoticed and unpunished, it is well to gather a little consolation and hope from the knowledge that in the very streets whose names now make us shudder there are peaceful homes where a dignified old age commands the respect of the roughest, and where virtue, cleanliness, and thrift shed their light around. If your readers doubt that any good thing can come out of Whitechapel, let them accompany a "lady almoner" to No.__ Buck's row, and call upon Mrs. P. They will find a little room, the picture of neatness and cleanliness, inhabited by an old woman of about seventy, in very feeble health, deaf, and almost blind, but always gentle and cheerful. She lives alone, having been a widow many years; her married son and daughter do for her what little they can. Until her sight failed she kept herself by brush work, having worked twenty five years for one employer. Her humble content and patient waiting for death teach the lessons that old age should. In a little court close by lives Mrs. M'C., a perfect picture of a beautiful old woman. She has occupied the same room for fifty two years, and it is a pattern of neatness. Some years a long lost son returned and promised his mother 5s a week. She at once voluntarily gave up the charitable help she had been receiving, and only her son's death and her own increasing infirmities have induced her to apply for it again. Such rare independence deserves to be recorded. In Hanbury street and Berner street similar bright spots may be found. In Fashion street, which has the reputation of being one of the three worst streets in London, two old sisters have lived for forty three years. They tell how "it used to be very respectable," and cannot bear to leave it even in its fall. Their landlady is kind to them, their neighbours respect if they do not imitate their thrift and cleanliness. It is in the belief that such homes are a strong influence for good among the East London poor, and that the old people who have made and love them, poor as they are, deserve a better fate than the workhouse, that the Tower Hamlets Pension Committee undertakes to help all thoroughly deserving cases brought to their notice in those districts (Whitechapel, Stepney, and St. George's in the East) where outdoor parish relief has been abolished. The pensions are raised by voluntary contributions, the whole of which go to the relief of the aged poor, the committee defraying its own expenses of management. The Hon. Treasurer is Mr. A.G. Crowder, 65 Portland place, W.

I am, Sir, yours faithfully,

P.D. Townsend.
28 Commercial street, E. October 15.

THE MORALS OF THE MURDERS.
TO THE EDITOR OF *THE ECHO*.

Sir,

The letter of the Rev. Hugh B. Chapman, which appeared in your issue of Saturday last, struck the correct key with reference to the recent murders.

At the same time, I would remind him that, however eloquent one may be in the pulpit or in the Press, such eloquence will be of no avail unless one is game enough to put their shoulders to the wheel, and to do all in their power to get such sentiments carried out into practical effect. The recent murders have had one effect: viz., to bring the condition of the residents in East London under public notice, and what is now wanted is for earnest men like Mr. Chapman to apply a practical remedy for the evils which exist. It is all very well to talk about the coming revolution; but what we should do, if we are in earnest, is to try and avert such a mishap, and, as a worthy City rector has well said, "It is far better to unloose the knot than to have it cut," a process always to be avoided, if possible.

The remedy is, as the saintly Bishop of Lincoln has truly said, "to disarm the so-called dangerous classes by improving their condition," and by bringing them out of their environment. Let all practical men, including clergy and statesmen, consider such plans as the better housing of the poor, the taxation of ground-rents and values, and a better distribution of the land which is the source of all wealth, and in general all schemes for the social improvement of the people. If this is done, good will have arisen out of evil, and the suffering of the poor in some degree alleviated. No one who has spent any time in East London can gainsay the fact that the poverty, the distress, the mode of life under which men exist compared with the West is enough to make one's heart ache and view the future with fear. What is wanted is more sympathy between men and men, less distinction between class and class, and for men to realise more than they do the Christian brotherhood.

Men of the East-end do not want patronage, they want sympathy and help to allow them to fight the battle of life, and if the Church, instead of giving so much attention to the science of ritual and to the propagation of dogma, turned its attention to the moral and social condition of mankind it would have a power which very few Churchmen now realise. The Church holds the key to the social problem, and it will be her own fault if she allows the coming Democracy to be atheistic instead of Christian. I would appeal to all earnest men to take the social questions of the day into their consideration, and by practical methods arrive at a solution of our present difficulties.

R.J. Bruton.
Peckham, Oct. 13

18 October 1888

TO THE EDITOR OF *THE TIMES*.

Sir,

As it would be a thousand pities if the good work which the Rev. Samuel A. Barnett has urged in your columns should be hindered by any misunderstanding as to the existence of the requisite machinery for carrying it through, permit me to emphasize the fact that though "The Tenements Dwellings Company" is doing good service in endeavouring to secure to the occupiers of tenement houses good and sanitary accommodation at reasonable rents, while at the same time proceeding on business principles, it does not attempt to touch those premises which are at present dedicated to vice and crime.

May I add that I believe that it is possible to bring about the desired reformation, while securing a moderate interest for the outlay, if an earnest attempt be made in the right direction.

I am &c.,

F. H. HARVEY-SAMUEL
Honorary Secretary and Solicitor to the Tenement Dwellings Company (limited).
88, Broadhurst-gardens, Hampstead, N.W.

TO THE EDITOR OF *THE TIMES*.

Sir,

Having been intimately acquainted with the neighbourhood, in which the recent unexampled atrocities were committed, for at least a generation, especially in connexion with efforts to reclaim outcasts from that terrible moral waste, I cannot refrain from giving expression to my conviction as to the effectual rooting out of the evils which have festered in certain parts of Spitalfields for so many years.

I respectfully submit that increased encouragement should be given to those moral aggressive agencies designed for domiciliary visitation in this locality, especially on the lines of the City Mission, Scripture Readers' Society, and Midnight Meeting Movement.

I have known the work of such agencies sufficiently long as to be enabled to speak confidently of their effectiveness, and there is one feature of the recent sad incidents which confirms this opinion. The victims were all women somewhat advanced in life. This can scarcely be regarded altogether as an accident. The fact is, the agencies referred to are continually reclaiming numbers of the younger victims drawn into that fearful locality. Those that remain become hardened into well-nigh irreclaimable evil-doers, and as such they form quite a colony.

My long experience in rescue work has confirmed the opinion that such centres of the fallen and criminal classes should be broken up. The reclaimed, of any age, out of that or similar districts should be removed into entirely new localities - indeed, if it were possible, companions should never be placed together in the same refuge or reformatory of any kind. Reformation in such cases depends almost entirely upon the breaking up of evil associations and surroundings.

Notwithstanding that all common lodging-houses are registered under a recent Act of Parliament, and visited from time to time by the sanitary officials, they still remain social abominations of the very worst kind, as I have proved from personal observation. Shocking as these recent murders have been, if they lead, as they ought to do, to a further amendment of the law, and an extension of proper supervision by night as well as by day, lasting good will be effected.

I have observed the rapid extension of model dwellings, especially on the east side of Commercial-street leading up to Thrawl-street, &c., and I am certain that if capital were employed to clear off the few acres still left in the neighbourhood referred to, and the land covered with better dwellings, not only would the capital invested pay a fair percentage, but, in addition, would secure to those who are obliged to resort to the lowest rented sleeping places, good sanitary accommodation as well as that privacy which is essential to the maintenance of morality.

From careful observation during the last 35 years, I know that when extreme poverty forces any unfortunate man or woman to locate themselves in the wretched common lodging-houses abounding in Flower and Dean-street, Thrawl-street, &c., demoralization inevitably and rapidly follows. Further, I maintain, in the interests of society generally, that the honest poor, homeless for a time, ought not to be feared, as it were, to herd themselves in such dangerous and degrading quarters.

I am, Sir, your obedient servant,

EDWARD W. THOMAS, Secretary.
London Female Preventive and Reformatory Institution
200, Euston-road, London.

19 October 1888

TO THE EDITOR OF *THE DAILY TELEGRAPH*.

SIR -

As the owner of the largest kennel of bloodhounds at present in existence, and taking a deep interest in the breeding and training of the animals, I can speak with some authority on the subject of utilising them for the purpose of tracing criminals. On the 4th of this month I received a communication from the Government on the subject, which resulted in an interview, at which I expressed my opinion in favour of a practical trial, and took two couples of my hounds to London for the purpose of testing them in the streets. I have since noticed a report of some trials having taken place in the parks, which I do not consider of much practical utility, since all breeders know that bloodhounds will follow a trail on grass or across country with a very little training.

What is wanted are hounds that will stick to the scent of the right man over paved streets. A writer in the *Field* suggests that raw meat or blood should be used as a method of training, but I consider this a doubtful plan, as in time of need the hound is not wanted to find the carcass of a sheep or bullock, and neither does he follow a scent for what he may get to eat at the end of it. He can be trained to follow the trail of a man from the man's own scent, as I am convinced, from several careful experiments, that each individual possesses a distinct scent to the bloodhound. This could be proved easily enough by starting a bicycle rider, who should first just pass his hand over the tyre of his wheel, which would be sufficient to carry the scent to the ground, after which he might be crossed and re-crossed by others, before laying the hounds on. Properly-trained hounds would then follow him to the end without swerving from the course.

I consider that bitches are better for town work than dogs, as they are more constant on the trail, and are not likely to raise their heads in passing other dogs. The most successful mode of training will be to find a few complaisant surgeons in constant surgical practice at the hospitals, on to whom the hounds might at first be laid immediately on leaving the hospital, the time being by degrees extended. This would be quite sufficient training, although it might be supplemented by practice in the streets either at night or in the early hours of the morning.

I am in favour of offering prizes to the owner of the hounds who may be declared the winners at competent trials. The police would soon find the usefulness of their new assistants, and, once let a capture be made by this means, and murders and burglaries would quickly become rarer. I have made a careful study of hounds generally, and I am satisfied that the bloodhound has the keenest power of scent of any breed, and is easily trained to hunt man without any artificial trails whatever. He is affectionate and intelligent, and is the best dog to keep as a companion, apart from his usefulness; and as a deterrent to crime his value is incalculable. I feel confident that if the police were to adopt his use, and keep him at the various metropolitan stations, good results would speedily follow.

Ten well-trained bloodhounds would be of more use than a hundred constables in ferreting out criminals who have left no trace beyond the fact of their presence behind them. I consider that the police have done all that they possibly could to discover the perpetrator of the Whitechapel murders, but they lack one important factor - namely, the power of scent, which the bloodhound possesses to perfection.

There is an idea - arising more from the name, I fancy, than anything - that the bloodhound is a savage animal, whereas he is one of the most docile of canine creatures.

I feel positive that, if I had been on the scene of the Mitre-square tragedy, even several hours after the occurrence, with a few of my hounds, that the man would have been captured, as after such mutilation the scent would have been sufficient to keep them on the track for miles. I consider that bloodhounds should be used by the police for the purpose of tracing criminals, and the training of them for this purpose should be under the direction of a careful man who understands hound-work generally.

The hounds should be kept at work daily until they are brought to a high state of perfection. This would be rapidly achieved, owing to their innate fondness for hunting.

I believe that the knowledge that bloodhounds are being kept on the spot has acted as a deterrent to the Whitechapel murderer. If not, and he meditates further atrocities, he will certainly have an opportunity of learning something about them that he did not know before.

I am, Sir, yours obediently,

H. M. MACKUSICK.
Merstham, Surrey, Oct. 18.

DISTRESS IN EAST LONDON.
TO THE EDITOR OF *THE MORNING ADVERTISER*.

SIR,

Very few people know to what an extent genuine poverty exists in this district; thick masses of poor people are living all around us, and, as a matter of fact, more than 60 per cent of the population are dependent on some form of charity, and of the remainder by far the greater proportion are mechanics and shop-keepers, who are only just able to make both ends meet. Some are utterly unable to bear the terrible strain, and go to swell the ranks of those who need assistance. For over 30 years I have laboured as the honorary pastor of a church in the Roman-road, Bow, and have been privileged to do much to relieve the terrible distress by which I am surrounded. Many hundred pairs of boots and clothing have been provided for the destitute children attending our Board schools, because the parents are crushed and enfeebled by painful surroundings. The district is carefully visited by mission agency, and the people relieved according to their several necessities. Our mission hall has long been a centre for good work in this respect. But, Sir, the means at my disposal are altogether inadequate to the winter's task, and I am compelled to appeal to your readers to help me with their contributions. The need for help was never greater than it is at present, and I am afraid that the approaching winter will witness an even greater amount of poverty than that to which we are unhappily accustomed. Any sums with which I may be entrusted shall be promptly acknowledged, and I can safely promise that in the disposal due care shall be exercised, so that the really deserving shall benefit. I have for many years made it a rule not to give relief in doles merely, which can only satisfy present needs, but rather to assist those who are struggling in such a way that they may be permanently benefited.

I am, Sir, yours &c.,

E. SCHNADHORST.
St. Stephen's-road, Bow, E., Oct. 18.

East End Poverty.
TO THE EDITOR OF *THE STAR*.

SIR,

Dr. Drysdale is to the fore again in your columns with his Malthusian solution of the social problem.

May I, sir, as a humble member of the army of workers, suggest to him, an experienced physician, that he has mistaken in over-population of the poor a symptom for the cause or origin of the great social disease.

How many of the poor creatures who are stived up in their dog hutches of dwellings have any sort of social environment calculated to excite any healthful motives of moral pleasure? I think most of them are forced to resort to the two things that bring about the symptoms complained of by Dr. Drysdale.

Remove them and the disease will find another outlet in perhaps a more inconvenient form to the classes whose very existence is the cause of theirs.

Yours, &c.,

9 Oct.
ULTRA RADICAL.

TO THE EDITOR OF *THE STAR*.

SIR,

Dr. Drysdale has hit upon the causes of East-end poverty in his letter to you: *i.e.*, drink and over-population. But how to apply the remedy, there's the rub. I believe it is legislation alone which can remedy both.

Whilst philosophers, preachers, and reformers have been proving the drink curse to be fraught with abounding social evils for several decades past, politicians have still allowed the miasmatic stream to flow unchecked, because the pockets of the wealthy and influential are interested, and decline to interfere.

A short Act should also prohibit the marriage of infants destitute of any means or powers of earning, and all parsons and registrars should be placed under a heavy penalty who married young pauper couples, and all under 21 at lowest.

The less reference to the example of France the better for our social and national life.

Yours, &c.,

SIGMA.

TO THE EDITOR OF *THE STAR*.

SIR,

Poverty Cause of Social Evil. - Would you be surprised that wealth has much to do with it? Go to Piccadilly-circus at midnight and discover the cause of women being there. It was in the first instance wealth! Decoyed by men of means from honest livelihoods. Few women are naturally so depraved, but men bring them down. Make your men virtuous, and this evil disappears. Make all total abstainers, and poverty disappears; but not otherwise. Poverty cannot or ought not to indulge in either of these evils. Men can live better without both.

Yours, &c.,

A CONSTANT READER.

26 October 1888

A WHITECHAPEL FUND
To the Editor of *The Times*

Sir,

I have begun to raise a fund, to which I invite contributions from your readers, with a view of powerfully bringing the teachings of Christianity to bear on the dark corner in Whitechapel which has been disgraced by such hideous crimes. If the Gospel sufficed to change the cannibal inhabitants of the Fiji Islands into a nation of Christian worshippers, it is sufficient, and alone sufficient, to turn the darkest spots on London into gardens of the Lord.

My desire is to apply the fund in support of the following agencies:

1. To provide a colporteur to go from house to house with Christian literature for sale. £40 or £50 a year paid to the Christian Colportage Association would provide such an agent.

2. An extra London City missionary, for which about £80 to £90 per annum would be needed to be sent to the London City Mission.

3. Another Bible woman or nurse in connexion with the London Bible and Domestic Female Mission, at a cost of about £40 per annum.

4. A mission house, to be the headquarters of this united effort, part of which might be used for girls' club rooms, &c., with a resident lady to work specially among the young women of the district, with a few beds attached.

May I plead for generous and immediate help to start these various agencies at once?

Contributions may be sent to the Dowager Lady Kinnaird, 1 Pall Mall East, S.W., or to the "Whitechapel Fund," care of Messrs. Barclay, Ransom and Co., 1 Pall Mall East, S.W.

Your obedient servant,

Mary J. Kinnaird.
1 Pall mall East, Oct. 24.

29 October 1888

WHITECHAPEL FUND
TO THE EDITOR OF *THE TIMES*

Sir,

Will you allow me, through your columns, to beg the Dowager Lady Kinnaird to reconsider her plans for the reformation of Whitechapel, and the general public to hold their hands until some consultation has been held with those who by living and working in the district know it thoroughly.

I ask this, because every single agency suggested for the amelioration of Whitechapel is already in existence.

The Church of England Scripture Readers' Society and the London City Mission have their agents visiting from house to house. The East End deaconesses and others are ministering to women. The East London Nursing Society supplies parish nurses to visit the sick. Parochial and other mission women are busily employed. Pure literature is being disseminated in various ways. The Girls' Friendly Society and many private individuals are interesting themselves in the girls.

One would suppose from Lady Kinnaird's letter that no Christian influence is being brought to bear upon the people.

I would, however, remind your readers that the Church is at work, and that not unsuccessfully, as can be easily proved. That Mr. George Holland representing "the unsectarians" has a large and powerful agency, and the more modern exponents of philanthropic effort are adequately represented by the Rev. S. Barnett and his coadjutors at Toynbee Hall.

It will, therefore, be seen that there is absolutely no need to start a new agency, and that religious people if nearly every possible shade of opinion have their representatives among us.

What then is needed? I reply, the strengthening of existing agencies, and the more active and sympathetic support of those who are devoting their best energies to making the lives of their poorer brethren happier and more hopeful.

I am your obedient servant,

Arthur J. Robinson
Rector of Whitechapel
Oct. 27

30 October 1888

A HOME FOR INEBRIATE WOMEN.
TO THE EDITOR OF *THE DAILY TELEGRAPH*.

SIR -

Would you be so good as to allow space for an appeal on behalf of a home for inebriate women, under the auspices of the "Women's Union of the Church of England Temperance Society." The urgent need for homes of this kind is not generally known, although all who work in the above-mentioned and kindred societies find it forced upon them at every turn.

One such home was opened, at 99, Southam-street, Westbourne Park, on June 12 last, the house having most generously been placed, rent free, at the disposal of the committee of management. This house contains ten beds, which are constantly full, and applications continue to come from all parts of England, to which the discouraging answer "We have no more room" has to be returned. It was intended, in the first instance, that this home should be a "shelter," to supplement the work of the police-court missionaries of the Church of England Temperance Society, but the applications from the country, as well as from London, were so numerous that the committee found it impossible to limit its benefits to police-court cases only. The committee now hope to open another home, as soon as they have the funds necessary for the purpose. They are most anxious to raise £500, towards which sum they have already received £50 from two anonymous donors. It is hoped that this second home may be made partly self-supporting by the payments of those who will be received there; but there must always of necessity be many expenses connected with such an undertaking.

The Church of England Temperance Society are desirous to keep the "shelter" as much as possible for the numerous cases from the police-courts, most of which, obviously, must be received free of charge; although it is hoped that washing and other work will by degrees be provided for those under the care of the home, which will bring in some slight addition to the funds. The work of the past few months has been very encouraging, and has given good reason to those in charge to be hopeful of seeing real and permanent good results, the improvement in the poor sufferers who have sought this shelter being most marked.

But the need of funds is most pressing. Subscriptions and donations may be sent to the treasurer, Mrs. G. Howard Wright, Mapperley Cottage, Weybridge; or to the office, 141, Palace-chambers, Bridge-street, Westminster, S.W.; or to me, Mrs. Temple, Fulham Palace, S.W.

I remain, sir, yours faithfully,

BEATRICE TEMPLE.
Fulham Palace, Oct. 29.

The Hallucination of Warren
TO THE EDITOR OF *THE STAR*

SIR,

I am much alarmed about poor Sir Charles Warren. Does he drink, do you think? Or can it be that he is the victim of mental hallucination? Perhaps both. In an article recently written by him to *Murray's Magazine*[61] he expresses himself so strangely that many of his friends (amongst whom I am proud to include myself) have become seriously frightened about him. We would not lose him; no, we love our Charles; knowing full well that did he die, such a combination of red tape, buckram, and wooden head were hard to match.

It appears, Mr. Editor, that we are really living on a volcano.

You have heard me say so in full senate, and no one believed; but now that I am corroborated by Sir Charles I shall repeat the offence next session. The first of the day dreams that afflict this mystic warrior is that London has been for many years past (in fact, till he entered office) exposed to the "sinister influence of a mob stirred up into spasmodic" (spasmodic is good) "action by restless demagogues."

By restless demagogues I conclude, sir, that Sir Charles refers to you and me, as we often have addressed the "sinister mob" in days gone by. He should not be so previous. To refer to a member of Parliament as a "restless demagogue," is no doubt praiseworthy, but to lift his ruthless pen against one who like yourself combines in his single person the sacred offices of popular representative and editor, this passeth all understanding.

London exposed to mob rule! London, the most peaceful of European cities, not excluding Reigiavik.

If our jaunty Chief Commissioner could see the Californian hoodlum or the Australian larrikin at play; if he had seen a New York street or a Paris boulevard after a street war, with shops wrecked, trees broken, and dead men as thick as flies on a bath bun at a railway station - then perhaps he would be warranted in getting up and snorting like an Indian pony.

How can an unarmed mob terrorise a town? how can a mob composed of starvelings like a London mob be dangerous to anyone but itself? Do London democrats carry pistols? If they did, perhaps last year Trafalgar-square would have looked different.

A London mob is the quietest, most pacific, underfed collection of human atoms it has ever been my lot to see.

The abject misery of the mob in contradistinction to the overfed appearance of the bourgeoisie is

---

[61] The publication of this article would subsequently result in Sir Charles Warren's resignation as Commissioner of Police.

the thing that appeals most strongly to any one who is not a pious soldier. Our military friend does not descend to instances of this mob coercion. No, I presume that particular instances would be too sociable and respective for his conversing, and that he prefers to vilify his countrymen in general terms. Besides, too, the instance of the park railings would hardly be a good one for a man who poses as a Radical to bring forward.

The second hallucination that troubles this gifted soldier, is that Trafalgar-square was cleared last year without loss of life. If I did not know the fixity of your religious principles, sir, and that you would hesitate to sully your columns with an oath, I should say, like Julius, "It's a damned lie."

Does Sir Charles forget the funeral of one Linnell (to which he was invited), a funeral at which a million people turned out? Has he forgotten the devices the police resorted to (no doubt in opposition to his orders) in order to get the body out of the relatives' hands. Does he pretend to forget the inscription on the coffin, "Killed by the police?" Has he forgotten the howls of execration that greeted him when at that time he was seen in the streets?

Was it not he who failed to lecture on Palestine?

Oh, Sir Charles, "without loss of life!" Who was Curwen. Was he not also buried publicly?

A soldier, even a pious one, may suffer from hallucination; the tightness of his uniform, no doubt, may impede circulation, and so produce brain disturbances.

But a lie and a public one. When he knows that these men were killed through his own folly. I question, sir, if even the position he holds at pious tea-fights authorises him to print what he knows to be untrue.

Then, his statement that "ex-Ministers have not hesitated to embarrass those in office by smiling (sic) on the insurgent mob."

Would they had done so. But, no, a Ministerial smile is such a scrumptious article, I would not have it wasted. And where was the "insurgent mob?" Fancy the rictus of Sir Harcourt in Trafalgar-square! It would be better than a square meal to the unemployed. Imagine, if you can, Mr. Shaw Lefevre grinning through a horse collar from the railings.

John Morley is an awkward smiler, too.

As to Sir Ughtred Shuttleworth, perish the thought; no one (not even Sir Charles) would dare to connect him with anything so indecent. But there were some who smiled, who smole. Where be the gay smilers? "Oh est le preux Charlemagne?"

I saw no smiling; no laugh of a Minister grated jarringly on my ears.

I saw a miserable mob trampled down for doing nothing. I saw all law and order outraged by Sir Charles Dogberry and Mr. Henry Verges (the Home Secretary), and so far from ex-Ministers smiling, they were too cowardly to say a word.

Go to, Sir Charles. Look not on the wine when it is red. The race suffers, as Chaucer says.

Let thy study be ever on the Bible. Pore not over Monsieur Lecoq. Try and see London as it is, with its awful miseries. Incline thine ear to the cry of the unemployed for bread.

Survey human misery no longer through a piece of flint glass (or maybe pebble), but with eyes of human sympathy. Be less of a soldier and more of a Christian. Such is the prayer of your earnest well-wisher.

R. B. CUNINGHAME GRAHAM[62]

---

[62] Robert Bontine Cunninghame Graham (1852-1936) was a radical socialist member of Parliament. He attended the Trafalgar Square demonstration of November 1887 (known as "Bloody Sunday") and was severely beaten by police called in by Sir Charles Warren to quell the disturbance. Graham was subsequently sentenced to six weeks' imprisonment for his participation in the demonstration, but for the remainder of his career he would continue to campaign for the rights of working people.

13 November 1888

THE EAST-END MURDERS AND WHAT IS TO BE DONE.
TO THE EDITOR OF *THE TIMES*.

Sir,

Occupying as I do the rectory-house of St. Botolph, Bishopsgate[63], which is agreeably situated, with Mitre-square within easy access at the back and Dorset-street in the front, flanked by Petticoat-lane on the east and Liverpool-street, which is the focus of harlotry, on the west, I confess that at this crisis I share with my neighbours in the horror of the situation. "Our hearts are disquieted within us, and the fear of death is fallen upon us," and we ask, What is to be done? Murder succeeds to murder, and for a time we are staggered. A number of people are arrested who ought to have been let alone, but gradually the excitement passes off, the faithful bloodhounds are sent back to their kennels, the tide of business flows on, and the murders seem to be forgotten; but I really do hope that the event of Lord Mayor's day will not be allowed to pass off so quietly, and that some measures will be adopted to assure our disquietude. But what is to be done? It is not so much the murders, ghastly as they are, that sadden and appall us, but it is the awful state of things which these murders reveal-the disorderly and depraved lives which these poor people lead. What is to be done to remedy this state of things? That is the problem to be solved. Having had some experience in these matters, and having lived among these people for nearly half a century, I venture to think that I speak with some authority, and I offer two suggestions. The first is that all those women who ply the meretricious trade should be registered, and if need be licensed. I know the cry that will be raised against this, but I ask, Are the interests of society to be sacrificed to a blatant prudery? Secondly, there should be a house to house visitation, which would throw light into these bleak dwellings. As a Christian minister I should like to see this carried out by devoted men living in these districts, and by their self-sacrifice and sympathy gaining the confidence of the inhabitants. This, however, would require organization and some leader to set it on foot. I should like to do it myself, but *non sum qualis eram*, and I cannot undertake it. Failing this, the work should be carried out by the police - police dressed as the "new police" were when they were first introduced by Sir Robert Peel, in the dress of civilians - men set apart for the work, going in and out among the people and mingling with them. As friends they would be in correspondence with the various philanthropic societies who would render assistance for rescue and relief. Of course there will be a cry raised against such a movement, which would be said to interfere with the rights of the Englishman. Every man's house is his castle, &c. What was poor Mary Ann Kelly's castle?

---

[63] This is the church commonly known as the "Prostitutes' Church." In the 1880s it was common for prostitutes to continually circumnavigate St. Botolph's while waiting for clients. As long as they kept moving they could not be arrested for solicitation. Mr. Rogers' progressive ideas on prostitution may have resulted from his familiarity with the "unfortunates" who plied their trade near St. Botolph's.

However, if judiciously carried out it would, I am sure, eventually become popular; at all events the plague would be stayed.

Your faithful servant,

WILLIAM ROGERS.
Rectory, Bishopsgate, E., Nov. 12.

14 November 1888

BLACK WINTER IN EAST LONDON.
TO THE EDITOR OF *THE MORNING ADVERTISER*.

Sir,

Black winter has already settled down on East London. My missionaries give a deplorable account of the distress. Many people are foodless and fireless. My blood curdles as I find decent, respectable people going without food for two days together. I think I am pretty well on guard against cadgers and imposters, after more than 12 years work at the East-end. Our stringent system of continuous and constructive visitation makes us acquainted with the poor as no other system can. But with funds run out I am powerless. If friends of the suffering care to send help, I will see that it is used to the best advantage.

I am, Sir, yours &c.,

W. EVANS HURNDALL
16, Cottage-grove, Bow, London, E.,
Nov. 9, 1888.

15 November 1888

Whitechapel.
TO THE EDITOR OF *THE STAR*.

SIR,

May I trouble you with a few words as to the conduct of the Home Secretary with regard to the East-end murders, speaking from a working-man's point of view? Could Mr. Matthews only hear what working-men generally think about his refusal to offer a reward, he would be able to form some idea of the injury he is doing his party, and which they will feel at the next election. The working class think, and rightly think, if a reward is offered and it does not lead to the conviction of the murderer no harm can have been done, and no money will have to be paid; on the other hand, it might lead to the man's conviction; and more, they argue that if the victim was some person of high standing in society a reward would have been offered long since. But life is life, and it is as much to the poor degraded victims of this fiend as it is to the highest in the land. A reward might bring forward evidence of the conduct of the murderer at his lodgings or in a hundred different ways.

With regard to the notice of pardon to anybody not the actual murderer, in the last case, it is childish. Degraded as the poor victim was, does Mr. Matthews think she would take a third person to witness her immorality?

Yours, &c.,

C. THOMAS.
Canterbury-place, Lambeth, S.E.,
12 Nov.

16 November 1888

TO THE EDITOR OF *THE DAILY TELEGRAPH.*

SIR -

Can nothing be done to prevent a set of hoarse ruffians coming nightly about our suburban squares and streets, yelling at the tops of their hideous voices, "Special Edition" - "Whitechapel" - "Murder" - "Another of 'em!" - "Mutilation!" - "Special Edition!" - "Beautiful - Awful - Murder!" and so on, and nearly frightening the lives out of all the sensitive women and children in the neighbourhood? Last evening (Wednesday), for instance, their cry was, "Special - Murder - Paper - Jack - The Ripper - Caught - Paper - Whitechapel - Paper - Got 'im at Last - Paper - Murder - Ripper - Paper - Murder - Got the Ripper - Paper - At Last."

These awful words were bawled out about nine o'clock in a quiet part of Kensington; and a lady who was supping with us was so greatly distressed by these hideous bellowings that she was absolutely too unnerved to return home save in a cab, because she would have to walk about a hundred or two yards down a quiet street at the other end of her journey by omnibus.

Now, I venture to ask, Sir, is it not monstrous that the police do not protect us from such a flagrant and ghastly nuisance?

I enclose my card, and beg to subscribe myself,

PEMBROKE-SQUARE.
Kensington, Nov. 15.

THE WHITECHAPEL MURDERS
To the Editor of the *St. James's Gazette*

Sir,

The "extraordinary statement" - very properly so headed - which appeared in today's papers about the Whitechapel murderer's cousin, whose conscience suddenly impelled him to make a confession to a fruiterer[64] from whom he had just chanced to buy twelve shillings' worth of rabbits, seems rather to lack finish. It omits to add how many rabbits the murderer's cousin got for his twelve shillings. In justice to the fruiterer this should have been told, and I think there might also have been some slight acknowledgement of the zeal and intelligence of the reporter who was con-

---

[64] Reference to Matthew Packer (1830-1907), a fruit-vendor who claimed to have sold grapes to a man and a woman he identified as Elizabeth Stride on the night of her murder. He made other sensational claims in late October and mid-November, and is generally regarded as an attention-seeker.

veniently at hand to take down the fruiterer's story and convey it promptly to the Home Secretary - and to the News Agencies. It has doubtless occurred to many people, and it is well known to the police, that extraordinary statements of this kind and the extraordinary proceedings of the amateur detectives who nightly patrol Whitechapel are of great help - to the murderer in evading discovery. Every wrongful arrest and every wild goose chase after the murderer's cousin on which the police are sent tends distinctly in the murderer's favour. You cannot play the fool in these ways with men, however efficient, without lessening their efficiency. And, unfortunately, just at present the police dare not, as they should, tell the amateur detectives to go home, and the murderer's cousin to make his confession, if he has any to make, at the nearest police station. If the murderer be possessed, as I imagine he is, with the usual cunning of lunacy, I should think it probable that he was one of the first to enroll himself amongst the amateur detectives.

As to the disgusting Jack the Ripper letter and post card of which facsimiles were published, the detective police are much less intelligent than I suppose them to be if they do not know where to look for the writer if they want him.

I am, sir, your obedient servant,

H.T.
November 15.

Another Protest.
TO THE EDITOR OF *THE STAR*.

SIR,

While willing to bow to superior judgement on this matter, I, too, would support Mrs. Langworthy by my protest against the wholesale publication of the details of Whitechapel. I have been asking myself over and over again what possible good can result from such publication. That harm does follow, as a consequence, we know from the horrid Newcastle imitation, and who can say for a certainty that the same fiend has been guilty of the whole series?

I quite agree that the detective department has totally collapsed; but although the press must to some extent fill the gap, yet is it necessary to fill our children's minds (for even children read newspapers now-a-days) with all the bestial details of these crimes? My reason for writing is that this very evening a child of mine called out to his sister "I am Jack the Ripper. Look out!" and I learn that even the street Arabs are making a game of it. We object to a "Zola" and tolerate an "Ouida," we allow in Ireland what we object to in Russia, and we tolerate a Hughes-Hallett under the very roof that rings with the eloquence of a Gladstone. Where is our consistency? Only the other day there was a huge outcry against the *Pall Mall Gazette* for publishing prurient details in which the welfare of our children was vitally concerned, and now the very papers (yours excepted, because it was not in existence then) which called out the loudest are publishing broadcast details which makes the *Pall Mall Gazette* take a back seat altogether. There is not the slightest doubt that murder begets murder, and horror begets horror; for weak minds brood over disgusting and vicious details until the frail thread of reason becomes too slight for the tension exercised, and the balance is unhinged.

For God's sake, sir, use your powerful influence to overcome the morbid tendencies of the age, or ere long we shall revert to the dark periods when human torture was rampant and the stake a potent force for the inculcation of ideas of a higher civilisation.

Yours, &c.,

J. ARTHUR ELLIOTT.
Liberal Club, Wood-green, 12 Nov.

LAW AND ORDER IN WHITECHAPEL.
TO THE EDITOR OF *THE TIMES*.

Sir,

Will you permit me, through your columns, to offer to the friends of law and order an opportunity of maintaining and extending those principles in the part of London that has become so notorious of late? Some two or thee years back a small Volunteer Cadet Corps was formed in Whitechapel for the boys of the neighbourhood. It's headquarters are the Whittington Club in Leman-street, and it is attached to the 1st Tower Hamlets Rifle Volunteer Brigade. In spite of the serious difficulties which necessarily attend a new experiment of this kind, it has hitherto held its own with good success and is very popular among the boys themselves, to some hundreds of whom it could now afford the means of physical exercise and discipline, greatly wanting among our city populations. Some of its members have passed into the Regular Forces, and it was inspected last July by Colonel Stracey, commanding the Scots Guards, who gave a most satisfactory report on the present condition of the corps. The working cost of the undertaking is not very great, consisting chiefly of expenses for drill instructors and bandmaster, purchase of uniforms, hire of drill-hall, and marches out; but considering the class of boys for whom the corps is intended it is impossible that it should be self-supporting. The officers, therefore, are obliged to ask for the co-operation of others in extending the influence of the movement, and securing the moral and physical advantages of regular training for a district where the history of the last few months and years has proved them to be so much needed.

Subscriptions may be sent to the Commanding Officer, 86, Leman-street, Whitechapel; or to the

Hon. C. W. Fremantle, C.B., the Royal Mint; or to the E.L.V.C. Fund, Messrs. Cox & Co.'s, 16 and 17, Charing-cross.

I am, Sir, &c.,

PAUL METHUEN, Colonel.
Toynbee-hall, Commercial-street, Whitechapel, Nov. 13.

WHAT IS TO BE DONE?
TO THE EDITOR OF *THE TIMES*.

Sir,

With Mr. Rogers, I am appalled more "by the disorderly and depraved lives" of our neighbours than by the actual murders. The acts of a madman are not matters for horror, and his escape is not sufficient reason for wholesale condemnation of the police. A series of courts such as Miller's-court, where rooms unfit for stables are let at 4s. a week, where the cries of murder are too common to arouse notice, where vice is the staple trade and drunkenness the chief resource - this fact should arouse horror, and ought to be remedied.

We may agree that elevation of character is the only radical remedy, and many will be willing to endure the sight of much suffering while Christian people rescue men and women one by one from selfishness and impurity. For my part, I believe that even order in the streets would be obtained at too great a cost if, by the adoption of one of Mr. Rogers' remedies, public opinion did less to educate the self-control which is the basis of character. He that believeth shall not make haste.

At the same time there is something which can be done. These houses are managed by agents; the landlords are ladies and gentlemen, and the rents ultimately reach their pockets. These landlords could enforce order, they could see that the rooms are fit for habitation, provided with locks and means of privacy, they could have a night watchman to prevent rows and the intrusions of the viscious, they could see that the tenants lived respectable lives, and they could prove themselves their friends in hours of need. You, Sir, in an article, expressed the wish that the names of the owners of the houses in this criminal quarter might be published. My hope is that, as they realize that the rents are the profits of vice, they will either themselves take direct action to improve this disgraceful condition of things, or sell their property to those who will undertake its responsibility.

I am truly yours,

SAMUEL A. BARNETT.
St. Jude's Vicarage, Commercial-street,
Whitechapel, E., Nov 13.

17 November 1888

SIR CHARLES WARREN AND MR. MATTHEWS.
TO THE EDITOR OF *THE TIMES*.

Sir,

With reference to the debate last night in the House of Commons, I trust I may state that I have never to my knowledge in any way contested the lawful authority of the Secretary of State over the Metropolitan police force; and the insinuation that I have in any way contested the administration of the police being subject to Parliament through the Secretary of State seems too ridiculous for me to contradict.

A period cartoon depicting the conflict between Warren and Matthews

In many cases, while accepting directions given me which were to all appearances contrary to the statute, I have entered a protest; and in thus protesting I have acted in accordance with the advice of the legal advisor appointed by the Secretary of State, the late Mr. J. Davis, formerly stipendiary magistrate of Sheffield.

I can only express my astonishment at the statements attributed to Mr. Matthews last night, and I venture to assert that an entirely different impression would be conveyed to the public mind about my action if the correspondence were to be made known.

I am, Sir, your obedient servant,

CHARLES WARREN.
44, St. George's-road, S.W. Nov. 16

21 November 1888

Dr. Tumblety and Isaac Golliday
To the Editor of THE EVENING STAR
(Washington, D.C.)

My attention was directed to an article in your paper of yesterday (Tuesday, November 20), regarding the arrest of Dr. Tumblety in London on suspicion of being connected with the Whitechapel murders. The notice revived sad memories of the mysterious disappearance of young Isaac Golliday, whom I had known from childhood, and who visited my house up to the time of his singular disappearance. He often spoke of Dr. Tumblety, and some one told me his father, Frederick Golliday, had tried to break up the friendship between his son and Dr. Tumblety, as he had a bad opinion of him. If I have been correctly informed, Isaac Golliday left his father's boarding-house after dark and was never seen or head of since. The last conversation I had with his father he had no clue as to his whereabouts. As Dr. Tumblety was not seen in Washington after Isaac Golliday's disappearance from home, it was hoped by his friends he had gone to Europe with the doctor and might possibly return. At the time of his disappearance he had about $100 in money and a watch valued at $180. Isaac Golliday was a nephew of ex-Congressmen Jacob and Edward Golliday of Kentucky.

Frederick Charrington

23 November 1888

Whitechapel
TO THE EDITOR OF *THE STAR*.

SIR,

I trust you will allow me, now that public attention is again aroused by another Whitechapel horror, to say I hope something will be done to reach those who are second only in criminality to the murderer himself - namely, the class of infamous scoundrels who are commonly known as "bullies." These are the wretches who live on the earnings of these poor women, and who in the midst of all this terror have driven them out to their awful doom that they may eat the bread of idleness and sink themselves still deeper with drink. Only a little while ago a young girl only 15 years of age came to us for protection from one of these fellows, and after we had placed her in charge of the matron of our home for fallen girls, she informed us that she had been decoyed into a house of ill-fame, and they threatened her (with an uplifted knife over her head) with murder if she dared try to escape. Now, I was only able to get this man and his wife six months' hard labor each on another indictment - namely, for harbouring a girl under 16 years of age for immoral purposes, as they were the keepers of the house. Happily, the law does now reach those who keep the houses, but I do hope before these horrors are forgotten as a nine days' wonder some member of Parliament will be led to press for a short Act of Parliament as an addition to the Criminal Law Amendment Act so that these scoundrels may be reached, as at present the police are utterly powerless, although these fellows are as well known as the public-houses, at the corners of which they are continually loafing and looking out for fresh victims to entrap, and where they may be seen at all hours of the day, and, if questioned, will pretend to be laborers out of work. Hoping that we shall at least have this one reform in our law, though others are also greatly needed.

Yours, &c.,

FREDERICK N. CHARRINGTON[65]
Great Assembly Hall, Mile-end, E.

---

[65] Frederick Charrington (1850-1936) was the wealthy heir of the Charrington Brewing family, a noted philanthropist and social activist.

1 December 1888

MITRE SQUARE.
TO THE EDITOR OF *THE CITY PRESS*.

SIR,

In your issue of Wednesday I read in "Notes and Queries" that Mitre-square has "criminally-historic" associations. "C.C." gives three incidents. I concur with him in two, but the last, which reads thus, "Twenty years ago two men blew up a house in the square," was not a criminal act, but the result of a pure accident. Permit me to briefly give particulars of the event. The house was No. 7 (site now occupied by warehouses), and stood in a south-east position, then occupied by a Mrs. Simmonds, who used to let the upper part as furnished apartments. The first floor was let to two foreigners, who at the time were experimenting with some material of an explosive nature, when one of them struck a match to light a cigar, and carelessly threw it down, and, coming into contact with the inflammable combustion, exploded, set fire to the house, the interior of which was destroyed, and the two unfortunate men lost their lives. The charred remains were placed in St. James's Church (which then stood immediately opposite) awaiting burial. Being a resident in the square at the time, I can substantiate the above facts.

I am, &c,

MITRE.

6 December 1888

IS JACK THE RIPPER A FRENCHMAN?
To the Editor of *the Pall Mall Gazette*

Sir,

I venture to offer you a few remarks upon the singular article which appeared in the *Pall Mall Gazette* last Saturday upon the Whitechapel murders.[66] Under some circumstances I might comment upon the inferences drawn by your contributor, "One Who Thinks He Knows," from the fact that straight lines, drawn through the point at which the outrages were committed cross one another, but, remembering that I am in a country where Mr. Ignatius Donnelly and his Great Cryptogram are the subjects of serious discussion, I, as a native of a frivolous land, abstain from saying more than that I am myself engaged in preparing a diagram by which I hope to prove that the crimes were really the work of a Unionist who is gradually marking out in the East end of London an exact reproduction of the Union Jack.

Now, Sir, to speak seriously, I do not at all deny that the assassin may be a Frenchman; there are plenty of French assassins in the world, and, though I venture to think that in London English assassins are more plentiful, I am willing to admit the possibility of "Jack the Ripper" being my compatriot. But I say that the arguments by which "One Who Knows" seeks to establish this are utterly baseless and absurd. Frenchmen may be, as he says "the worst linguists in the world," but if he were a better "linguist" himself he would know that bad "linguists" may know their own language, and in this respect, Frenchmen may be compared favourably with any other people. As to his assertion that they constantly make mistakes in gender, it is simply untrue. There are a few substantives, such as "hotel," "ouvrage," &c., which have a feminine sound to the ear, and as to which some utterly uneducated French people fall into the error of applying to them feminine articles or adjectives; such a person might therefore talk of "une hotel juive," or "une ouvrage juive," but no French man, woman, or child would ever mistake a feminine for a masculine substantive, and the idea that they could, under any circumstances, write Juives for Juifs when using the word as a substantive is enough to make a Frenchman hold his sides with laughter. Perhaps "One Who Thinks He Knows" also thinks that the uneducated Frenchman speaks of femmes when he means hommes!

Your contributor refers for proof of his assertions to the "voluminous correspondence of Napoleon III." As I have not had access to this source of information - and, indeed, though tolerably conversant with the literature of my country, now hear for the first time of its existence - I should be much obliged if "One Who Thinks He Knows" would send you for publication a few extracts from

---

[66] Reference to "The Whitechapel Demon's Nationality: and Why He Committed the Murders" by One Who Thinks He Knows (Roslyn Donston Stephenson), published December 1st 1888 in the *Pall Mall Gazette*. See the appendix to read this article in its entirety.

this "voluminous correspondence" containing examples of mistakes in gender. He would be a doing a kindness to a poor French professor, who has always held that Napoleon III did much harm to his country, but who has hitherto held him guiltless of having introduced into its literature a new form of grammatical error.

I remain, Sir, your obedient servant,

A FRENCHMAN
December 4.

12 December 1888

JACK THE RIPPER'S MOTIVE
To the Editor of the *Pall Mall Gazette*

Sir,

Although the anxiety to solve the Whitechapel mystery is, for the nonce, allayed, if not extinct, it may interest students of human nature to hear of a somewhat similar case in which the murderer, when discovered, was found to be actuated by a less extraordinary motive that that of solving necromantic problems, attributed to the Whitechapel monster by the writer of "Who is the Whitechapel Demon?", published in your issue of the 6th. inst. Forty or fifty years ago, my grandfather, a Portuguese judge at Coviltra, convicted a man for the murder of sixteen women by stabbing them in the abdomen. For the space of twelve months the inhabitants of the town had been in a state of wild panic at the periodical repetition of such hideous and objectless crimes, as in no case could pillage or lust be ascribed as the cause; the victims, in many cases, being penniless octogenarians. At last the miscreant was caught in flagrante delicto, and on trying him for wilful murder Judge Joao de Campes received from him the confession that he had done it solely to enjoy the fun of watching the grimaces the poor women made in their agony! I have no details of the criminal's modus operandi, as it occurred long before my time; I had in fact forgotten this episode in my grandfather's judicial career until the accounts of the London ghastly tragedies brought to my mind the conviction that should the East end murderer ever be brought to justice, which I do not anticipate, it will be ascertained that his motive has been either a morbid taste of the very same kind, or an exaggerated longing for notoriety, coupled with the love of excitement that feeds on perusing the different versions of his deeds, his intentions, and the means he employs to defeat the combined intellects of the detective administrations of London, which last feat, be it said, might make anybody a little proud.

Yours faithfully

Esther Delaforce
9 Courthope villa, Wimbledon
December 8.

28 December 1888

THE POPLAR MYSTERY
TO THE EDITOR OF *THE DAILY NEWS*.

Sir,

In reading your article on the Poplar mystery[67], in which the surgeon and the police differed in opinion as to the cause of the woman's death, I am of opinion that the police view is the correct one, for I had a very similar case some years ago when practising in Barnsley. A young man, about 35 years of age, who was much addicted to drinking, had an acute attack of rheumatism in the knee. I kept him in bed free from drink until he was able to walk, when he determined to attend the funeral of a member of the same club, and he promised me that he would refrain from spirits until he returned home. He was lodging with a very respectable middle aged couple. They went to bed early, as the husband had to go early to his work. The lodger had a latch key, and would come in when he pleased. It was a four room cottage. The front door opened into the parlour, with the kitchen behind it. He returned home after the public houses were closed, passed into the kitchen, and left his necktie and pin on the table, and returned to secure the front, when he dropped close to the door, where the landlord found him, raised him up, and put him in a chair, and came for me, when I found he had been dead for some hours. I gave notice to the police for a coroner's inquest, and the coroner ordered the surgeon of the police to make a post mortem examination. When the body was stripped there was a mark found on his neck as if he had been strangled, and the surgeon charged the landlord with doing it. I attended the post mortem, when the surgeon called my attention to the mark on the neck. I accounted for it by his having on a tight collar the pressure from which, in consequence of the position in which he was found, had forced the blood out of the capillaries; hence the mark. I removed the skull cap, and when we examined the base of the brain we found the ventricles were filled with serum, proving that death was caused by serious apoplexy. I found that between his going to the funeral and returning he drank ten glasses of whisky, and had nothing to eat. It is probable that this unfortunate woman was in the same predicament with regard to drink and want of food as my patient, and that serious apoplexy was the cause of death.

Andrew Rowan,
Physician and Surgeon,
35 High street, Lewisham.

---

[67] Reference to the murder of Rose Mylett, December 20th 1888. There were conflicting opinions as to whether Mylett was murdered or died of accidental asphyxiation. The verdict at the inquest was murder.

Appendix

The Whitechapel Demon's Nationality: and Why He Committed the Murders
by "One Who Thinks He Knows"[68]

Published in the *Pall Mall Gazette*, December 1st 1888

In calmly reviewing the whole chain of facts connected with these daring and bloodthirsty atrocities, the first thing which strikes one is the fact that the murderer was kind enough to (so to speak) leave his card with the Mitre-square victim. But this most important clue to his identity, which 'he who runs may read', seems to have baffled the combined intellects of all grades of the police. This admits of no question, because we find in all the journals a note from Sir C. Warren to the effect that 'no language or dialogue is known in which the word "Jews" is spelt "Juwes".'

O! most sapient conclusion! Let us see what *we* can make of the word.

It will be remembered that a chalk inscription (which it is not denied was written by the murderer) was found on the wall in Mitre-square, just above the body of the murdered woman. It ran as follows: "The Juwes are the men who will not be blamed for nothing', and was evidently intended to throw suspicion on the Jews. This writing was seen by the police by means of artificial light, and was unfortunately obliterated by them before daylight. *Hinc illae lachrymae!!*

Why did the murderer spell the word Jews 'Juwes'? Was it that he was an uneducated Englishman who did not know how to spell the word; was he in reality an ignorant Jew, reckless of consequences and glorying in his deeds; or was he a foreigner, well accustomed to the English language, but who in the tremendous hurry of the moment unconsciously wrote the fatal word in his native tongue?

The answers to these three queries, on which the whole matter rests, are easy. Juwes is a much too difficult word for an uneducated man to evolve on the spur of the moment, as any philologist will allow. Any ignorant Jew capable of spelling the rest of the sentence as correctly as he did, would know, certainly, how to spell the name of his own people. Therefore, only the last proposition remains, which we shall now show, in the most conclusive manner, to be the truth.

To critically examine an inscription of this kind, the first thing we naturally do is not to rest satisfied with reading it in print, but to make, as nearly as we can, a facsimile of it in script, thus:-

Juwes

---

[68] Almost certainly Roslyn Donston Stephenson.

Inspection at once shows us, then, that *a dot* has been overlooked by the constable who copied it, as might easily occur, especially if it were placed at some distance, after the manner of foreigners.

Juives

Therefore we place a dot above the *third* upstroke in the word Juwes, and we find it to be *Juives*, which is the French word for Jews. Strictly Juives and grammatically speaking, of course, it is the feminine form of *Juifs* and means 'Jewesses.' But in practice it will be found that (French-men being notoriously the worst linguists in the world) most Frenchmen who are not either litterateurs or men of science are very inaccurate as to their genders. And almost all the ouvrier and a large majority of the bourgeois class use the feminine where the word should be masculine. Even the Emperor Napoleon III was a great sinner in this respect, as his voluminous correspondence amply shows.

Therefore, it is evident that the native language - or, to be more accurate, the language in which this murderer *thinks - is* French. *The murderer is, therefore, a Frenchman.*

It may here be argued that both Swiss and Belgians make French almost their mother tongue; but Flemish is the natural and usual vehicle for the latter, while the idiosyncrasy of both those nationalities is adverse to this class of crime.

On the contrary, in France, the murdering of prostitutes has long been practised, and has been considered to be almost peculiarly a French crime.

Again, the grammatical construction of the sentence under examination is distinctly French in two points - first, in the double negative contained; and, secondly, in the employment of the definite article before the second noun. An Englishman or an American would have said, 'The Jews are men who, &c.' But the murderer followed his native idiom 'Les Juifs sont *des* hommes' in his thoughts, and when putting it into English rendered *des homes* 'the' men'.

Again, neither Belgians nor Swiss entertain any animosity to the Jews, whereas the hatred of the French proletarian to them is notorious.

The ground for research being thus cleared and narrowed, the next question is, what is the motive? Speculation has been rife, the cries are many; almost every man one meets, who is competent to form an opinion, having a different one.

And in endeavouring to sift a mystery like this one cannot afford to throw aside *any* theory, however extravagant, without careful examination, because the truth might, after all, lie in the most unlikely one.

There seems to be no doubt that the murderer, whether mad or not, had a distinct motive in his mutilations; but one possible theory of that motive has never yet been suggested. In the nineteenth century, with all its enlightenment, it would seem absurd, were it not that superstition dies hard, and some of its votaries do undoubtedly to this day practice unholy rites.

Now, in one of the books by the great modern occultist who wrote under the *nom de plume* of 'Eliphaz Levy', 'Le Dogme et Rituel de la Haute Magie,' we find the most elaborate directions for working magical spells of all kinds. The second volume has a chapter on Necromancy, or black magic, which the author justly denounces as a profanation. Black magic employs the agencies of evil spirits and demons, instead of the beneficent spirits directed by the adepts of *la haute magie*. At the same time he gives the clearest and fullest details of the necessary steps for evocation by this means, and it is in the list of substances prescribed as absolutely necessary to success that we find the link which joins modern French necromancy with the quest of the East-end murderer. These substances are in themselves horrible, and difficult to procure. They can only be obtained by means of the most appalling crimes, of which murder and mutilation of the dead are the least heinous. Among them are strips of the skin of a suicide, nails from a murderer's gallows, candles made from human fat, the head of a black cat which has been fed forty days on human flesh, the horns of a goat which has been made the instrument of an infamous capital crime, and a preparation made from a certain portion of the body of a *harlot*. This last point is insisted upon as essential and it was this extra-ordinary fact that first drew my attention to the possible connection of the murderer with the black art.

Further, in the practice of evocation the sacrifice of human victims was a necessary part of the process, and the profanation of the cross and other emblems usually considered sacred was also enjoined. In this connection it will be well to remember one most extraordinary and unparalleled circumstance in the commission of the Whitechapel murders, and a thing which could not by *any* possibility have been brought about fortuitously. Leaving out the last murder,-committed indoors, which was most probably not committed by *the* fiend of whom we speak, we find that the sites of the murders, six in number, form a perfect cross. That is to say, a line ruled from No. 3 to No. 6, on a map having the murder sites marked and numbered, passes *exactly* through Nos. 1 and 2, while the cross arms are accurately formed by a line from No. 4 to 5. The seventh, or Dorset-street murder, does not fall within either of these lines, and there is nothing to connect it with the others except the mutilations. But the mutilations in this latter case were evidently not made by any one having the practical knowledge of the knife and the position of the respective organs which was exhibited in the other six cases, and also in the mutilated trunk found in the new police-buildings, which was probably the first of the series of murders, and was committed somewhere on the lines of the cross, the body being removed at the time. Did the murderer, then, designing to offer the mystic number of seven human sacrifices in the form of a cross - a form which he intended to profane - deliberately pick out beforehand on a map the places in which he would offer them to his infernal deity of murder? If not, surely these six *coincidences* are the most marvellous event of our time.

To those persons to whom this theory may seem somewhat far-fetched, we would merely remark that the French book referred to was only published a few years ago; that thousands of copies were sold; that societies have been formed for the study and practice of its teachings and philosophy; and, finally, that within the last twelve months an English edition has been issued. In all things history repeats itself, and the superstitions of yesterday become the creeds of today.

Index – By Author

Note: Because of the prevalent use of initials, pseudonyms, etc. the author index is ordered alphabetically by first letter and not last name. * Authors/letters marked with an asterisk indicate that the original newspaper source provided only a summary of the letter, not the complete text.

A Clairvoyant

Daily Telegraph*
October 4th 1888.
Detection Suggestions - Spiritualism
106

A Constant Reader

"East-End Women"
Echo
October 2nd 1888.
Social Conditions
89

Star
October 19th 1888.
Social Conditions
188

A Country Doctor

Times
September 11th 1888.
Theories - Mania and Lunacy
15

A Fabian

"The Moral of the Murders"
Star
October 16th 1888.
Immorality
178-179

A Frenchman

"Is Jack the Ripper a Frenchman?"
Pall Mall Gazette
December 6th 1888.
Theories - Frenchman
209-210

A Frightened Woman

"A Strange Omission"
Echo
October 6th 1888.
Press Criticism
143-144

A Girl Radical

"Whitechapel"
Star
October 15th 1888.
Social Conditions
176-177

A Mariner

Daily Telegraph*
October 1st 1888.
Detection Suggestions - Registration of Lodging House Inhabitants
84

A Metropolitan Registrar of Births and Deaths

"A Safe Four Per Cent"
Daily Telegraph
September 24th 1888.
Artisans Dwellings
60-61

A Mother

Daily Telegraph*
October 5th 1888.
Municipal Shelters
119

A Poor Woman

Daily Telegraph*
October 1st 1888.
Home Secretary - Criticism
86

A Practical Philanthropist

"A Safe Four Per Cent"
Daily Telegraph
September 22nd 1888.
Artisans Dwellings
48-49

A Publican

Morning Advertiser
October 3rd 1888.
Detection Suggestions - Deputization of Lodging House Keepers
104

A Reader

"Whitechapel Murders"
Irish Times
October 12th 1888.
Detection Suggestions - False Confessions
166

A Scotchman

Daily Telegraph*
October 1st 1888.
Bloodhounds
84

A Surgeon

Daily Telegraph*
October 1st 1888.
American Anatomist
84

Daily Telegraph*
October 1st 1888.

Detection Suggestions -
Rubber Boots
86

A Terrified Woman

*Daily Telegraph**
October 3rd 1888.
Suspicious Persons
96

A Time Expired

"Soldiers as Policemen"
Evening News
September 20th 1888.
Detection Suggestions -
Soldiers as Policemen
41

A Working Man

"Crime in Whitechapel"
Star
September 7th 1888.
Police Criticism
9

A. Eubule Evans

"The Personal Appearance
of the East-End Murderer"
Pall Mall Gazette
October 6th 1888.
Detection Suggestions -
Criminal Types
131-132

A. Laing

"Nuisances in Whitechapel"
Echo
September 12th 1888.
Pernicious Art and Literature
20

A.E. Gower

*Daily Telegraph**
October 1st 1888.
Detection Suggestions -
Rubber Boots
86

A.J.M.

"Woman Killing No Murder"
Daily News
October 6th 1888.
Violence Against Women
142

A.P.

"Woman Killing No Murder"
Daily News
October 4th 1888.
Violence Against Women
114

A.W.

*Daily Telegraph**
October 5th 1888.
Police Criticism
119

Abbott, Earle, and Ogle

"A Disgraceful Scene"
Echo
September 13th 1888.
Pernicious Art and
Literature
22

Albert Bachert

Evening News
September 6th 1888.
Theories - Pimps
8

Alfred C. Calmour

*Daily Telegraph**
October 5th 1888.
Detection Suggestions -
Sewers
120

Alfred Hoare

"The East-End"
Times
October 6th 1888.
Artisans Dwellings
136-137

Amateur Detective

*Daily Telegraph**
October 5th 1888.
Theories - Slaughterman
119

Amelia Mackintosh

"In Praise of the Silly Season"
Pall Mall Gazette
August 31st 1888.
Miscellaneous
6

An East-Ender

"A Disgraceful Scene"
Echo
September 11th 1888.
Pernicious Art and
Literature
16

"The Non-Detection
of Crime"
Star
September 12th 1888.
Police Criticism
21

An Elderly Gentleman

"The Whitechapel Murders"
Times
October 15th 1888.
Mistaken Identity
175-176

An Englishwoman

*Daily Telegraph**
October 5th 1888.
Municipal Shelters
119

An Inquirer

"A Safe Four Per Cent"
Daily Telegraph
September 22nd 1888.
Artisans Dwellings
49-52

An Observer Waiting

"Our Detective System"
Star
September 14th 1888.
Police Criticism
26

An Old Detective

Daily Telegraph*
October 1st 1888.
Detection Suggestions - Women's Clothing
86

An old police constable under Sir Richard Mayne

"Sir Charles Warren's Appointment"
Evening News
August 8th 1888.
Charles Warren
5

Andrew Rowan

"The Poplar Mystery"
Daily News
December 28th 1888.
Rose Mylett
212

Anglo-Texan

Daily Telegraph
October 6th 1888.
Theories - American
128

Archd. Forbes

"The Motive of the Murders"
Daily News
October 3rd 1888.
Theories - Venereal Disease
99-102

Arthur J. Robinson

"Whitechapel Fund"
Times
October 29th 1888.
Missionary Work
190

Beatrice Temple

"A Home for Inebriate Women"
Daily Telegraph
October 30th 1888.
Municipal Shelters
191

Bloodhound

Daily Telegraph
October 4th 1888.
Bloodhounds
107-108

Daily Telegraph*
October 5th 1888.
Theories - Not One But Many
120

C. Thomas

"Whitechapel"
Star
November 15th 1888.
Rewards
198

C.F.A.G.

"The Whitechapel Murders"
Echo
September 14th 1888.
Detection Suggestions - Timing of the Murders
26

C.H.

"Whitechapel"
Star
October 5th 1888.
Police Criticism
126

C.L.M.

Daily Telegraph
October 1st 1888.
Detection Suggestions
88

C.R. Drysdale, M.D.

"The Poverty of the East-end of London"
Star
October 9th 1888.
Social Conditions
157

Canis

Daily Telegraph
October 4th 1888.
Theories - An Upper-Class City Dweller
108-109

Carita

Daily Telegraph
October 3rd 1888.
Municipal Shelters
98

Charles Ed. Jerningham

"The Coroner and the Whitechapel Murderer"
Pall Mall Gazette
September 29th 1888.
American Anatomist
71-72

Charles Warren

Times
October 4th 1888.
Police Criticism
116-118

"Sir Charles Warren and Mr. Matthews"
Times
November 17th 1888.
Police Criticism
203-204

Citizen

Daily Telegraph*
October 1st 1888.

Bloodhounds
84
*Daily Telegraph**
October 5th 1888.
Rewards
120

Civis

"The Metropolitan Police"
Daily Telegraph
September 22nd 1888.
Police Criticism
52-53

Clergyman

*Daily Telegraph**
October 3rd 1888.
Theories - Gangs
96

Cockney

"The Whitechapel Murders"
Echo
October 4th 1888.
Lenient Sentences
115

Compton

"The Homes of the Criminal Class"
Times
October 6th 1888.
Lodging Houses
139-140

Editor's Note: Possibly the same person as George Hy. Compton, see letter of Daily Telegraph, October 3rd 1888.

Constance Howell

"Woman Killing No Murder"
Daily News
October 9th 1888.
Violence Against Women
150

D.

"The Detection of Crime"
Times
October 11th 1888.
Police Criticism
158-159

D. Everett

Daily Telegraph
October 1st 1888.
Detection Suggestions - Rubber Boots
89

D.C.L.

*Daily Telegraph**
October 1st 1888.
Home Secretary - Criticism
86

D.H.

"Woman Killing No Murder"
Daily News
October 6th 1888.
Violence Against Women
141-142

David Sime, M.D.

Daily Telegraph
October 4th 1888.
Theories - Mania and Lunacy
110

Detective

*Daily Telegraph**
October 3rd 1888.
Theories - Gangs
96

Disgusted

"The Haunts of Vice and Crime"
Echo
October 1st 1888.
Brothels and Prostitution
77

Dobra

"Shelters for the Homeless"
Star
October 12th 1888.
Municipal Shelters
167-168

E. Bannister

"A Safe Four Per Cent"
Daily Telegraph
September 24th 1888.
Artisans Dwellings
59-60

E. Fairfield

Times
October 1st 1888.
Lodging Houses
74

E. Schnadhorst

"Distress in East London"
Morning Advertiser
October 19th 1888.
Social Conditions
186-187

E. Swabey

Evening News
September 20th 1888.
Theories
39-40

E.A. Harvey

Daily Telegraph
October 5th 1888.
Police Criticism
124

E.P.

"The Bloodhound as a Detective"
Morning Advertiser
September 15th 1888.
Bloodhounds
27

E.R.B.C.

Daily Telegraph
October 6th 1888.
Theories - Cabman
127

E.R.L.

Daily Telegraph
October 5th 1888.
Municipal Shelters
122

Edgar Sheppard, M.D.

Times
October 1st 1888.
Theories - Mania and Lunacy
78-79

Edmund Lawrence

"Police Organization"
Times
September 18th 1888.
Police Criticism
30-31

Edward Dillon Lewis

*Daily Telegraph**
October 4th 1888.
Theories - Foreigner
107

Times
October 4th 1888.
Theories - Foreigner
111-112

Edward W. Thomas

Times
October 18th 1888.
Artisans Dwellings
183-184

Edward Wilson

"The Recent Murders in London"
Irish Times
October 9th 1888.
Rewards
150-151

Edwin Brough

"The Old English Bloodhound or Sleuthound and his Capabilities as a Man-Hunter"
Times
October 8th 1888.
Bloodhounds
145-147

Times
October 11th 1888.
Bloodhounds
158

Ellerford

*Daily Telegraph**
October 5th 1888.
Rewards
120

Ernest Fisher

"Policemen's Boots"
Echo
October 5th 1888.
Detection Suggestions - Rubber Boots
125

Esther Delaforce

"Jack the Ripper's Motive"
Pall Mall Gazette
December 12th 1888.
Theories
211

Ex-Constable C. Baddelby

Daily Telegraph
October 6th 1888.
Detection Suggestions - Plain Clothes Police
129

Ex-Convict

"The Whitechapel Murder Mystery"
Pall Mall Gazette
October 8th 1888.
Theories - A Local
147-148

F. Schaffter

Daily Telegraph
October 6th 1888.
Theories - American
130

F. W. Devereux Long

Daily Telegraph
October 1st 1888.
Police Criticism
88

F.C.

*Daily Telegraph**
October 5th 1888.
Theories - Civil Servant
119

F.G. Debenham

Times
September 29th 1888.
Artisans Dwellings
68

F.H. Harvey-Samuel

Times
October 18th 1888.
Artisans Dwellings
183

F.H.H.

"The Murders in Whitechapel"
Echo
September 12th 1888.
Theories - A Woman
17

F.T.

*Daily Telegraph**
October 5th 1888.
Detection Suggestions - Empty Warehouses
120

Fair Play

"A Word for the Police"
Star
October 1st 1888.
Police Criticism
75

Fleet-street

*Daily Telegraph**
October 4th 1888.
Detection Suggestions -
Similar Murders in
America
106

Florence Fenwick Miller

"Woman Killing No Murder"
Daily News
October 1st 1888.
Violence Against Women
82-84

Frances Power Cobbe

"Detectives"
Times
October 11th 1888.
Detection Suggestions -
Female Detectives
160

Fred Wellesley

Times
October 1st 1888.
Detection Suggestions
74

Fred. W. P. Jago

Times
October 3rd 1888.
Detection Suggestions -
Fingerprinting
91-93

Frederick N. Charrington

"Whitechapel"
Star
November 23rd 1888.

Brothels and Prostitution
207

Fredk. J. Money, M.D

Daily Telegraph
September 26th 1888.
Lodging Houses
64

G. Bernard Shaw

"Blood Money to
Whitechapel"
Star
September 24th 1888.
Social Conditions
57-59

G. Standerwick

*Daily Telegraph**
October 3rd 1888.
Detection Suggestions -
Female Detectives
96

G. Walker

Daily Telegraph
October 5th 1888.
Lodging Houses
120-121

G.C.

*Daily Telegraph**
October 3rd 1888.
Pernicious Art and Literature
96

G.E.K.

Daily Telegraph
October 1st 1888.
Detection Suggestions
87

G.H.H.

"Slaughtering the Jews"
Evening News
September 11th 1888.
Anti-Semitism
12

G.R.H.

Daily Telegraph
October 1st 1888.
Rewards
86-87

Gamma

"At Last"
Times
September 22nd 1888.
Artisans Dwellings
53

Geo. Hy. Compton

Daily Telegraph
October 3rd 1888.
Police Criticism
99

George Fox

*Freeman's Journal and Daily
Commercial Advertiser*
October 1st 1888.
American Anatomist
76-77

George H. Giddine

Daily Telegraph
October 6th 1888.
Municipal Shelters
129

**George Lusk and
Joseph Aarons**

"The Murders in the East
End"
Daily Telegraph
October 1st 1888.
Rewards
75

H. Delahooke

"Police Supervision"
Times
October 13th 1888.
Police Criticism
173

H. M. Harewood

*Star**
September 17th 1888.
Police Criticism
28

H.C.W.

*Daily Telegraph**
October 1st 1888.
Detection Suggestions - Rubber Boots
86

H.E. Bell

*Daily Telegraph**
October 5th 1888.
Theories - Fish Cleaner
119

H.E.W.

"Whitechapel Murder"
Echo
September 15th 1888.
Inquests
29

H.J. Cushing

Daily Telegraph
October 6th 1888.
Bloodhounds
128

H.M. Mackusick

Daily Telegraph
October 19th 1888.
Bloodhounds
185-186

H.P.B.

Times
October 5th 1888.
Rewards
125

H.R.

Daily Telegraph
October 5th 1888.
Pardons
122

H.T.

"The Whitechapel Murders"
St. James Gazette
November 16th 1888.
Detection Suggestions - Amateur Detectives
199-200

H.Y.P.

Daily Telegraph
October 6th 1888.
Theories - American
130

Henry Bax

"The East End Tragedies"
Echo
October 4th 1888.
Detection Suggestions - Rubber Boots
116

"Policemen's Boots"
Echo
October 6th 1888.
Detection Suggestions - Rubber Boots
143

Henry Brudenell Bruce

"The East End"
Times
October 1st 1888.
Lodging Houses
73

Henry Fennell

"Bloodhounds as Detectives"
Times
October 13th 1888.
Bloodhounds
172-173

Henry Harrison

*Daily Telegraph**
October 5th 1888.
Theories - Slaughterman
119

Henry Sutherland, M.D.

Lancet
September 22nd 1888.
Theories - Mania and Lunacy
54-55

Henry White

Times
October 1st 1888.
Rewards
79-80

Herbert F. Scott

*Daily Telegraph**
October 3rd 1888.
Detection Suggestions - Rubber Boots
96

Hermann Adler

"The Murder Near Cracow"
Times
October 3rd 1888.
Jews and Anti-Semitism
93-94

Hope

Daily Telegraph
October 3rd 1888.
Rewards
96-97

Hugh B. Chapman

"The Moral of the Murders"
Star
October 13th 1888.
Immorality
169-170

Inquirer

*Daily Telegraph**
October 4th 1888.
Detection Suggestions -

Spiritualism
106

J. Arthur Elliott

"Another Protest"
Star
November 16th 1888.
Pernicious Art and Literature
200-201

J. Flynn

Echo
October 2nd 1888.
Bloodhounds
90

J. Morris

*Daily Telegraph**
October 5th 1888.
Police Criticism
119

J. S. Whichelow

"A Safe Four Per Cent"
Daily Telegraph
September 26th 1888.
Artisans Dwellings
63

J.E. Waller

"The Dangers of Whitechapel"
Star
September 17th 1888.
Police Criticism
27-28

J.F.S.

Times
September 14th 1888.
Social Conditions
26

J.G. Newfield

"Bloodhounds"
Echo
October 3rd 1888.
Bloodhounds
104

J.M.S. Brooke

Times
October 1st 1888.
Chloroforming
78

J.P.

Times
September 19th 1888.
Inquests
36

J.P.H.

"The Sensationalism of Our Day"
Star
October 12th 1888.
Press Criticism
167

James Sharpless

"Whitechapel-Road Murder"
Echo
September 5th 1888.
Social Conditions
7

James Stuart

"The London Police"
Daily News
October 16th 1888.
Police Criticism
180

Jas. Risdon Bennett

Times
September 28th 1888.
American Anatomist
67

Jo. Perrott

Daily Telegraph
October 5th 1888.
Police Criticism
123

John Bell Sedgwick

Daily Telegraph
October 5th 1888.
Theories - Mania and Lunacy
123

John Wheelwright

"Blood Money to Whitechapel"
Star
October 3rd 1888.
Social Conditions
105

Justice

"Woman Killing No Murder"
Daily News
October 3rd 1888.
Violence Against Women
103

Justice and Equality

"Audi Alteram Partem"
Star
October 9th 1888.
Women's Rights
155-157

K.T.A.

"Stories of Crime"
Times
September 22nd 1888.
Pernicious Art and Literature
54

Kate Mitchell

"Woman Killing No Murder"
Daily News
October 6th 1888.
Violence Against Women
140-141

L. Forbes Winslow

Times
September 12th 1888.
Theories - Mania and Lunacy
19

Lancet
September 22nd 1888.
Theories - Mania and Lunacy
56

L.F.S. Maberly

"Bloodhounds as Detectives"
Morning Advertiser
September 14th 1888.
Bloodhounds
25

L.K.

Daily Telegraph
October 5th 1888.
Municipal Shelters
124-125

L.R. Thomson

Times
October 3rd 1888.
Detection Suggestions - Rubber Boots
91

M. Cursham Corner

"The Whitechapel Atrocities"
East London Observer
September 15th 1888.
Street Lighting
28-29

M. Gaster, Ph.D

Times
October 3rd 1888.
Jews and Anti-Semitism
94-95

M. Van Thul

"The Tower Gardens"
Evening News
August 8th 1888.
Miscellaneous
5

M. Williams

*Daily Telegraph**
October 5th 1888.
Police Criticism
119

M.H.

*Daily Telegraph**
October 5th 1888.
Detection Suggestions - Sewers
120

M.P.

*Daily Telegraph**
October 3rd 1888.
Police Criticism
96

M.S.

*Daily Telegraph**
October 5th 1888.
Theories - American
119

Mary H. Steer

"Ratcliff Highway Refuge"
Times
October 11th 1888.
Municipal Shelters
160-161

Mary J. Kinnaird

"A Whitechapel Fund"
Times
October 26th 1888.
Missionary Work
189

Matron

*Daily Telegraph**
October 5th 1888.
Municipal Shelters
119

Medicus

"The Whitechapel Horrors"
Evening News
September 11th 1888.
Theories - Epilepsy
13-14

Mentor

*Daily Telegraph**
October 4th 1888.
Street Lighting
107

Michael Mack

"A French Chapter of Whitechapel Horrors"
Times
October 6th 1888.
Detection Suggestions - Similar Murders in France
137-138

Michael Zeffertt

"The East End"
Jewish Chronicle
October 12th 1888.
Jews and Anti-Semitism
164

Mitre

"Mitre Square"
City Press
December 1st 1888.
Mitre Square
208

Morton Latham

Times
October 3rd 1888.
Street Lighting
91

Nemo

Times
October 4th 1888.
Theories - Malay
112-113

No Theory

"No Theory"
Daily News
October 3rd 1888.
Detection Suggestions - Avoid Theories
102-103

"Mr. Forbes's Theory"
Daily News
October 4th 1888.
Detection Suggestions - Avoid Theories
113-114

Observer

Daily Telegraph
October 3rd 1888.
Detection Suggestions - Points on a Map
97

Daily Telegraph
October 5th 1888.
Theories - American
121

One More Unfortunate

*Daily Telegraph**
October 1st 1888.
Detection Suggestions - Registration of Lodging House Inhabitants
84

One of the X Division

*Daily Telegraph**
October 1st 1888.
Detection Suggestions - House to House Searches
86

One Who Knows

Times
September 29th 1888.
Lodging Houses
69-70

*Daily Telegraph**
October 1st 1888.
Detection Suggestions - Registration of Lodging House Inhabitants
84

Onlooker

"The East End Atrocity"
Evening News
September 20th 1888.
Social Conditions
39

Owen Banford

*Daily Telegraph**
October 3rd 1888.
Detection Suggestions - Female Detectives
96

P.D. Townshend

"Can Anything Good Come Out of Whitechapel?"
Pall Mall Gazette
October 17th 1888.
Government Pensions
181

P.Q.R.S.

Evening News
September 13th 1888.
Theories - Mania and Lunacy
23

Paul Methuen

"Law and Order in Whitechapel"
Times
November 16th 1888.
Organization for Boys
201-202

Percy Lindley

Times
October 1st 1888.
Bloodhounds
79

"Bloodhounds in London"
Pall Mall Gazette
October 6th 1888.
Bloodhounds
132-133

"Bloodhounds as Detectives"
Times
October 16th 1888.
Bloodhounds
179-180

Pro Caritate

"Metropolitan Immorality"
Echo
October 3rd 1888.
Social Conditions
105

Progress

"London Police - A Suggestion"
Echo
October 6th 1888.
Detection Suggestions - Bicycles
143

R. B. Cuninghame Graham

"The Hallucination of Warren"
Star
October 30th 1888.
Charles Warren
192-194

R. Johns

Daily News
October 1st 1888.
Police Criticism
80

R. Macdonald

Daily Telegraph
October 4th 1888.
Theories - Drugged then Murdered
110-111

R. Roberts

Daily Telegraph*
October 4th 1888.
Street Lighting
106-107

R.C. Bedford

"Whitechapel"
Times
October 9th 1888.
Municipal Shelters
154

"Whitechapel"
Times
October 13th 1888.
Social Conditions
170

R.E. Lawford Webb

Daily Telegraph
October 6th 1888.
Detection Suggestions - Fruit Vendors
127

R.H. Winter

"A Shelter For Females"
Morning Advertiser
October 13th 1888.
Municipal Shelters
174

R.H.T.

Daily Telegraph
October 4th 1888.
Detection Suggestions - Opium Dens
109

R.J. Bruton

"The Morals of the Murders"
Echo
October 17th 1888.
Social Conditions
182

R.N. Fowler

"The Repression of Immorality"
Morning Advertiser
October 8th 1888.
Immorality
148-149

Ratepayer

"Police Incompetence"
Evening News
September 12th 1888.
Police Criticism
20

"A Safe Four Per Cent"
Daily Telegraph
September 21st 1888.
Artisans Dwellings
42-46

"The Police and the Murders"
Star
September 10th 1888.
11

Reform

"London Detective Force"
Daily Telegraph
September 21st 1888.
Police Criticism
46-47

Reformer

"The Whitechapel Murders"
Echo
September 10th 1888.
Intemperance
11

"The East End Horrors"
Evening News
September 12th 1888.
Whitechapel
17

Revenge

Daily Telegraph*
October 4th 1888.
Detection Suggestions
106

Rowland Addams Williams

"The Whitechapel Murders"
Times
September 26th 1888.
Inquests
62

S.

"The Whitechapel Murders"
Star
September 13th 1888.
Theories - Similar Murders in Westphalia
24

Daily Telegraph*
October 4th 1888.
Detection Suggestions - Spiritualism
106

S. Smithers

Daily Telegraph*
October 4th 1888.
Detection Suggestions - Similar Murders in America
106

S.G.O.

"At Last"
Times
September 18th 1888.
Social Conditions
32-34

"Unfortunates"
Times
October 6th 1888.
Social Conditions
133-135

S.M.

Daily Telegraph*
October 3rd 1888.
Detection Suggestions - Female Detectives
96

Samuel A. Barnett

"At Last"
Times
September 19th 1888.
Social Conditions
36-38

"The East End"
Times
September 29th 1888.
Artisans Dwellings
68

"What Is to Be Done?"
Times
November 16th 1888.
Landlords
202

Samuel Hayward

"The Whitechapel Murders"
East London Observer
September 29th 1888.
Municipal Shelters
70

Daily Telegraph
October 6th 1888.
Municipal Shelters
131

Samuel Montagu

"The Jews and Animal Killing"
Echo
October 11th 1888.
Jews and Anti-Semitism
162

Sigma

Star
October 19th 1888.
Social Conditions
188

Spes

Daily Telegraph*
October 1st 1888.
Detection Suggestions
86

Spiritualist

Daily Telegraph*
October 4th 1888.
Detection Suggestions -
Spiritualism
106

St. Aubin Hamilton

Daily Telegraph*
October 3rd 1888.
Theories - Gangs
96

St. John Carr

Daily Telegraph*
October 1st 1888.
Bloodhounds
84

Sydney Hodges

"The Whitechapel
Murder"
Echo
September 21st 1888.
Detection Suggestions -
Photographing the Retina
47

T. Jones

Daily Telegraph*
October 5th 1888.
Police Criticism
119

T. L. Selder

Daily Telegraph*
October 3rd 1888.
Theories - Gangs
96

T. Wentworth Grant

"The Duties of the Police"
Times
October 9th 1888.
Police Criticism
155

T.B.B.

Daily News
October 1st 1888.
Police Criticism
81

T.W.S.

Daily Telegraph*
October 5th 1888.
Municipal Shelters
119

The Secretary of the St. Jude's District Committee

Daily News
September 11th 1888.
Vigilance Committees
14-15

Thomas Hancock Nunn and Thomas G. Gardiner

"Whitechapel"
Times
October 6th 1888.
Vigilance Committees
135-136

Thos. J. Barnardo

"The Children of Common
Lodging Houses"
Times
October 9th 1888.
Lodging Houses
151-153

Town Clerk

"A Safe Four Per Cent"
Daily Telegraph
September 27th 1888.
Artisans Dwellings
65-66

Ultra Radical

"East End Poverty"
Star
October 19th 1888.
Social Conditions
187

Index – By Author

Vindex
*Daily Telegraph**
October 5th 1888.
Police Criticism
119

Violet Greville
"An Appeal From the East End"
Daily Telegraph
October 12th 1888.
Social Conditions
165-166

W. Evans Hurndall
"Peril in East London"
Daily Telegraph
September 18th 1888.
Social Conditions
35

"Black Winter in East London"
Morning Advertiser
November 14th 1888.
Social Conditions
197

W. Gearon
*Star**
September 17th 1888.
Lodging Houses
28

W. Grist
"The Sleuthhound as a Tracker"
Morning Advertiser
October 12th 1888.
Bloodhounds
164-165

W. Nicholls
"Letter From the Husband"
Lloyd's Weekly
September 9th 1888.
Mary Ann Nichols
10

W.E. Corner
"Two Practical Suggestions"
Echo
October 4th 1888.
Detection Suggestions - Rubber Boots
115

W.H.
*Daily Telegraph**
October 5th 1888.
Rewards
120

W.H. Bakes
*Daily Telegraph**
October 4th 1888.
Detection Suggestions - Similar Murders in America
106

W.J.W.
"More Police Wanted"
Echo
September 11th 1888.
Detection Suggestions
15-16

W.M. Adamson
Times
October 13th 1888.
Social Conditions
170-172

W.M.R.
*Daily Telegraph**
October 3rd 1888.
Theories - Gangs
96

W.S.
*Daily Telegraph**
October 1st 1888.
Detection Suggestions - Rubber Boots
86

W.S. Pilling
Daily Telegraph
October 4th 1888.
Calls for Prayer
109

Walter Hazell
"Friendless and Fallen in Whitechapel"
Times
October 6th 1888.
Municipal Shelters
138-139

Watch
"Plain Clothes Detectives"
Echo
September 13th 1888.
Detection Suggestions - Plain Clothes Police
22-23

Waterside
Daily Telegraph
October 4th 1888.
Theories - Sailor
108

Wideawake
*Daily Telegraph**
October 5th 1888.
Pardons
120

William Rogers
"The East-End Murders and What Is To Be Done"
Times
November 13th 1888.
Registration of Prostitutes
195-196

Williams Buchanan, B.A.
"Bloodhounds"
Echo
October 2nd 1888.
Bloodhounds
90

Working Man

*Star**
September 17th 1888.
Inquests
28

X

Daily Telegraph
October 3rd 1888.
Theories - Mania and
Lunacy
98

X.Y.Z.

*Daily Telegraph**
October 4th 1888.
Theories - Revenge
106

Index – By Topic

* Authors/letters marked with an asterisk indicate that the original newspaper source provided only a summary of the letter, not the complete text.

American Anatomist

Jas. Risdon Bennett
Times
September 28th 1888.
67

"The Coroner and the Whitechapel Murderer"
Charles Ed. Jerningham
Pall Mall Gazette
September 29th 1888.
71-72

A Surgeon*
Daily Telegraph
October 1st 1888.
84

George Fox
Freeman's Journal and Daily Commercial Advertiser
October 1st 1888.
76-77

Artisans Dwellings

"A Safe Four Per Cent"
Ratepayer
Daily Telegraph
September 21st 1888.
42-46

"A Safe Four Per Cent"
A Practical Philanthropist
Daily Telegraph
September 22nd 1888.
48-49

"A Safe Four Per Cent"
An Inquirer
Daily Telegraph
September 22nd 1888.
49-52

"At Last"
Gamma
Times
September 22nd 1888.
53

"A Safe Four Per Cent"
A Metropolitan Registrar of Births and Deaths
Daily Telegraph
September 24th 1888.
60-61

"A Safe Four Per Cent"
E. Bannister
Daily Telegraph
September 24th 1888.
59-60

"A Safe Four Per Cent"
J. S. Whichelow
Daily Telegraph
September 26th 1888.
63

"A Safe Four Per Cent"
Town Clerk
Daily Telegraph
September 27th 1888.
65-66

F.G. Debenham
Times
September 29th 1888.
68

"The East End"
Samuel A. Barnett
Times
September 29th 1888.
68

"The East-End"
Alfred Hoare
Times
October 6th 1888.
136-137

Edward W. Thomas
Times
October 18th 1888.
183-184

F.H. Harvey-Samuel
Times
October 18th 1888.
183

Bloodhounds

"Bloodhounds as Detectives"
L.F.S. Maberly
Morning Advertiser
September 14th 1888.
25

"The Bloodhound as a Detective"
E.P.
Morning Advertiser
September 15th 1888.
27

A Scotchman*
Daily Telegraph
October 1st 1888.
84

Citizen*
Daily Telegraph
October 1st 1888.
84

Percy Lindley
Times
October 1st 1888.
79

St. John Carr*
Daily Telegraph
October 1st 1888.
84

J. Flynn
Echo
October 2nd 1888.
90

"Bloodhounds"
Williams Buchanan, B.A.
Echo
October 2nd 1888.
90

"Bloodhounds"
J.G. Newfield
Echo
October 3rd 1888.
104

Bloodhound
Daily Telegraph
October 4th 1888.
107-108

H.J. Cushing
Daily Telegraph
October 6th 1888.
128

"Bloodhounds in London"
Percy Lindley
Pall Mall Gazette
October 6th 1888.
132-133

"The Old English Bloodhound or Sleuthound and his Capabilities as a Man-Hunter"
Edwin Brough
Times
October 8th 1888.
145-147

Edwin Brough
Times
October 11th 1888.
158

"The Sleuthhound as a Tracker"
W. Grist
Morning Advertiser
October 12th 1888.
164-165

"Bloodhounds as Detectives"
Henry Fennell
Times
October 13th 1888.
172-173

"Bloodhounds as Detectives"
Percy Lindley
Times
October 16th 1888.
179-180

H.M. Mackusick
Daily Telegraph
October 19th 1888.
185-186

Brothels and Prostitution

"The Haunts of Vice and Crime"
Disgusted
Echo
October 1st 1888.
77

"Whitechapel"
Frederick N. Charrington
Star
November 23rd 1888.
207

Calls for Prayer

W.S. Pilling
Daily Telegraph
October 4th 1888.
109

Charles Warren

"Sir Charles Warren's Appointment"
An old police constable under Sir Richard Mayne
Evening News
August 8th 1888.
5

"The Hallucination of Warren"
R. B. Cuninghame Graham
Star
October 30th 1888.
192-194

Chloroforming

J.M.S. Brooke
Times
October 1st 1888.
78

Detection Suggestions

"More Police Wanted"
W.J.W.
Echo
September 11th 1888.
15-16

C.L.M.
Daily Telegraph
October 1st 1888.
88

Fred Wellesley
Times
October 1st 1888.
74

G.E.K.
Daily Telegraph
October 1st 1888.
87

Spes*
Daily Telegraph
October 1st 1888.
86

Revenge*
Daily Telegraph
October 4th 1888.
106

Detection Suggestions - Amateur Detectives

"The Whitechapel Murders"
H.T.
St. James Gazette
November 16th 1888.
199-200

Detection Suggestions - Avoid Theories

"No Theory"
No Theory
Daily News
October 3rd 1888.
102-103

Index – By Topic 237

"Mr. Forbes's Theory"
No Theory
Daily News
October 4th 1888.
113-114

Detection Suggestions - Bicycles

"London Police - A Suggestion"
Progress
Echo
October 6th 1888.
143

Detection Suggestions - Criminal Types

"The Personal Appearance of the East-End Murderer"
A. Eubule Evans
Pall Mall Gazette
October 6th 1888.
131-132

Detection Suggestions - Deputization of Lodging House Keepers

A Publican
Morning Advertiser
October 3rd 1888.
104

Detection Suggestions - Empty Warehouses

F.T.*
Daily Telegraph
October 5th 1888.
120

Detection Suggestions - False Confessions

"Whitechapel Murders"
A Reader
Irish Times
October 12th 1888.
166

Detection Suggestions - Female Detectives

G. Standerwick*
Daily Telegraph
October 3rd 1888.
96

Owen Banford*
Daily Telegraph
October 3rd 1888.
96

S.M.*
Daily Telegraph
October 3rd 1888.
96

"Detectives"
Frances Power Cobbe
Times
October 11th 1888.
160

Detection Suggestions - Fingerprinting

Fred. W. P. Jago
Times
October 3rd 1888.
91-93

Detection Suggestions - Fruit Vendors

R.E. Lawford Webb
Daily Telegraph
October 6th 1888.
127

Detection Suggestions - House to House Searches

One of the X Division*
Daily Telegraph
October 1st 1888.
86

Detection Suggestions - Opium Dens

R.H.T.
Daily Telegraph
October 4th 1888.
109

Detection Suggestions - Photographing the Retina

"The Whitechapel Murder"
Sydney Hodges
Echo
September 21st 1888.
47

Detection Suggestions - Plain Clothes Police

"Plain Clothes Detectives"
Watch
Echo
September 13th 1888.
22-23

Ex-Constable C. Baddelby
Daily Telegraph
October 6th 1888.
129

Detection Suggestions - Points on a Map

Observer
Daily Telegraph
October 3rd 1888.
97

Detection Suggestions - Registration of Lodging House Inhabitants

A Mariner*
Daily Telegraph
October 1st 1888.
84

One More Unfortunate*
Daily Telegraph
October 1st 1888.
84

One Who Knows*
Daily Telegraph
October 1st 1888.
84

Detection Suggestions - Rubber Boots

A Surgeon*
Daily Telegraph
October 1st 1888.
86

A.E. Gower*
Daily Telegraph
October 1st 1888.
86

D. Everett
Daily Telegraph
October 1st 1888.
89

H.C.W.*
Daily Telegraph
October 1st 1888.
86

W.S.*
Daily Telegraph
October 1st 1888.
86

Herbert F. Scott*
Daily Telegraph
October 3rd 1888.
96

L.R. Thomson
Times
October 3rd 1888.
91

"The East End Tragedies"
Henry Bax
Echo
October 4th 1888.
116

"Two Practical Suggestions"
W.E. Corner
Echo
October 4th 1888.
115

"Policemen's Boots"
Ernest Fisher
Echo
October 5th 1888.
125

"Policemen's Boots"
H. Bax
Echo
October 6th 1888.
143

Detection Suggestions - Sewers

Alfred C. Calmour*
Daily Telegraph
October 5th 1888.
120

M.H.*
Daily Telegraph
October 5th 1888.
120

Detection Suggestions - Similar Murders in America

Fleet-street*
Daily Telegraph
October 4th 1888.
106

S. Smithers*
Daily Telegraph
October 4th 1888.
106

W.H. Bakes*
Daily Telegraph
October 4th 1888.
106

Detection Suggestions - Similar Murders in France

"A French Chapter of Whitechapel Horrors"
Michael Mack
Times
October 6th 1888.
137-138

Detection Suggestions - Soldiers as Policemen

"Soldiers as Policemen"
A Time Expired
Evening News
September 20th 1888.
41

Detection Suggestions - Spiritualism

A Clairvoyant*
Daily Telegraph
October 4th 1888.
106

Inquirer*
Daily Telegraph
October 4th 1888.
106

S.*
Daily Telegraph
October 4th 1888.
106

Spiritualist*
Daily Telegraph
October 4th 1888.
106

Detection Suggestions - Timing of the Murders

"The Whitechapel Murders"
C.F.A.G.
Echo
September 14th 1888.
26

Detection Suggestions - Women's Clothing

An Old Detective*
Daily Telegraph
October 1st 1888.
86

Francis Tumblety

"Dr. Tumblety and Isaac Golliday"
Authot unknown
Washinton Evening Star
November 21st 1888.
205

Government Pensions

"Can Anything Good Come Out of Whitechapel?"
P.D. Townshend

Pall Mall Gazette
October 17th 1888.
181

Home Secretary - Criticism

A Poor Woman*
Daily Telegraph
October 1st 1888.
86

D.C.L.*
Daily Telegraph
October 1st 1888.
86

Immorality

"The Repression of Immorality"
R.N. Fowler
Morning Advertiser
October 8th 1888.
148-149

"The Moral of the Murders"
Hugh B. Chapman
Star
October 13th 1888.
169-170

"The Moral of the Murders"
A Fabian
Star
October 16th 1888.
178-179

Inquests

"Whitechapel Murder"
H.E.W.
Echo
September 15th 1888.
29

Working Man*
Star
September 17th 1888.
28

J.P.
Times
September 19th 1888.
36

"The Whitechapel Murders"
Rowland Addams Williams
Times
September 26th 1888.
62

Intemperance

"The Whitechapel Murders"
Reformer
Echo
September 10th 1888.
11

Jews and Anti-Semitism

"Slaughtering the Jews"
G.H.H.
Evening News
September 11th 1888.
12

"The Murder Near Cracow"
Hermann Adler
Times
October 3rd 1888.
93-94

M. Gaster, Ph.D
Times
October 3rd 1888.
94-95

"The Jews and Animal Killing"
Samuel Montagu
Echo
October 11th 1888.
162

"The East End"
Michael Zeffertt
Jewish Chronicle
October 12th 1888.
164

Landlords

"What Is to Be Done?"
Samuel A. Barnett
Times
November 16th 1888.
202

Lenient Sentences

"The Whitechapel Murders"
Cockney
Echo
October 4th 1888.
115

Lodging Houses

W. Gearon*
Star
September 17th 1888.
28

Fredk. J. Money, M.D
Daily Telegraph
September 26th 1888.
64

One Who Knows
Times
September 29th 1888.
69-70

E. Fairfield
Times
October 1st 1888.
74

"The East End"
Henry Brudenell Bruce
Times
October 1st 1888.
73

G. Walker
Daily Telegraph
October 5th 1888.
120-121

"The Homes of the Criminal Class"
Compton
Times
October 6th 1888.
139-140

"The Children of Common Lodging Houses"
Thos. J. Barnardo
Times
October 9th 1888.
151-153

Mary Ann Nichols

"Letter From the Husband"
W. Nicholls
Lloyd's Weekly
September 9th 1888.
10

Missionary Work

"A Whitechapel Fund"
Mary J. Kinnaird
Times
October 26th 1888.
189

"Whitechapel Fund"
Arthur J. Robinson
Times
October 29th 1888.
190

Mistaken Identity

"The Whitechapel Murders"
An Elderly Gentleman
Times
October 15th 1888.
175-176

Mitre Square

"Mitre Square"
Mitre
City Press
December 1st 1888.
208

Municipal Shelters

"The Whitechapel Murders"
Samuel Hayward
East London Observer
September 29th 1888.
70

Carita
Daily Telegraph
October 3rd 1888.
98

A Mother*
Daily Telegraph
October 5th 1888.
119

An Englishwoman*
Daily Telegraph
October 5th 1888.
119

E.R.L.
Daily Telegraph
October 5th 1888.
122

L.K.
Daily Telegraph
October 5th 1888.
124-125

Matron*
Daily Telegraph
October 5th 1888.
119

T.W.S.*
Daily Telegraph
October 5th 1888.
119

George H. Giddine
Daily Telegraph
October 6th 1888.
129

Saml. Hayward
Daily Telegraph
October 6th 1888.
131

"Friendless and Fallen in Whitechapel"
Walter Hazell
Times
October 6th 1888.
138-139

"Whitechapel"
R.C. Bedford
Times
October 9th 1888.
154

"Ratcliff Highway Refuge"
Mary H. Steer
Times
October 11th 1888.
160-161

"Shelters for the Homeless"
Dobra
Star
October 12th 1888.
167-168

"A Shelter For Females"
R.H. Winter
Morning Advertiser
October 13th 1888.
174

"A Home for Inebriate Women"
Beatrice Temple
Daily Telegraph
October 30th 1888.
191

Organization for Boys

"Law and Order in Whitechapel"
Paul Methuen
Times
November 16th 1888.
201-202

Pardons

H.R.
Daily Telegraph
October 5th 1888.
122

Wideawake*
Daily Telegraph
October 5th 1888.
120

Pernicious Art and Literature

"A Disgraceful Scene"
An East-Ender
Echo
September 11th 1888.
16

"Nuisances in Whitechapel"
A. Laing
Echo
September 12th 1888.
20

"A Disgraceful Scene"
Abbott, Earle, and Ogle
Echo
September 13th 1888.
22

"Stories of Crime"
K.T.A.
Times
September 22nd 1888.
54

G.C.*
Daily Telegraph
October 3rd 1888.
96

"Another Protest"
J. Arthur Elliott
Star
November 16th 1888.
200-201

Police Criticism

"Crime in Whitechapel"
A Working Man
Star
September 7th 1888.
9

"The Non-Detection of Crime"
An East-Ender
Star
September 12th 1888.
21

"Police Incompetence"
Ratepayer
Evening News
September 12th 1888.
20

"Our Detective System"
An Observer Waiting
Star
September 14th 1888.
26

H. M. Harewood*
Star
September 17th 1888.
28

"The Dangers of Whitechapel"
J.E. Waller
Star
September 17th 1888.
27-28

"Police Organization"
Edmund Lawrence
Times
September 18th 1888.
30-31

"London Detective Force"
Reform
Daily Telegraph
September 21st 1888.
46-47

"The Metropolitan Police"
Civis
Daily Telegraph
September 22nd 1888.
52-53

F. W. Devereux Long
Daily Telegraph
October 1st 1888.
88

"A Word for the Police"
Fair Play
Star
October 1st 1888.
75

R. Johns
Daily News
October 1st 1888.
80

T.B.B.
Daily News
October 1st 1888.
81

Geo. Hy. Compton
Daily Telegraph
October 3rd 1888.
99

M.P.*
Daily Telegraph
October 3rd 1888.
96

Charles Warren
Times
October 4th 1888.
116-118

A.W.*
Daily Telegraph
October 5th 1888.
119

"Whitechapel"
C.H.
Star
October 5th 1888.
126

E.A. Harvey
Daily Telegraph
October 5th 1888.
124

J. Morris*
Daily Telegraph
October 5th 1888.
119

Jo. Perrott
Daily Telegraph
October 5th 1888.
123

M. Williams*
Daily Telegraph
October 5th 1888.
119

T. Jones*
Daily Telegraph
October 5th 1888.
119

Vindex*
Daily Telegraph
October 5th 1888.
119

"The Duties of the Police"
T. Wentworth Grant
Times
October 9th 1888.
155

"The Detection of Crime"
D.
Times

October 11th 1888.
158-159

"Police Supervision"
H. Delahooke
Times
October 13th 1888.
173

"The London Police"
James Stuart
Daily News
October 16th 1888.
180

"Sir Charles Warren and Mr. Matthews"
Charles Warren
Times
November 17th 1888.
203-204

Press Criticism

"A Strange Omission"
A Frightened Woman
Echo
October 6th 1888.
143-144

"The Sensationalism of Our Day"
J.P.H.
Star
October 12th 1888.
167

Registration of Prostitutes

"The East-End Murders and What Is To Be Done"
William Rogers
Times
November 13th 1888.
195-196

Rewards

G.R.H.
Daily Telegraph
October 1st 1888.
86-87

"The Murders in the East End"
George Lusk and Joseph Aarons
Daily Telegraph
October 1st 1888.
75

Henry White
Times
October 1st 1888.
79-80

Hope
Daily Telegraph
October 3rd 1888.
96-97

Citizen*
Daily Telegraph
October 5th 1888.
120

Ellerford*
Daily Telegraph
October 5th 1888.
120

H.P.B.
Times
October 5th 1888.
125

W.H.*
Daily Telegraph
October 5th 1888.
120

"The Recent Murders in London"
Edward Wilson
Irish Times
October 9th 1888.
150-151

"Whitechapel"
C. Thomas
Star
November 15th 1888.
198

Rose Mylett

"The Poplar Mystery"
Andrew Rowan
Daily News
December 28th 1888.
212

Social Conditions

"Whitechapel-Road Murder"
James Sharpless
Echo
September 5th 1888.
7

J.F.S.
Times
September 14th 1888.
26

"At Last"
S.G.O.
Times
September 18th 1888.
32-34

"Peril in East London"
W. Evans Hurndall
Daily Telegraph
September 18th 1888.
35

"At Last"
Samuel A. Barnett
Times
September 19th 1888.
36-38

"The East End Atrocity"
Onlooker
Evening News
September 20th 1888.
39

"Blood Money to Whitechapel"
G. Bernard Shaw
Star
September 24th 1888.
57-59

"East-End Women"
A Constant Reader
Echo
October 2nd 1888.
89

Index – By Topic   **243**

"Blood Money to Whitechapel"
John Wheelwright
Star
October 3rd 1888.
105

"Metropolitan Immorality"
Pro Caritate
Echo
October 3rd 1888.
105

"Unfortunates"
S.G.O.
Times
October 6th 1888.
133-135

"The Poverty of the East-end of London"
C.R. Drysdale, M.D.
Star
October 9th 1888.
157

"An Appeal From the East End"
Violet Greville
Daily Telegraph
October 12th 1888.
165-166

"Whitechapel"
R.C. Bedford
Times
October 13th 1888.
170

W.M. Adamson
Times
October 13th 1888.
170-172

"Whitechapel"
A Girl Radical
Star
October 15th 1888.
176-177

"The Morals of the Murders"
R.J. Bruton
Echo
October 17th 1888.
182

A Constant Reader
Star
October 19th 1888.
188

"Distress in East London"
E. Schnadhorst
Morning Advertiser
October 19th 1888.
186-187

Sigma
Star
October 19th 1888.
188

"East End Poverty"
Ultra Radical
Star
October 19th 1888.
187

"Black Winter in East London"
W. Evans Hurndall
Morning Advertiser
November 14th 1888.
197

Street Hawkers

Author Unknown
Daily Telegraph
November 16th 1888.
199

Street Lighting

"The Whitechapel Atrocities"
M. Cursham Corner
East London Observer
September 15th 1888.
28-29

Morton Latham
Times
October 3rd 1888.
91

Mentor*
Daily Telegraph
October 4th 1888.
107

R. Roberts*
Daily Telegraph
October 4th 1888.
106-107

Suspicious Persons

A Terrified Woman*
Daily Telegraph
October 3rd 1888.
96

Theories

E. Swabey
Evening News
September 20th 1888.
39-40

"Jack the Ripper's Motive"
Esther Delaforce
Pall Mall Gazette
December 12th 1888.
211

Theories - A Local

"The Whitechapel Murder Mystery"
Ex-Convict
Pall Mall Gazette
October 8th 1888.
147-148

Theories - A Woman

"The Murders in Whitechapel"
F.H.H.
Echo
September 12th 1888.
17

Theories - American

M.S.*
Daily Telegraph
October 5th 1888.
119

Observer
Daily Telegraph
October 5th 1888.
121

Anglo-Texan
Daily Telegraph
October 6th 1888.
128

F. Schaffter
Daily Telegraph
October 6th 1888.
130

H.Y.P.
Daily Telegraph
October 6th 1888.
130

Theories - An Upper-Class City Dweller

Canis
Daily Telegraph
October 4th 1888.
108-109

Theories - Cabman

E.R.B.C.
Daily Telegraph
October 6th 1888.
127

Theories - Civil Servant

F.C.*
Daily Telegraph
October 5th 1888.
119

Theories - Drugged then Murdered

R. Macdonald
Daily Telegraph
October 4th 1888.
110-111

Theories - Epilepsy

"The Whitechapel Horrors"
Medicus
Evening News
September 11th 1888.
13-14

Theories - Fish Cleaner

H.E. Bell*
Daily Telegraph
October 5th 1888.
119

Theories - Foreigner

Edward Dillon Lewis*
Daily Telegraph
October 4th 1888.
107

Edward Dillon Lewis
Times
October 4th 1888.
111-112

Theories - Frenchman

"Is Jack the Ripper a Frenchman?"
A Frenchman
Pall Mall Gazette
December 6th 1888.
209-210

Theories - Gangs

Clergyman*
Daily Telegraph
October 3rd 1888.
96

Detective*
Daily Telegraph
October 3rd 1888.
96

St. Aubin Hamilton*
Daily Telegraph
October 3rd 1888.
96

T. L. Selder*
Daily Telegraph
October 3rd 1888.
96

W.M.R.*
Daily Telegraph
October 3rd 1888.
96

Theories - Malay

Nemo
Times
October 4th 1888.
112-113

Theories - Mania and Lunacy

A Country Doctor
Times
September 11th 1888.
15

L. Forbes Winslow
Times
September 12th 1888.
19

P.Q.R.S.
Evening News
September 13th 1888.
23

Henry Sutherland, M.D.
Lancet
September 22nd 1888.
54-55

L. Forbes Winslow
Lancet
September 22nd 1888.
56

Edgar Sheppard, M.D.
Times
October 1st 1888.
78-79

X
Daily Telegraph
October 3rd 1888.
98

David Sime, M.D.
Daily Telegraph
October 4th 1888.
110

John Bell Sedgwick
Daily Telegraph
October 5th 1888.
123

Theories - Not One But Many

Bloodhound*
Daily Telegraph
October 5th 1888.
120

Theories - Pimps

Albert Bachert
Evening News
September 6th 1888.
8

Theories - Revenge

X.Y.Z.*
Daily Telegraph
October 4th 1888.
106

Theories - Sailor

Waterside
Daily Telegraph
October 4th 1888.
108

Theories - Similar Murders in Westphalia

"The Whitechapel Murders"
S.
Star
September 13th 1888.
24

Theories - Slaughterman

Amateur Detective*
Daily Telegraph
October 5th 1888.
119

Henry Harrison*
Daily Telegraph
October 5th 1888.
119

Theories - Venereal Disease

"The Motive of the Murders"
Archd. Forbes
Daily News
October 3rd 1888.
99-102

Vigilance Committees

The Secretary of the St. Jude's District Committee
Daily News
September 11th 1888.
14-15

"Whitechapel"
Thomas Hancock Nunn and Thomas G. Gardiner
Times
October 6th 1888.
135-136

Woman Killing No Murder

"Woman Killing No Murder"
Florence Fenwick Miller
Daily News
October 1st 1888.
82-84

"Woman Killing No Murder"
Justice
Daily News
October 3rd 1888.
103

"Woman Killing No Murder"
A.P.
Daily News
October 4th 1888.
114

"Woman Killing No Murder"
A.J.M.
Daily News
October 6th 1888.
142

"Woman Killing No Murder"
D.H.
Daily News
October 6th 1888.
141-142

"Woman Killing No Murder"
Kate Mitchell
Daily News
October 6th 1888.
140-141

"Woman Killing No Murder"
Constance Howell
Daily News
October 9th 1888.
150

Whitechapel

"The East End Horrors"
Reformer
Evening News
September 12th 1888.
17

Women's Rights

"Audi Alteram Partem"
Justice and Equality
Star
October 9th 1888.
155-157

Acknowledgements

This modest book would never have been possible without the diligent – some would say obsessive – work of those who have volunteered their time, money and energy to the Casebook Press Project. The project was the brainchild of the late Adrian Phypers, an historian and London tour guide who had researched and written extensively on the subject of Jack the Ripper. His enthusiasm for contemporary press coverage of the Whitechapel murders fueled my own, and over a span of nearly four years he and a group of volunteers meticulously transcribed and proofread hundreds of articles which are now freely available to any researcher at the www.casebook.org website.

Although Adrian is no longer with us, his passion for contemporary press reports lives on with the project he founded. As of the time of writing, over four thousand articles from 270 different newspapers have been transcribed and contextually indexed on the *Casebook* web site, with more being added every month.

Over the years, dozens of people have volunteered for the Casebook Press Project. One in particular deserves special recognition. Chris Scott, an author and researcher currently living in Ramsgate, England, has transcribed and contributed so many articles to the project that I've simply lost count. How he's managed to do all of this typing without succumbing to carpal tunnel syndrome, I'll never know.

There are many other volunteers, who I will try to list here as best I can from my (limited) memory, in no particular order. They've all been instrumental in the success of this project, and the debt of gratitude owed to them, from myself and from anyone who has ever used the press report library in their research, is simply incalculable. Thank you to David O'Flaherty, Nina Thomas, Alex Chisholm, Alan Sharp, Lyn Hollifield, Jennifer Pegg, Jim DiPalma, Neil MacMillan, John Malcolm, Tim Riordan, Stephen Long, Debra Arif, Jana Oliver, Matfelon, Adam Went, Coral Kelly, Robert Linford and many others who have lent their typing fingers along the way. And a big thank you goes out to Norma Buddle, whose generous donations helped us continually expand to new and different papers.

I'd also like to thank Thomas Schachner, editor of www.jacktheripper.de, for the cover design and Karen Kurt Teal, Rosemary Van Arsdel and Robert Clack for their help in bringing together illustrations for the finished volume. And of course my thanks to Dan Norder for his time and patience in producing this book.

All proceeds from sales of this book will directly benefit the Casebook Press Project.

Printed in the United States
55433LVS00004B/4